Why John Wrote a Gospel

WHY JOHN WROTE
A GOSPEL

Jesus—Memory—History

Tom Thatcher

WESTMINSTER
JOHN KNOX PRESS
LOUISVILLE · KENTUCKY

Except where noted, all Scripture translations are the author's.

Book design by Sharon Adams
Cover design by Jennifer K. Cox
Cover photograph courtesy of Bill Jacobson/Getty Images

First edition
Published by Westminster John Knox Press
Louisville, Kentucky

This book is printed on acid-free paper that meets the American National Standards Institute Z39.48 standard. ∞

PRINTED IN THE UNITED STATES OF AMERICA

06 07 08 09 10 11 12 13 14 15 — 10 9 8 7 6 5 4 3 2 1

Library of Congress Cataloging-in-Publication Data is on file at the Library of Congress, Washington, D.C.

ISBN-13: 978-0-664-22905-4
ISBN-10: 0-664-22905-0

Then
when he was raised from the dead,
his disciples remembered
that he said these things,
and they believed the Scriptures
and the word[s] that Jesus spoke. . . .
But these things have been written
so that *you* may believe.

(John 2:22; 20:31)

[T]he text
is no longer
a support for memory,
but its replacement.
(Fentress and Wickham, *Social Memory*, 10)

Contents

Prescript

Why Ask Why John Wrote a Gospel? or, What Difference Does This Make?

About halfway through my work on this manuscript, I began to realize that a book so short and so sweeping would need many caveats, or at least some contextualization. But rather than couching such comments in methodological digressions, long histories of research, and dense footnotes, I decided that it would be easier, clearer, and much less boring simply to trace the path of my thinking in a preface. What follows here, then, is the series of steps that brought me to this point, refracted through the lens of my own understanding of the problems under consideration and my memory of the way I've come to think as I do about those problems. I seek, in other words, to provide you a fair and accurate description of my perceptions and logic, and apologize to those who will object to my caricature of the issues. They may not look the same to you, but I think it only fair for you to know how they look to me. By the way, even if you are a person who doesn't know much about the Johannine literature or memory theory or orality theory or Jesus studies, you still should probably read the rest of this preface, rather than just skipping to the first chapter, just to give you a brief introduction to what we'll be talking about.

In 1995, as a doctoral student, I was privileged to attend my first meeting of the Bible in Ancient and Modern Media Section at the Society of Biblical Literature (SBL) convention in Philadelphia. Actually, having now been to a dozen SBL conventions, I cannot precisely remember the year or the city. But I recall very clearly the room in which the session was held, because there I saw, in the same place and at the same time, four of my heroes—John Miles Foley, Dan Ben-Amos, Werner Kelber, and Joanna Dewey. The first two are giants in the field of folkloristics, and my interdisciplinary interests had elevated all four to a point of authority at least equal to the texts of the Christian canon—indeed, superior to those texts, as the lens through which I viewed almost everything in the Bible. Doubtless because of my great awe in the presence of this pantheon, I cannot remember the contents of any of their presentations. I do, however, clearly recall the last ten minutes of the "open discussion" at the end of the meeting, after all members of the general audience except myself and a guy from New Zealand had left the room. I remember those closing moments, because in them I was privileged to ask Prof. Kelber a question, and he actually took time to answer.

"Professor Kelber," I asked, "what difference would Mark's original audience have seen between his Gospel and the oral traditions he used? In other words, what did he think was going to happen with all this information, once he wrote it down?" My inquiry went something along those lines, but was probably actually much less coherent. I was nervous and inarticulate. I have since learned that Graham Stanton had already posed the same question much more clearly and concisely twenty years earlier: "To what extent did Mark's decision to *write* a gospel lead automatically to a change of perspective?"[1] What happened in the move from oral Jesus tradition to written text? What motivated that shift, and how did that shift reshape the tradition itself and the church's reception of that tradition, the Christian understanding of Jesus? For if the transition to literacy is of no interpretive value—if the production of the Gospels is insignificant to the nature of the contents of those texts—then the interpretive significance of Mark's composition history is exhausted by a simple form-critical chronology of the development of "the tradition," with the written text as the final link in the chain. Once the line from Jesus through tradition to written text has been drawn, the game is over—*unless* there is something inherently significant in the very act of *writing* Jesus' story, something that would make us read the Gospels in a different way. And for me, it was and is impossible to think that this move from the gospel to a Gospel was not perceived to be significant by the early Christians.

Admittedly, all these broader implications were not entirely clear to me at the moment I asked Prof. Kelber my seminal question. Yet I remember his answer word for word: "I'm not yet sure how to answer that." And I am certain now that this was not because Prof. Kelber did not know how to answer, but simply because I didn't know how to ask. Since that time, I have been seeking for a better way to pose the question.

I share this experience to identify the constellation of interpretive problems that has been at the forefront of my thinking for the past decade, the core constellation that underlies the book you are now reading. I became interested in folkloristics and orality theory during my last year of seminary, and since that time I have been on a quest for the answers to two basic questions. First, Why did Matthew, Mark, Luke, and John write Gospels? I now understand, acutely, that these are actually four distinct questions, and I'm still not sure how to answer at least three of them. But to take one example: Mark's oral culture was dramatically different from my own literate culture, in ways that can be listed and described. A great deal of modern anthropological theory, supported by many clear examples from the ancient primary evidence, makes this fact indisputable. So what? What does that have to say about the way I understand Mark's motive for writing a Gospel, and how should I interpret his book based on that understanding?

My second guiding question has been equally ambitious: Did any of these people who wrote Gospels have a "historical interest in Jesus," and what does it mean to say that they did or did not? Clearly, any attempt to reconstruct a historical Jesus from the Gospels requires a preliminary set of assumptions about how early Christians thought about the past. But even those who are disinterested in a "historical Jesus" per se still must answer this question if they wish to interpret the Gospels against their historical setting, because the evangelists' views of their subject and the perceived relationship between their stories and that subject must have shaped their presentation. Did Mark have a "historical interest" in Jesus? I remain convinced that the answer must be yes, but also convinced that the word "historical" cannot be defined in any way close to what I thought it meant when I first formed the question over a decade ago.

Early on in my pursuit, I had a sense that the answer to these two questions—Why were the Gospels written? In what sense do they evidence a "historical interest" in Jesus?—must have something to do with "Jesus traditions," whatever those might be. Perhaps more precisely, I sensed that the roots of these two questions were intertwined at some deep level, and that an understanding of Jesus traditions would be the spade that could unearth and disentangle them. But I was surprised to discover that definitions of "Jesus tradition" are scarce, vague, and often inconsistent in biblical studies—inconsistent in the work of different scholars and sometimes even within the writings of one person.

My thinking was, and still is, that biblical scholars could escape this ambiguous approach to "Jesus tradition" by seeking the wisdom of contemporary orality theorists and experts in folklore. But I realized some while ago that, while these approaches point to a solution, their inherent limitations torment any student of Christian origins who tries to harness them. Specifically, while contemporary folkloristics emphasizes the significance of the answer to my first question—something very important *does* happen in the shift from tradition to text—it doesn't provide that answer. Ruth Finnegan and John Miles Foley can tell biblical scholars why the transition from orality to literacy is important, and what oral traditions look like before and after specific performances are committed to writing, but we obviously cannot expect them to work out all the implications of their conclusions for problems in our own field. Even worse, many folklorists refuse to answer my second question out of humble admission that they don't have the right tools for the job. They're interested in how traditions work, not necessarily in whether people who tell traditional stories are actually relating "facts" about the past. As an interpretive method, folkloristics gave me a glimpse of the promised land but left me to die on the mountain, forever seeing yet blind to the specific reasons why the Gospels were written and what difference it makes to interpretation.

Aside from my inability to make my methods answer my questions, my journey has been hindered by the many traps and snares that lie in that part of the canon where I spend most of my time. While most people have approached my guiding problems through Mark, almost at the very beginning my pursuit took a strange turn through the dark woods of the Gospel of John. Truthfully, I was never that interested in the Johannine literature, but my doctoral adviser, Gerald Borchert, was working on a commentary on John, and his enthusiasm and the convenience of following behind him led me to do a dissertation that applied a folklore model to the Fourth Gospel. Since then I've focused much of my energy on the Johannine Jesus tradition, and this has raised another set of problems, related not so much to the nature of the biblical text or the application of folkloristics to that text as to the nature of biblical scholarship.

The Gospel of John was, like Matthew, Mark, and Luke, treated as a memoir of Jesus at least until the 180s CE. That impression changed somewhat with Clement of Alexandria, who labeled John the "spiritual gospel" and postured it as a supplement to the Synoptics—both a supplement to the content of Jesus' story, providing information the others deleted, and, more important, a sort of theological supplement to the others, revealing the deep spiritual/christological truth behind the events of history. The most remarkable thing about Clement's postulate is the fact that it stands as the majority view to this day. Indeed, it is hard to identify any thesis in any academic discipline that has held consensus so long as Clement's claim that John is a "spiritual gospel" (although of course our modern understandings of that moniker differ somewhat from Clement's emphasis). And the durability of this thesis problematizes any attempt to say anything about the interface between John's Jesus tradition and the text of the Fourth Gospel, simply because scholars have had difficulty identifying parts of this "spiritual" text that might reflect traditional content. That is, scholars have had a hard time determining what parts of the Gospel of John are "traditional" in any sense of the word, as opposed to things the author simply worked up out of his theological imagination.

Of course, it isn't odd that readers since Clement have found it easy to affirm his theorem, for the Gospel of John, much more than Matthew, Mark, and Luke, portrays, in Käsemann's words, "the earthly life of Jesus merely as a back-drop for the Son of God proceeding through the world."[2] But at the same time, it seemed, and still does seem, odd to me that the "spiritual gospel" label has led us to overlook two key facts. First, John is the only early Gospel that explic-itly claims (and more than once) to offer the reader a direct, firsthand witness to the preresurrection Jesus. In my view, this fact must become significant at some point in any discussion of the tension between John's theology and his historical consciousness, even if we decide that it isn't significant to discussions of the Fourth Gospel's historicity. And I should also say that it seems to me that we have to come to a definite conclusion about John's historical consciousness before we can discuss the Gospel of John's historicity, rather than vice versa.

Second, John is the only evangelist, and one of the very few Christian writ-ers at any point in history, who articulated a distinct theory about what "the Jesus tradition" was and how it operated. Whatever else he may have thought about Christ, John had a very clear sense that his presentation of Jesus was based on someone's memory, and an explicit theory of how that memory worked. Further, he openly states on more than one occasion that the disci-ples' original memories of Jesus were inadequate, and admits that those mem-ories have been thoroughly reworked. And, remarkably, he seems to see no tension whatsoever between this admission and the validity of his claims about Jesus. As punishment for this lack of insight, or perhaps for the fact that he doesn't seem to be bothered by this problem, for nineteen centuries John has worn the label "spiritual gospel" like a scarlet letter, the cost of his complete honesty about the nature of the claims he is making.

Such was my pilgrimage up to about 2001. At that point I was seeking answers to the questions, Why did John write a Gospel? and Did John have any historical interest in Jesus, and if so how should that interest be defined? and was realizing that the analytical methods which interested me could not fully answer these questions. In fact, by that point in time I had a strong sense that I wasn't making much progress because I wasn't asking the questions the right way.

Then I met Alan Kirk, who introduced me to an emerging discipline called Social Memory theory—emerging not just in reference to biblical studies, but in a more general sense. As it exists today, Social Memory theory is usually dated back to the seminal work of Maurice Halbwachs in the 1920s. But the discipline really caught on and began to grow only in the 1980s and 1990s. I had never heard of Social Memory theory before Alan brought it to my atten-tion, and I still don't know half as much about it as I need to. Yet I think I know enough to see what I was missing without it.

As the name of the discipline suggests, Social Memory theory is essentially concerned with the social dimensions of memory, specifically with the ways that present social realities impact the way that groups envision and use the past. "Memory" is taken in the broadest possible sense here to include any means by which groups attempt to preserve the past, construct the past, or evoke the past, including oral traditions, rituals, trends and styles, bodily practices and habits, and written texts. Social approaches to memory are grounded on at least two key premises: first, that "remembering" is a complex phenomenon that cannot be reduced to the recall of data by isolated individuals; second, that the interplay between the past and present understandings of the past is always a complex phenomenon, and ultimately a group phenomenon. As such, Social Memory theory draws its energy, insights, and vocabulary from a wide range of fields, including psychology, sociology, anthropology, neurology, linguistics, philosophy, and history—basically, any discipline that deals in any way with anything that human beings do with the past.

I realized immediately that this approach held the key to my quest, because it suddenly became possible to view the guiding questions from a new angle. Social Memory theory seemed especially relevant to the Johannine tradition, because John himself uses "memory" and the related term "witness" to describe the connection between his Gospel and the historical Jesus.

Since my initiation into the mysteries of this new discipline, my thinking about John and his tradition has followed the lines of three new and improved questions. First, what is "memory," and what does John mean when he talks about the disciples' "memories" of Jesus or "witness" to Jesus? Second, if that's what "memory" is, what is "history," and how do written history books relate to living memories (what biblical scholars generally call "tradition")? Are history books, like the Gospel of John, the same as memory—just a permanent version of recollections that people have stored in their brains? Or are they something else? Third, if history books and memory differ, why do people write history books? What's the point of doing that? Why write a book about Jesus?

Essentially, these three questions have led me to conceptualize my ongoing pursuit in a different way, which boils down to approaching the problem of tradition and text from the opposite direction. In other words, I realized that I had been working with a model of tradition that moved from Jesus to memory to traditions to written Gospels, an approach I inherited from my parents and grandparents in the guild of biblical studies. But from the perspective of the actual evidence, this approach looks at the problem backward. For the single indisputable piece of data about the Johannine Jesus tradition (or the Markan Jesus tradition, or the Matthean, or the Thomasine) is this: *somebody at some point in time decided to write that tradition down in a book.*

This point has become so significant to my thinking that I need to unpack it a bit. The single thing we can prove about any ancient Gospel, the single historical fact that we can know with absolute certainty, is that some early Christian decided to write his or her thoughts about Jesus down on paper. As such, the only absolutely firm starting point for investigation does not lie with Jesus, the Jesus tradition, or the history of the early church; the only firm starting point lies at the other end of the line, with the existence of the written texts themselves. What would happen, I wondered, if I started my inquiry into the Gospel of John from that single, certain fact and worked backward? Specifically, what happens if the investigation started not with questions about Jesus or oral traditions, but rather with the question, Why did John—living as he did in a culture where most people couldn't read, fewer could write, and no one regretted that fact at all—write down his ideas about Jesus? Why did John write a Gospel? Why does the Fourth Gospel exist?

The answer to this question, Why did John write a Gospel?—at least my preliminary answer—constitutes the remainder of this book. And my current belief is that a solid explanation of the reasons why the Gospels were written can take us a long way around some of the impasses in understanding Jesus traditions, and in understanding the relationship between those documents and the historical Jesus.

This, then, is the story of my pilgrimage, my personal history of research, that brings us to the moment in which you find yourself reading this preface. Before you join me for the rest of the journey, I must make two disclaimers. Both relate to foundational assumptions that may emerge from time to time along the way, despite my best efforts to suppress them. I suppress them simply because I don't think they would impact my conclusions either way, but you may think they're more important than that. In any case, perhaps by bringing them into the light at this early stage I can persuade them to go back to the closet until we're done.

First, my current view of the authorship of the Fourth Gospel: I think that the Beloved Disciple, who appears in the upper room the night before Jesus' death and at several other places in the Gospel of John, was a real person, albeit portrayed now as a legendary figure to meet specific needs in the Fourth Evangelist's situation. In my view, this Beloved Disciple, whose specific identity is of no significance to my argument, was an associate of the historical Jesus and the source of the information in the Fourth Gospel, at least the bulk of it. I am generally inclined, at the present time, to think that this person is probably also the mysterious "Elder" mentioned in 2 John and 3 John. I do not, however, believe that this person "wrote" the Gospel of John, any more than I think that Pilate took a piece of charcoal and "wrote" "INRI" on Jesus' cross (John 19:22). I take the word "wrote" at John 21:24 as synonymous with modern uses of the word "published." That is, if you were to say that "Thatcher published a book on memory and history in John," no one would take that to mean that I did all the proofreading, designed the cover, bound the book, and distributed it. I did "write" this book, but I did not produce the physical product that you now hold in your hands, and, for all you know, I didn't even type it. The statement that I "wrote" this book simply means that I was responsible for its contents. Similarly, I think that the Beloved Disciple was responsible for at least the bulk of the Fourth Gospel's content, and that one or several of his followers, whom I here (collectively) call "John," was/were the person(s) who actually wrote down the Gospel of John and published it among the Johannine churches (at least among the Johannine churches who were willing to listen to it).

Whether or not John used sources other than the Beloved Disciple—a Signs Gospel, or the Synoptics, or a Sayings Source, or other free-floating oral traditions—I do not know for certain but would generally say, "I doubt it," and would certainly say, "We can't prove it from the text if he/she/they did." As a general rule, I tend to say "I doubt it" about things that can't be proved with certainty from the text—meaning, of course, "certain" to me. But I would also say, in terms of this particular study, "This issue makes no difference whatsoever," because personal recollections, reports from eyewitnesses, and documentary sources are all facets of the same jewel within the theoretical orientation of this book.

I need to stress this point, because I want to make it clear from the outset that the conclusions I advocate here would, in my view, remain relevant regardless of one's specific views of the Fourth Gospel's authorship. Specifically, I am interested in the shift from memory/tradition to written text that produced the Fourth Gospel and in the motives behind that shift, and every approach to the authorship question has to deal with that issue. Many scholars today support versions of the traditional view that the Fourth Evangelist was a direct associate of Jesus, perhaps the apostle John, and that the Fourth Gospel is this person's autobiographical memoir. Yet even in this model, the Gospel of John is placed at the end of a long period of oral preaching and is treated as a repository for a primitive witness to Jesus, generally with no specific explanation of why John eventually felt compelled to commit his vision to writing.[3] The present book also seeks to transcend the problem of possible literary sources. Advocates of the view that John utilized written sources—whether the Synoptics or sources now lost—believe that materials from these sources were revised, conflated, and supplemented in the production of the Fourth Gospel.[4] If this is indeed what happened, it remains relevant to ask why John felt it necessary to produce a new written Gospel that would combine information culled from a Signs Gospel or the Gospel of Luke or other documents with supplemental traditional material. Essentially, I am concerned with John's recycling of traditional materials and the motives behind his decision to commit these traditional materials to writing, regardless of the specific source (oral, written, or personal recollection) of any particular unit of that tradition.

Second, from time to time you may wonder what any of this might say about the "historicity" of the Gospel of John or of specific sections of that text. While I will talk about John's historical consciousness, this book does not address the historicity issue, not even implicitly, and no part of my argument should be taken as an attempt to support or challenge any of John's claims about Jesus. As I noted, my thinking here is driven primarily by contemporary approaches to oral tradition and ancient literacy and by that branch of Social Memory theory that focuses on the politics of commemoration, what's at stake in the ways we construct images of the past. These methods do not and, in my view, cannot say anything definitive about the historicity issue, although their implications could doubtless be developed in that direction. But I personally would not be interested in pursuing those implications right now, simply because at this point in my career I am more interested in the interpretation of the Bible than in trying to prove whether Jesus did or did not do something.

At the same time, though, I do believe that the question of the Fourth Gospel's "historicity"—what that term means and how it could be measured—really does make a difference for how we interpret that book, at least for how we would interpret it in historical perspective. When we are looking at Jesus and John's claims about Jesus, it makes a huge difference what we think we're looking for. If we're looking for something that John doesn't care to provide, we obviously aren't going to find it. And since recent biblical scholarship hasn't been looking for what John says he's providing, categorically, it's been very comfortable to conclude that we don't need to look there. What we've been looking for is hard, objective, historical "facts" about Jesus, and John hasn't been much use, because he doesn't seem to believe that such things are important. The ultimate problem, as I noted above, is that John has been marginalized simply because he admits what every Gospel writer was doing. My point in this book is not necessarily to affirm that marginalization nor to counter it, but rather to explain what John thought "memories" about Jesus were, how those memories are related to history books, and how that line of thinking made it logical for him to write a Gospel.

One last point. I owe a great debt of thanks to many people, but space will permit me to mention only a few of them: Alan Kirk, my good friend and colleague who introduced me to Social Memory theory and who is, in so many ways, a wonderful person; Dick Horsley, who has encouraged both Alan and me immensely with his gracious enthusiasm and whose vision opened my eyes to the potential of this approach; Barry Schwartz, who has invested a remarkable amount of time in my understanding and who has guided me on the journey through memory and kept me honest all the while; Gerald Borchert, my *Doktorvater*, who introduced me to the Johannine literature and to whom I am forever grateful for guidance at a key juncture in my career; Werner Kelber, who left footprints big enough for so many of us to walk in; Robert Fortna and Bob Kysar, who are two of the best men alive today, and whose wisdom has been my guiding light on many occasions. I must also thank the library staff at the College of Mt. St. Joseph in Cincinnati for being my gracious hosts as I worked on this project. Actually, I never told them who I was, and I know they often wondered about me as I came into the library day after day in the middle of summer and in the dead of winter breaks, when no other living soul disturbed their secret work among the books. I should have introduced myself, but quiet places are so hard to find these days, and I didn't want to loose that sanctuary. Let me now say to all of you Mount people how much I appreciated your hospitality.

Finally, in this and everything I am forever thankful to, and grateful for, my wife Becky, my son Aaron, and my daughter Julie, who are truly and in so many ways the only reasons I am alive today.

PART 1

The Question—Why Write a Gospel?

1

Why Did John *Write* a Gospel?

This book will offer a new answer to the question, Why did John write a Gospel? In traditional categories of analysis, such as we find in study Bibles and at the beginning of commentaries, this concern generally falls under the heading "purpose." What was John's purpose in, or reason for, producing this text?

Obviously, this is not a new topic or a novel problem, and in one sense this study is just another pebble in the mountain of recent attempts to reconstruct the background of the Johannine literature. The huge number of essays, monographs, and introductory chapters produced on this topic in the last century reflects the current lack of consensus on several key historical issues:

- the identity of "John," the author of the Fourth Gospel[1]
- John's connections to Jesus' "Beloved Disciple" (John 13:23; 19:26; 20:2; 21:7) and to "the Elder" of 2 John and 3 John
- whether there were, perhaps, many "Johns," a series of authors and editors who revised and expanded the text over time to produce the version that exists today
- the historical sources available to John, ranging from personal recollections to oral traditions to lost documents to the Synoptic Gospels
- whether or not there was a distinct "Johannine community," a limited circle of Christians with unique experiences and a peculiar Jesus tradition, to whom John was writing
- whether the Fourth Gospel was written only for this Johannine community, or for the benefit of all Christians

The proliferation of proposals on these problems is sustained by the vagueness of the available historical data. The present study will therefore take as its

3

point of departure the single indisputable fact about the Fourth Gospel's historical background: that John decided to commit his view of the gospel, his version of Jesus' story, to writing. This concrete block of foundational data will be treated here as a natural law, buttressed by a hypothesis that, though theoretically subject to debate, has been so widely accepted since the time of the ancient church that it wears a halo of moral certitude: this author, John, wrote his book about Jesus in a setting of conflict (or, at least, of perceived conflict). The juxtaposition of these two basic facts—that the Gospel of John was *written*, and that it was written during a *conflict* over the identity of its protagonist—is, in itself, sufficient to generate a definitive theory about the purposes of the Fourth Gospel. This is especially the case when these two facts are viewed against the backdrop of contemporary approaches to the interface between memories, traditions, and written history books.

> The juxtaposition of these two basic facts—that the Gospel of John was *written*, and that it was written during a *conflict* over the identity of its protagonist—is, in itself, sufficient to generate a definitive theory about the "purpose" of the Fourth Gospel.

WHY DID JOHN WRITE A GOSPEL?

At first glance, any attempt to offer a "new" perspective on the reasons why John wrote a Gospel must be viewed as a lost cause, for the topic is addressed in detail in every textbook, commentary, and Sunday school curriculum on the Johannine literature. Closer examination, however, reveals that almost all of these studies focus on the word *Why* in the above question, arguing that John's peculiar vision of Jesus was forged in the context of his unique experiences and assuming that he wrote a Gospel because he wanted to preserve this vision for posterity. John wrote a Gospel, it is argued, because he wished to establish the legitimacy of his group's messianic-Jewish beliefs after their excommunication from the synagogue; and/or because he wished to counter the heretical teachings of the proto-quasi-gnostic Antichrists mentioned in the Epistles of John; and/or because he wanted to persuade inquiring Jews to accept Jesus as the Christ; and/or because he wished to portray his community's Jesus tradition as equal or superior to the gospel messages of other Christian communities, especially those churches that aligned themselves with Peter; and so forth. It is generally assumed that a coherent theory on these issues is synonymous with the motivations that led the Fourth Evangelist to write the Gospel of John. In other words, answers to the question "Why did John write a Gospel?" generally begin with a theory about the author's/authors' circumstances and end with an assumption that John wrote in reaction to those circumstances.

To illustrate this point, it will be helpful to briefly review the way this approach plays itself out in an actual study of the Johannine literature. I will take as a specimen Alan Culpepper's popular 1998 textbook, *The Gospel and Letters of John*. Culpepper opens his survey of John's background and purposes by asking, "What Is [the Gospel of] John? Is John best understood as history, theology, or literature?" The question is admittedly difficult to answer, and the options are not mutually exclusive. The novice reader is therefore assured that "as we wrestle to understand [the Gospel of] John and discern the extent to which it is history, we will learn that the evangelist is writing for a particular believing community facing a specific set of historical conditions."[2] Primary among these historical conditions was the Johannine community's recent experience of "conflict and persecution." At least some of the Johannine Christians were Jews who had been excommunicated from their synagogue(s) because of "the emergence of a high Christology [among their ranks], their acceptance of non–Jewish converts [i.e., they allowed Gentiles to become Christians], and differing attitudes regarding the Jewish revolt of A.D. 66–70."[3] Sometime after these traumatic events, the Johannine churches were split by the "Antichrist" schism mentioned in the Johannine Epistles, which led to an internal "struggle to define correct doctrine . . . [and] to define authority and positions of leadership."[4] Culpepper reasonably concludes that the Gospel of John was written in the context of these two major conflicts— external threats from the Jews, internal threats from the Antichrists—in order "to bring the reader into an intimate confrontation with Jesus, to which the reader will [hopefully] respond with faith."[5]

Culpepper's analysis offers an imminently plausible explanation for the unique themes of the Johannine literature, and his study is cited here simply because it summarizes so many major issues so well and so concisely. I have used this book as a required course text more than once. But can his approach adequately explain why John wrote a Gospel?

Most scholars—including those who do not accept Culpepper's specific conclusions—would agree that it can, on the basis of a key assumption about the relationship between the historical circumstances of the Gospels and the writing of the Gospels: "theological developments are often precipitated by social crises." Following this principle, Culpepper suggests that the "Beloved Disciple and his own disciples shaped the emerging Gospel tradition in light of the liturgical, polemical, apologetic, and catechetical needs" of their early Christian community.[6] Some version of this theorem underlies all current theories about the background of the Fourth Gospel, including those that argue that the book was written for a specific Johannine community and those that

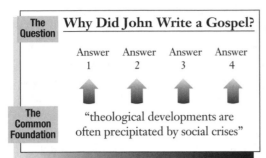

argue that John was writing for all Christians in the church at large. Indeed, the above quote is an excellent summary of biblical scholarship's approach to all Jesus traditions and all Gospels: Mark shaped his Gospel message to meet the "liturgical, polemical, apologetic, and catechetical needs" of his church; Luke to meet the needs of his church; Matthew of his church; Thomas of his; and so on. The inherent usefulness of this principle and the validity of its underlying assumptions will not be addressed here—indeed, both will be assumed for purposes of this study. The situational nature of all rhetoric suggests that texts are inherently dialogic, tailored to meet the needs of specific social contexts and anticipating particular responses within those contexts. Hence it is entirely reasonable to argue that John, like every other early Christian, developed the contours of his thinking and preaching about Jesus in response to some historical situation.

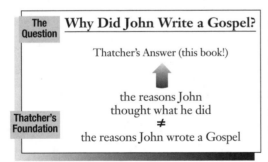

But at the same time, it is important to stress what the argument that "theological developments are often precipitated by social crises" *cannot* explain: it cannot explain why the Gospel of John, or the Gospel of Mark, or the Gospel of Thomas, or any other ancient Gospel, was *written*. In other words, the theorem that the unique theological and literary themes of the Fourth Gospel were developed in the context of specific historical circumstances cannot necessarily be extended to explain why the Gospel of John exists today.

By way of analogy, the conclusions advocated in this book are an expression of my (Tom Thatcher's) personal convictions about the Johannine literature, and about the correct interpretation of several key passages from the Gospel of John and the Johannine Epistles. These convictions were developed through my study of the texts under consideration and my interactions with the arguments of others, and all this research was played out within the arena of my total life experience. Such research and such experiences may therefore be viewed as formative events in the development of my views on the issues I am now discussing. But neither my research, nor my life experiences, nor the views I have developed about the Johannine literature in response to them, can explain why I wrote the book that you are now reading. To answer the question, Why did Tom Thatcher write this book? it would be necessary to further explore why I might feel compelled to commit my views about these or any other issues to writing. But such an inquiry would immediately depart from the aspects of my experience that have led me to believe something about the Gospel of John. Similarly, any inquiry into the reasons why John wrote a book about Jesus must depart from the aspects of John's experience that led him to believe something about Jesus.

Culpepper's analysis, typical of current approaches to the background of the Gospel of John and all other Gospels, focuses on the word *Why* in the question that opened this chapter: *Why* did the Fourth Evangelist write the Gospel of John? The answer is taken to be self-evident: the Gospel of John was written to address specific historical circumstances, its nuances reflecting its author's peculiar theological agenda. Such an approach assumes that writing a Gospel was, for John and other early Christians, a natural response to these circumstances. Yet scholars who adopt this approach generally do not explain *why* this was a natural response. In other words, the connection between John's reaction to his situation and his decision to record that reaction in a book is generally vaguely conceived and/or seen as a secondary issue.

Culpepper's study is again illustrative. Shortly after their initial excommunication, he says, "the [Johannine] Community was persecuted by the Pharisaic authorities from the synagogue ([John] 15:18–16:2). The writing of the [Fourth] Gospel . . . was in part a response to this persecution."[7] Notably, Culpepper does not explain the connection between the terms "writing" and "response" in this statement, and does not attempt to support such a connection in his broader analysis. The second sentence in the quote above may therefore be interpreted in two different ways, depending on whether emphasis is placed on the word "writing" or on the word "response." If emphasis is placed on the word "writing"—"The *writing* of the [Fourth] Gospel . . . was in part a response to this persecution"—Culpepper simply means that the first edition of the Gospel of John was written "*during* this persecution," that the text was produced at a particular moment in history when the author was being persecuted by synagogue authorities. This conclusion is supported by several Johannine theological themes that seem especially relevant to such a historical context. On the other hand, if emphasis is placed on the word "response"—"The writing of the [Fourth] Gospel . . . was in part a *response* to this persecution"—Culpepper is highlighting the point noted above, that the unique theological themes of the Fourth Gospel may be viewed as products of the author's experiences of excommunication from the synagogue and, later, of internal community debates. But however Culpepper's statement is interpreted, it remains an assumption about, rather than an explanation of, why the Gospel of John was *written* as a response to any particular set of circumstances.

Culpepper's arguments, then, are sufficient to explain the origin of many peculiar nuances of John's theology, and of several unique narrative motifs in the Fourth Gospel. Such arguments may also be sufficient to offer a relative date for the composition of the first draft of the text, at least relative to the history of John's Christian community, if not relative to general history. Further, Culpepper's arguments are entirely sufficient to explain why John and/or the Beloved Disciple and/or the followers of either or both of these individuals preached and taught about Jesus the way they did. In fairness, it must be stressed that these are Culpepper's primary concerns, and that the question of the relationship between the development of John's theology and John's motives for writing a Gospel is simply not an issue within the scope of his study.

But even if all of Culpepper's arguments—or any arguments of a similar type—were accepted without debate, they would remain inadequate to explain why any person involved in the Johannine trajectory of early Christianity felt it necessary to preserve their unique vision of Jesus *in writing*. Why did John choose to write a Gospel in response to his difficult situation, rather than, say, preaching a sermon? Or assassinating the leading local Pharisees? Or organizing a mass suicide for all Christians in the area? Or filing a protest with the Roman authorities? Or simply giving in, rejecting Christ, and returning to the Jewish fold? Why, from all these and many other options, did John choose to write a Gospel in response to his situation? In other words, in answering the question, Why did John write a Gospel? Culpepper actually discusses why the Gospel of John exists *as it does today* but does not explain why the Gospel of John *exists*.

Why Did John Write a Gospel?

Three key questions:

 Why did John decide to commit his version of Jesus' story to writing, when most people in his culture couldn't read?

 Why did John think a written text was necessary, when he believed that the Spirit would preserve Jesus' memory?

 How did a written Gospel serve John's purposes?

The present study, by contrast, will focus on the word *write* in the above question: Why did John choose to commit his version of Jesus *to writing*, at a point in time when it was expensive and difficult to do so, and when the vast majority of people in his oral culture could not read? Why, especially, did he choose to do this when he apparently believed that the memory of Jesus could be preserved indefinitely without the support of written texts? Finally and primarily, what rhetorical moves were involved in the very act of writing the Gospel of John—what was, to resurrect Marshall McLuhan, the "message in the medium" of the Fourth Gospel? These and related questions will guide our discussion.

2

Writing as Archive:
The Fourth Gospel
and the Medicine of Memory

In order to explain why John wrote a book about Jesus, it will be necessary to discuss the reasons why anyone anywhere would choose to commit events from the remembered past to writing. Translated into the jargon of biblical studies, this means that we must explain the motives behind the shift from oral Jesus tradition to written Gospels, from "the gospel" to "the Gospels." But before diving into John's thinking and circumstances, it will be helpful first to dip our toe into the ways that biblical scholars have typically understood the dynamic interaction between eyewitness memories of Jesus, early traditions about Jesus, and the written Gospels based on these memories and traditions. The paradigm described below is foundational to the way biblical scholars have approached the question, Why did John (or anyone) write a Gospel?

FROM TRADITION TO GOSPELS:
THE CONSENSUS VIEW

From the early centuries of the church, the existence of the Gospels has been explained through a broad set of assumptions about the relationship between memory, traditions, and written history books, assumptions that undergird a disarmingly simple story of the composition-history of these texts. This paradigm views "memory" as a filing cabinet for past experience, and the act of "remembering" as a process of retrieving and reviewing bits of data "like checked baggage from storage."[1] We observed, felt, or did something before now, and when we review our mental notes about that situation we say we

11

"remember what happened," however inaccurately. This approach to memory is quite ancient. Augustine, for example, describes "the huge repository of the memory" as a vast network of "storage-places" for "the images of things perceived by the senses" and, in the case of ideas and concepts, "the [conceptual] realities themselves."[2] One can pull these images and concepts from the brain for mental mastication much "the same way that cattle can bring food back from the stomach for chewing the cud."[3] As a logical corollary, one technically could not "remember" something from outside the realm of personal experience, something not "perceived by the senses"—it would naturally be impossible to re-collect what we did not collect in the first place. In terms of the present study, Augustine's model of memory can easily be interpreted as a prooftext for the modern view that the memory of Jesus is "a finite activity" limited to his original disciples and associates, those people who could recall objective empirical data from their direct personal encounters with him.[4]

Yet according to the Gospels, even before his death Jesus' followers began to tell stories about him and the Kingdom of God that he proclaimed (see Matt. 10:1–40; Luke 10:1–17; John 1:40–45). Through their proclamation a new kind of "memory" of Jesus emerged. Jesus' associates remembered things they had actually seen him do and heard him say, and his friends and enemies later recalled these personal experiences and described them to their own disciples. The second-generation Christians remembered and preached the information contained in these stories but had no firsthand experience of their contents, giving birth to that elusive entity known as "the Jesus tradition."

The "Jesus tradition" is a critical concept in modern biblical studies, for it represents a fatal rupture between the Gospels as they exist today and the disciples' original memories of Jesus. Whereas the associates of Jesus could make "personal memory claims" because they themselves figured as characters in the image of the past, those who repeated Jesus tradition could make only "cognitive memory claims," secondhand statements about past events that they knew did not involve them.[5] Each time the stories were repeated and new links were added to the chain of tradition, the memories became more cognitive and less personal, more removed from the original experience. Over time, it became impossible for Christians to determine the original source of the information, making the story of Jesus more and more a matter of faith and less and less a question of the remembered past. Eventually, these individual strains of tradition were recorded in writing, producing the various Gospels that exist today (and, before them, any written sources from which their authors may have drawn). Under this model, the written Gospels are viewed as "an adjunct to memory"—essentially an extension of the early Christian tradition, now preserved in a more permanent form—and the evangelists functioned as "remembrancers," people who preserved the past for the benefit of posterity.[6]

This categorical distinction between original memory and written Gospel, separated by the great gulf of tradition, creates the interpretive problem that has necessitated the quests for a historical Jesus. Even eyewitnesses sometimes confuse fact and fantasy, and this tendency is magnified as information is passed from one person to another. It is therefore necessary to subject the Gospels to a variety of tests to determine whether they are "authentic, credible recountings of events."[7] Through careful and critical analysis, one can remove alien elements from the written accounts and reconstruct the original firsthand witness, producing a virtual memory of Jesus for modern investigators. This is a complicated business, yet not substantially different from our attempts to remember the fourth item on the mental list of things we were told to pick up at the grocery store. In terms of analytical method, the question, "Did Jesus really say, 'A prophet has no honor in his hometown'?" is not much different from, "Did she really say, 'Spaghetti sauce'?" for both are variations on the same underlying theme: is my memory correct? Such an inquiry assumes, of course, that "true history . . . is not made but found," that there was once a relatively fixed and accurate recollection of Jesus against which the available sources can be measured to reconstruct the actual past.[8]

In (too) general terms, then, it may be said that biblical scholarship has tended to view the composition-history of the Gospels as a three-act drama—Act I: Memory; Act II: Tradition; Act III: Writing—with two intermissions, the shift from memory to tradition and the shift from tradition to written text. The book

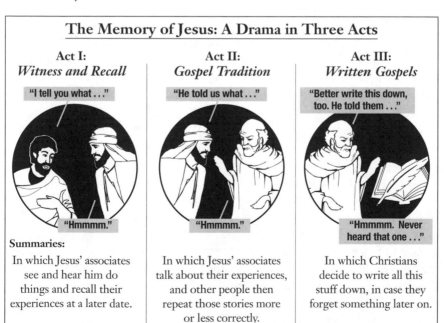

The Memory of Jesus: A Drama in Three Acts

Act I: *Witness and Recall*	Act II: *Gospel Tradition*	Act III: *Written Gospels*
"I tell you what . . ."	"He told us what . . ."	"Better write this down, too. He told them . . ."
"Hmmmm."	"Hmmmm."	"Hmmmm. Never heard that one . . ."

Summaries:

| In which Jesus' associates see and hear him do things and recall their experiences at a later date. | In which Jesus' associates talk about their experiences, and other people then repeat those stories more or less correctly. | In which Christians decide to write all this stuff down, in case they forget something later on. |

you are now reading is concerned with the motives behind the second shift: Why did John choose to commit his particular memory/tradition of Jesus to writing?

Viewed through the consensus paradigm, the answer to this question appears obvious. John wrote a Gospel to preserve memories and/or traditions about Jesus because he knew that important details would eventually be forgotten if they weren't written down. Returning to our earlier discussion, Culpepper's comment, "The writing of the [Fourth] Gospel . . . was in part a response to this persecution," seems to assume this foundational principle. His conclusion may therefore be paraphrased, "John developed his unique theological perspective in response to persecution from the synagogue and conflicts with the Antichrists, and he wrote a Gospel to preserve this perspective for later generations of the church." In the end, the written text of the Gospel of John is simply a more permanent version of John's teaching, a primitive recording of his voice. The Fourth Gospel is thus a record of John's response to his situation, but not an aspect of his response to that situation—not something that he did as a strategy to address the immediate needs of the moment, aside from the general need to help people remember to pick up a loaf of bread.

THE SUPPORTING EVIDENCE

The consensus view of memory, tradition, and written Gospels is compelling, not only because it is disarmingly simple, but also because it enjoys support from a growing body of recent anthropological literature and, further back, from the testimony of the church fathers and perhaps even from the text of the Gospel of John itself. I will survey this supporting evidence briefly in order to outline the type of issues that must be addressed in offering a new answer to the question, Why did John write a Gospel?

Following the seminal work of Milman Parry in the 1920s, a large number of studies have explored the interface between orality and writing in traditional societies. Oral cultures (ancient and modern) adopt and utilize literacy in a variety of ways, depending on the specific group's organization and worldview. In almost every instance, however, it appears that writing develops first and primarily as an aid to memory, a repository of cultural information that might otherwise be forgotten. No less a thinker than Socrates, living at the moment of transition from orality to literacy in ancient Greece, called writing the "medicine of memory" (μνήμης φάρμακον) and noted that documents could be used to supplement recall by "remind[ing] him who knows the matter about which they are written."[9] As time goes by, memories falter, witnesses disappear, traditions are distorted through transmission, and rituals are

The Gospels as "History Remembered"

 Note the view of "memory," and the implied relationship between "memory," "history," and written Gospels, expressed in the following comments by leading Jesus scholar John Dominic Crossan:

- On the Gospels' claim that darkness fell over the land as Jesus hung on the cross:

"To explain those accounts as **'history remembered'** means that **Jesus' companions observed** the darkness, **recorded it in memory, passed it on** in tradition, **and recalled it when writing** their accounts."

—Crossan, *Who Killed Jesus?* 2

- On the Gospels' accounts of Jesus' death:

"To describe the passion story as 100 percent **history remembered** means that **everything happened exactly as narrated** so that it is, as it were, **a court transcript** of the proceedings against Jesus combined with **a journalist's factual description** of the surrounding events."

—Crossan, *Who Killed Jesus?* 4

Key:

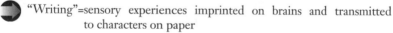 "History"="what happened"

 "Memory"=sensory experiences of what happened imprinted on brains

 "Writing"=sensory experiences imprinted on brains and transmitted to characters on paper

reshaped. Writing, however, is durable, and it is easy to preserve written information, at least easier than to preserve oral traditions and local litanies. For this reason, the earliest written documents in almost every culture are generally functional texts, such as business receipts and tax records, that maintain data critical to social interaction and cohesion.

One can imagine a similar functional necessity at the origins of the Gospels (and their hypothetical literary sources): written texts helped the early Christians remember traditional information about Jesus, thereby preserving his memory against the vicissitudes of amnesia and orality and safeguarding data that were critical to their ongoing community existence. Writing creates a sense of permanence around its contents, and from this it may be deduced that the early Christian communities adopted writing to create permanence, to store information about Jesus that might otherwise be forgotten.

This phenomenon—the use of documents to store and preserve information—may be referred to as the "archive function" of writing. Viewed from the perspective of the archive function, written texts are essentially parallel to memory—or, more specifically, the contents of written texts are essentially synonymous with the contents of memory—and reading these texts is an act of surrogate recall.

The logic of the archive approach to writing was clearly appealing to the early Christian commentators, who were themselves immersed in an oral culture and who imagined that the Gospels were written to permanently preserve what Papias (fl. 130–150 CE), borrowing a Johannine term, called "the living and abiding [μενούση] voice" of the original memory of Jesus (*Eccl. Hist.* 3.39.4). According to Eusebius (fl. 320s CE), Papias claimed that the Gospel of Mark was written to preserve the words of Peter, whose disciples wished to obtain "through writing a memory of the word that had been given to them through [oral] teaching" so that they could archive this information for future reference after the apostle's death (*Eccl. Hist.* 2.15.1). Matthew, being a tax collector and therefore presumably trained in writing, was apparently able to pen his own text, but again for the purpose of preserving his oral message. "Matthew first preached to Hebrews," Eusebius explains, "and when he was about to go on to others he gave in writing the gospel according to himself in his native language [Aramaic], thus through the text leaving his presence to those from whom he was being sent" (*Eccl. Hist.* 3.24.6). The apostle John later realized that some teachings and events from early in Jesus' ministry were not recorded in the Synoptics, and wrote the Fourth Gospel so that these memories would not be permanently lost (*Eccl. Hist.* 3.24.7–8). Eusebius's comments clearly emphasize the archive function of writing: the early Christians wrote Gospels because they wished to preserve the first disciples' actual memories of Christ. While his specific conclusions about the authorship of the canonical Gospels no longer represent the majority view of biblical scholarship, the logic of Eusebius's argument still dominates discussions of these texts as sources for the historical Jesus. Are the Gospels reliable archives of Jesus? Do they preserve accurate memories or not?

From the perspective of the archive function, the Gospel of John is simply a permanent version of the Fourth Evangelist's oral preaching and teaching, and reading that book is not very different from a sermon believers might have heard in one of John's churches. At least two passages in the Fourth Gospel could be taken as evidence that John's first readers also held this view: John 19:31–35 and John 21:20–25. Both passages are critical to any discussion of memory and history in the Fourth Gospel.

John 19:31–35 is one of only two ancient accounts of the *crurifragium* (cf. *Gospel of Peter* 4:1–5). This scene finds Jesus hanging on a cross at Calvary between two criminals. In order to hasten their deaths so that the corpses will not become a source of impurity during the Passover festival, a squad of Roman soldiers comes to break their legs. But Jesus, to their surprise, has already expired, an observation they test by driving a spear into his side. This produces a flow of water and blood, satisfactory evidence of his demise.

The Crurifragium (John 19:31-35)

31Then the Jews, since it was the Day of Preparation, asked Pilate that their legs should be broken and they should be taken away, so that the bodies would not remain on the cross on the Sabbath (for that Sabbath was a great day). 32Then the soldiers came and broke the legs of the first man, and then of the other, who had been crucified with him [Jesus]. 33But when they came to Jesus they did not break his legs because they saw that he had already died. 34Instead, one of the soldiers drove a spear into his side, and immediately water and blood came out. 35And the one who saw this has testified, and his testimony is true, and that one knows that he speaks the truth, so that you also may believe.

As fluid runs from Jesus' mutilated body, the narrator breaks into the story to assure the reader that "the one who saw this has testified, and his testimony is true, and that one knows that he speaks the truth, so that you also may believe" (John 19:35). Based on the immediate antecedent in the context, it appears that "the one who saw this" event is the Beloved Disciple, who is standing near the cross and to whom Jesus has just entrusted his bereaved mother (19:25–27).[10] Because the Fourth Gospel portrays the Beloved Disciple as a close associate of the historical Jesus, verse 35 "is most naturally understood as the writer's [= John's] appeal to the [eyewitness] evidence of someone . . . on whose authority he ventures to relate so remarkable a fact."[11] Some commentators go so far as to suggest that in verse 35 the Beloved Disciple is actually revealing himself as the author of the book. Carson, for example, argues that "here the witness [to Jesus' death] and the [Fourth] Evangelist are one, and the most compelling assumption . . . is that he [the author] is also the beloved disciple."[12]

Whether or not the Beloved Disciple is here portrayed as the author of the Fourth Gospel or only as the source of the author's information, the text clearly associates itself closely with the testimony of an eyewitness, an individual who could recall personal empirical experiences of Jesus. "Someone," John says, "*saw* this happen (ὁ ἑωρακὼς), and that person sometimes pulls the images of what he saw out of his brain and shows them to us as well."[13] Read in this light, John 19:35 seems to claim that the story of Jesus' death as recorded in the Gospel of John is equivalent to an autobiographical recollection of a peculiar circumstance connected with that event. One could therefore cite this passage as evidence that John views at least some portions of his Gospel as a memory archive, a surrogate recall that places readers of the text in a position similar to that of the Beloved Disciple and other associates of the historical Jesus.

A second, and very similar, passage from the Gospel of John seems to confirm this interpretation. John 21:15–23 describes another episode involving the mysterious Beloved Disciple.

John 21:20–24

[20]Peter, turning around, sees the disciple whom Jesus loved following (the one who leaned on his breast at the supper and asked, "Lord, who is the one betraying you?"). [21]Then Peter, seeing this man, says to Jesus, "Lord, what about this man?" [22]Jesus says to him, "Should I wish for him to remain until I come, what is that to you? You follow me." [23]Then this saying went out among the brothers, that that disciple would not die. But Jesus did not say to him that he would not die, but rather, "Should I wish for him to remain until I come, what is that to you?" [24]This is the disciple who testifies about these things and who wrote them, and we know that his testimony is true.

On this occasion, the resurrected Jesus is walking with Peter along the shore of the Sea of Galilee, and at some point they discuss Peter's ultimate fate (John 21:19). Confronted with the sobering prospect of a violent death, Peter asks Jesus about the future of the Beloved Disciple, who is following some distance behind them. Jesus refuses to answer the question directly and instead urges Peter to focus on his own pastoral calling: "If I want him [the Beloved Disciple] to remain [μένειν] until I come, what is that to you?" (v. 22). This oblique reply apparently created confusion at a later point in the life of the church, leading some to believe that "that [Beloved] Disciple would not die" before Christ's second coming (v. 23). John, attempting to squelch this rumor, clarifies that "Jesus did *not* say, 'He [the Beloved Disciple] will not die'; rather, [he said], 'If I want him to *remain until I come*, what is that to you?'" (v. 23). John then reasserts the validity of the Beloved Disciple's witness to Jesus: "This is the disciple who testifies [ὁ μαρτυρῶν] to these things and who wrote [ὁ γράψας] them, and we know that his testimony is true" (v. 24; cf. 19:35).

The significance of John 21:24 to discussions of the authorship of the

Fourth Gospel is universally recognized, and for this reason the verse is surrounded with controversy. As Brown notes, and as my translations above indicate, "the best Greek textual witnesses [= the most reliable ancient manuscripts of the Fourth Gospel] coordinate a present and an aorist participle."[14] Thus, the disciple in question "is testifying" *now*, at the present time, about what he saw; he also "wrote" these things down at some point in the past, or at least "caused them to be written down" by a secretary or by one of his own disciples.[15] What does this statement imply about the relative dates of the Beloved Disciple's death and the authorship of the book? Is he still alive and preaching, or has he passed on and left the book to replace his living presence?

At the most literal level, John 21:24 seems to suggest that the Beloved Disciple was still alive when the Gospel of John was written, and perhaps even that the Beloved Disciple was the author of the book.[16] Brown, however, argues that this reading "do[es] not do justice to the sense of crisis in v. 23," and insists that the overall meaning of the passage is clearer if the Beloved Disciple had already passed on by the time these words were written. In Brown's view, some of the Beloved Disciple's followers were "disturbed by the death of their great master since they expected him not to die" before the second coming of Christ.[17] The causes of such "disturbance" would be obvious, as this event would raise at least two crucial questions. Does the fact of the Beloved Disciple's death threaten the integrity of Jesus' prophetic word about his fate, since he clearly did not "remain until I come"? Or did Jesus actually "come" in some secret way before the Beloved Disciple's death, the same concern that had troubled Paul's churches at Thessalonica several decades earlier (2 Thess. 2:1–2)? John answers both questions at once by assuring his readers that, whatever Jesus meant by this cryptic statement, he did not mean that the Beloved Disciple would never die, nor that this person's life or death would somehow be a special sign of the second coming.[18]

But whether John 21:24 suggests that the Beloved Disciple was alive or dead at the time the book was written, it clearly emphasizes what John must have seen as the greatest potential risk in the spread of rumors about that individual: Does the fact of the Beloved Disciple's (imminent or recent) death mean that we can no longer trust his witness? If the Beloved Disciple was wrong about Jesus' comments about his own personal situation, how could anyone trust the credibility of other aspects of his testimony? John's reinterpretation of Jesus' saying waylays such questions by stressing that the Beloved Disciple's memory of Jesus' words was not incompatible with his own (past or impending) fate. One can therefore still confidently assert that the Beloved Disciple's "testimony is true" and, consequently, can accept the Fourth Gospel as "true" because it is a permanent written record of that testimony.

For purposes of the present study, then, John 21:24 seems to portray the contents of the Fourth Gospel as a persisting repository of the Beloved Disciple's witness and memory. If the Beloved Disciple were very old or, especially, if he had recently died, it is logical to imagine that his own disciples would wish to preserve the words of their departed teacher for future reflection, and that they would claim for the written version of his witness an "ecclesiastical authority" equal to firsthand memories of Jesus.[19] From this perspective, the present tense participle ὁ μαρτυρῶν means that the Beloved Disciple continues to "testify" about Jesus in the form of what has been written, making the Fourth Gospel synonymous with that individual's personal recollections: "This is the one who is still testifying even through what he wrote." Following this logic (but not this translation), Barrett portrays the Gospel of John as an authoritative, ongoing extension of the Beloved Disciple's presence in the community. "He [the Beloved Disciple] was not to survive, a living witness of Christ, till the *parousia* [second coming], but he was, through the written gospel, to constitute himself the permanent guarantor of the church's tradition and of the word of Jesus."[20] By citing this written Gospel and expounding upon it, the Beloved Disciple's followers could continually capitalize on the authority of his memory of Jesus and keep that memory alive for future generations of the church.

The view that the Gospel of John was written in specific historical circumstances to archive and preserve John's unique view of Jesus for posterity thus draws support from three distinct quarters: the testimony of the ancient church fathers, the field research of modern anthropologists and literacy specialists, and two key passages in the Gospel of John itself (John 19:35 and 21:24). The powerful convergence of these spheres of authority would render any alternate explanation of the Fourth Gospel's existence utterly vain, were it not for a single, simple fact: John himself did not subscribe to this theory of memory and writing. Specifically, John does not understand Christian memory to be simple recall of past experience, does not acknowledge any sharp distinction between "memory" and "tradition," and does not believe that written texts would be necessary to preserve the memory of Jesus for posterity.

In order to explore these claims further and to describe John's own perspective on memory and writing, part 2 will analyze in detail several passages from the Johannine literature that explicitly discuss both the nature and preservation of the disciples' memories of Jesus.

PART 2

John's Memory of Jesus

3

The Persistence of John's Memory

As chapter 2 has shown, the consensus view that Gospels were written primarily to archive their respective authors' traditions and/or personal memories of Jesus is persuasive. The church fathers advocated this approach, and further support may be drawn from anthropological research and from the text of the Fourth Gospel itself. Fortunately for modern readers, this evidence is consistent with our own experience of the Gospels as permanent records of early stories about Jesus, and it is easy to project this experience backward and transform it into an author's motive. As such, the Gospels may be treated as sacred filing cabinets, and the Fourth Gospel specifically may be treated as a record of John's unique response to a particularly difficult situation.

But while the Fourth Gospel has clearly preserved the Johannine image of Jesus for almost two millennia, the archive model runs aground on John's own theory of memory and writing. First, John does not understand the memory of Jesus to be simple autobiographical "recall." John does not, in other words, think that his portrait of Jesus is equivalent to the disciples' initial empirical experiences of Jesus, and he does not treat his accounts of those experiences as raw recollections of moments from Jesus' life. Despite John's persistent emphasis on "witness," the Gospel of John does not claim to be based on simple facts about the historical Jesus pulled directly from the brains of his associates. It claims to be based on something much better. Second, regardless of John's theory of the nature of memories, he does not seem to believe that written archives are necessary to preserve them. Instead, the Holy Spirit will operate in the church to preserve the memory of Jesus, making the existence of a written Gospel unnecessary for the persistence of the tradition over time.

John's theory of the nature of memories and the persistence of memory makes it unlikely that he wrote a Gospel primarily to preserve information about Jesus, and this perspective is reflected in the explicit purpose statements in his book.

The remainder of this chapter will attempt to support these claims by analyzing several key passages that reflect John's approach to memories and written Gospels. Chapter 4 will continue this discussion by situating John's perspective within its broader social context.

JOHN ON THE NATURE OF MEMORY

For John, the disciples' "memory" of Jesus is a complex combination of witness, recall, faith, and Scripture. This is perhaps most obvious in John's version of the temple incident, the story of Jesus' disruption of animal vending and currency exchange in the temple courts during a Passover festival (John 2:13–22).

In John's account of this episode, which differs from the Synoptic Gospels drastically in its overall narrative context and slightly in its specific internal details (see Mark 11:1–19; Matt. 21:1–17; Luke 19:29–48), "the Jews" demand a miraculous sign from Jesus to authorize his radical actions (cf. Matt. 21:15–16). Jesus responds by challenging them to "Destroy this temple, and in three days I will raise it" (John 2:19). As is typically the case in the Fourth Gospel, the Jews are astonished by Jesus' apparently flippant attitude, and can only point out the absurdity of his proposition: "This temple has been under construction for forty–six years, and you will raise [ἐγερεῖς] it in three days?!?" One can only imagine that things went downhill from there, but the conclusion of the story is suspended as John interrupts to offer an interpretation of the event. "But he [Jesus] said this about the 'temple' of his body. Then when he was raised [ἠγέρθη] from the dead, his disciples remembered [ἐμνήσθησαν] that he said these things, and they believed the Scripture and the word [= the saying in v. 19] that Jesus spoke" (2:21–22).

From the perspective of narrative criticism, John's explanation of Jesus' comment about the temple is entirely satisfactory, serving as a coherent foreshadowing of John 19:42–20:1. Jesus' dead body will, indeed, lie in the tomb three days—from the day of Preparation (Friday) until the first day of the week (Sunday)—before being "raised." One might argue that the Beloved Disciple, and/or John himself, and/or some other associate of Jesus who was the ultimate source of John's information (or the ultimate source for John's written sources), witnessed both events—Jesus' comment about his temple/body and Jesus' subsequent resurrection after three days—and brought these discrete

The Temple Incident (John 2:13–22)

13The Passover of the Jews was near, and Jesus went up to Jerusalem. 14And in the temple he found people selling oxen and sheep and doves, and the currency-exchangers at their seats. 15And making a whip from cords he drove them all from the temple, along with the sheep and the oxen, and he poured out the coins of the money changers and threw over the currency tables. 16And he said to the dove sellers, "Take these things out of here! Do not make my Father's house a house of business!" 17His disciples remembered that it has been written, "Zeal for your house will consume me." 18Then the Jews answered and said to him, "What sign do you show us that you can do these things?" 19Jesus answered and said to them, "Destroy this temple, and in three days I will raise it." 20The Jews said to him, "This temple has been under construction for forty-six years, and you will raise it in three days?" 21But he said this about the "temple" of his body. 22Then when he was raised from the dead, his disciples remembered that he said this, and they believed the Scripture and the word[s] that Jesus had spoken.

memories together in his mind.[1] At the very least, it seems obvious that John is making such a claim here, whether or not that claim is credible. Both the temple saying and the resurrection would theoretically fall within the finite corpus of the disciples' autobiographical recollections, the question being whether the Fourth Gospel is an accurate record of genuine recollections in this particular instance.

But this line of inquiry would overlook the fact that John does not portray the disciples' memory of the temple incident as a simple act of recall prompted by the analogy between the number of days Jesus lay in the tomb and an earlier remark about his body. For this memory was accompanied by the disciples' "belief" ($\dot{\epsilon}\pi\dot{\iota}\sigma\tau\epsilon\upsilon\sigma\alpha\nu$), a belief not in the veracity of their own recollections but rather in the words that Jesus spoke on that occasion and messianic passages from the Hebrew Bible (John 2:22). John also seems to think that this subsequent recollection/belief displaced the disciples' initial memories of Jesus' actions, or at least altered those initial memories, for the presentation implies that they were unable to comprehend the true meaning of Jesus' words at the time those words were imprinted on their brains.[2] Their first memory was shaped by one understanding, or misunderstanding, of Jesus' actions and comments, and this initial impression was later reconfigured in view of the disciples' subsequent understanding after Jesus' resurrection. In other words, the disciples now "remember" the temple incident in a form radically different from the shape that experience would have taken in their initial

POINT ←→ COUNTERPOINT:
JOHN ON MEMORY, TRADITION, AND GOSPELS

Tonight's Topic:
The Consensus View—John as Archive of Memory

The Consensus View: Pro	*The Consensus View: Con*
• "The church fathers believed that the Gospels were written to preserve eyewitness testimony about Jesus, and those guys were a lot closer to the facts than we are today."	• "John doesn't equate the disciples' 'memory' of Jesus with their recall of empirical experiences they had with Jesus. When John says 'witness,' it's not exactly what we mean by 'eyewitness testimony.'"
• "Anthropologists report that most cultures adopt literacy for the functional necessity of preserving critical information that might otherwise be forgotten."	• "John believes that the Holy Spirit helps you remember what you need to know about Jesus. So why bother to write a book that almost nobody could read, anyway?"
• "John 19:35 and 21:24 clearly indicate that John himself saw the Fourth Gospel as a repository of recollections about Jesus."	• "John 19:35 and 21:24 don't say that the Gospel of John is an archive of info about Jesus. They actually show that the book was written to serve the author's rhetorical purposes."
• "I'm not sure I see the relevance of this discussion if we're trying to answer the question, *Why* did John write a Gospel?	• "Once you figure out why John *wrote* a Gospel, it will become clear *why* John wrote a Gospel."

"So what's your agenda here, anyway? Just tell me that."

"Talk about agendas . . ."

consciousness, so different that it could scarcely be called a "memory" in the conventional sense of the word. Their recollections are not a snapshot image of the past.

The peculiar mode of memory described at John 2:22 surfaces once again in John's story of Jesus' triumphal entry into Jerusalem, an event that immediately precedes the temple incident in the Synoptics but follows it by some ten chapters in the Fourth Gospel (John 12:12–16).

The Triumphal Entry (John 12:12–16)

[12]The next day, the great crowd that had come to the feast, upon hearing, "Jesus is coming into Jerusalem," [13]took the branches from the palm trees and came out to meet him and cried out, "Hosanna! Blessed is he who comes in the name of the Lord, and the King of Israel!" [14]But Jesus, finding a donkey, sat on it, just as it has been written, [15]"Do not fear, daughter of Zion! Behold, your King is coming, seated on the colt of a donkey!" [16]At first, his disciples did not know these things, but when Jesus had been glorified, then they remembered that these things had been written about him and that they did these things to him.

As the disciples observe Jesus' journey on the donkey and listen to the crowds proclaiming him "King of Israel," they are apparently at a loss to comprehend what they see and hear. "At first, his disciples did not know [ἔγνωσαν] these things," John says, "but when Jesus had been glorified, then they remembered [ἐμνήσθησαν] that these things had been written about him and that they did these things to him" (12:16). "At first" (τὸ πρῶτον) here must mean "at the time this happened," and since the disciples later "remembered" the incident, John's assertion that they "did not know these things" must mean that their first memories differed from their later understanding. In other words, the disciples' initial neurological impressions of the event were flawed and were reconfigured and corrected in light of subsequent events.[3]

Here again, then, John portrays his "witness" to Jesus, or at least the disciples' "memory" of Jesus, as a complex cognitive interaction between (a) the disciples' autobiographical recollections of an ambiguous event involving themselves and Jesus, (b) their subsequent awareness of Jesus' destiny, and (c) a messianic reading of a passage from the Hebrew Bible, in this instance Zechariah 9:9 (loosely quoted in v. 15). Notably, John uses the same Greek verb (μνημονεύω) to describe both the disciples' recollection of the actual event and the subsequent interpretation of the Scripture that clarified the experience for them.

While John 2:22 and 12:16 are John's only explicit references to the disciples'

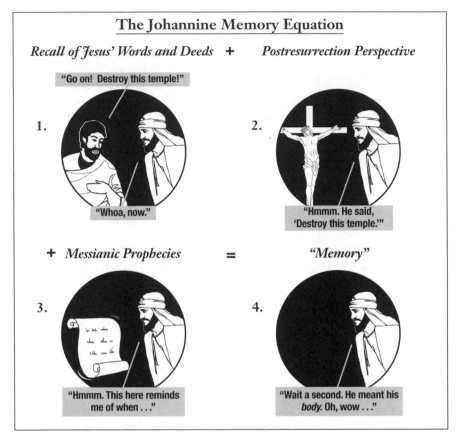

The Johannine Memory Equation

Recall of Jesus' Words and Deeds   **+**   *Postresurrection Perspective*

1. "Go on! Destroy this temple!" / "Whoa, now."

2. "Hmmm. He said, 'Destroy this temple.'"

+ *Messianic Prophecies*   **=**   *"Memory"*

3. "Hmmm. This here reminds me of when . . ."

4. "Wait a second. He meant his *body.* Oh, wow . . ."

"memory" (μνημονεύω) of Jesus, the same perspective is reflected in other passages that do not specifically use this terminology. Notably, both of these verses are blanket statements about all the disciples (not just the Beloved Disciple), a blanket that is spread broader by the fact that John refers obliquely to "the Scripture" at 2:22 but does not, in fact, cite any specific passage of the Hebrew Bible that would make the temple incident a unique situation.[4] Indeed, vague references to "Scripture" are not uncommon in the Fourth Gospel, even when John is citing the Hebrew Bible to prove key theological points (see John 7:38; 17:12; 19:28; 19:36; 20:9). Perhaps in these cases, as in 2:22, John is pointing his reader not to specific passages from the Bible but rather to a mode of recall, a way of remembering ambiguous things that Jesus said and did against the backdrop of the sacred text. Further, like the temple incident and the triumphal entry, almost everything Jesus says and does in the Fourth Gospel is portrayed as intentionally ambiguous, ambiguous not only to his enemies but also to his followers, as they themselves indicate on several occasions (see John 4:33; 6:7, 60; 8:33; 13:22, 36; 14:5, 8, 22; 16:17–18).[5] As such, the recasting of the disciples' memory after Jesus' death must have been thorough, wide enough to cross the vast distance between their previous ignorance and their subsequent comprehension. John's remarks on the temple incident and the triumphal entry could therefore presumably be extended to similar situations in the Fourth Gospel that do not explicitly mention "memory" or "the Scriptures" yet reflect the same perspective as John 2 and 12.

Three passages that do not refer explicitly to the disciples' "memory" of Jesus yet seem to reflect the perspective of John 2:22 and 12:16 will be noted here as examples: John 7:37–39; 12:31–33; and 13:6–11.

Traces of Memory

JOHN 7:37–39

37On the last day, the great day of the feast, Jesus stood and cried out, saying, "Should anyone thirst, let them come to me, and let the one who believes in me drink." 38Just as the Scripture says, "From his belly there will flow rivers of living water." 39But he said this about the Spirit, which those who believe in him were going to receive. For the Spirit was not yet [given], because Jesus was not yet glorified.

JOHN 12:31–33

[Jesus said,] 31"Now this world is under judgment, now the ruler of this world will be cast out. 32And I, should I be lifted up from the earth, will draw all people to myself." 33But he said this to signify the type of death he was about to die.

JOHN 13:6–11

6Then [Jesus] comes to Simon Peter. He [Peter] says to him, "Lord, are you going to wash my feet?" 7Jesus answered and said to him, "Now you do not understand what I am doing, but you will know after these things." 8Peter says to him, "You will never wash my feet!" Jesus answered him, "If I don't wash you, you have no part with me." 9Simon Peter says to him, "Lord, not only my feet, but also my hands and head!" 10Jesus says to him, "The one who has bathed has no need except to wash his feet, but rather he is wholly clean. And you [plural] are clean, but not all of you." 11For he knew the one betraying him; because of this he said, "Not all of you are clean."

Each of these three passages implies that the disciples' memories of Jesus are more than a mechanical recall of the words he spoke on some occasion. Although the account of Jesus' comment about "living water" at John 7:37–39 does not refer explicitly to the disciples' "memory" of that statement, the explanatory note at verse 39 implies that the disciples were later forced to reconfigure their initial recollections of his words, for only after Jesus' "glorification" was it possible to understand that he was alluding to the Spirit. Similarly, when Jesus says at 12:32, "I will draw all people to myself" after being "lifted up," the explanation in verse 33 that he was thus referring to his crucifixion suggests that the disciples reworked their memory of his comment in view of a significance it could have possessed only after his death. Their subsequent recall of the saying was thus somewhat different from, and in John's view better informed than, their first memory of Jesus' words. And when Jesus tells the disciples in the upper room that they do not need a bath because they are already clean and then adds, "But not all of you," the aside in verse 33 clearly reshapes the saying in terms of what the disciples later understood, after Judas had betrayed him.

In these three cases, as with John 2:22 and 12:16, the disciples' memories of Jesus—the initial recollections of those people who witnessed his actions, based on their empirical experiences—must have been altered in light of the deeper understanding to follow. This deeper understanding of the events recounted in these texts was, further, clearly enhanced through conflation with passages from the Hebrew Bible. Jesus himself cites the Scriptures in John 7, again in a vague way; the Johannine theme of Jesus' "lifting up" at 12:32 is drawn explicitly from Numbers 21:8–9, as Jesus himself indicates at John 3:14–15; finally, John understands Judas's treason to be a fulfillment of Psalm 41:9 (see John 13:18). Hence, while John does not explicitly refer to the disciples' "memory" of any of these events, his presentation seems to imply that their original recall was reconfigured to fit their subsequent knowledge of Jesus' identity and destiny and their subsequent understanding of the Bible.

Of course, it is nothing new to say that John's Jesus tradition was a mixture of eyewitness testimony, biblical interpretation, and post-Easter faith, all packaged in distinct theological themes. But it is important here to note that *John himself was completely conscious of this fact.* If a modern scholar were to travel back in time, meet John over coffee at a café in Ephesus, and confront him by saying, "Why, what you call 'witness' is nothing but a hodgepodge of memories, personal beliefs, and Bible verses strung together on a postresurrection thread," John could only reply, "That's exactly what I said it was."

John might further point out that this scholar's discomfort does not arise from anything inherent in the text of the Fourth Gospel, but rather from the fact that John flagrantly blurs the modern distinction between two categories of remembrance, "memory" and "tradition." Traditions, because they are secondary to personal experience and because they mix genuine recollections with subsequent community beliefs, indeed require one to "believe" (John

2:22), to accept the veracity of someone else's testimony about the past. Memories, in the modern scholar's paradigm, do not require those who recall them to "believe," even when we acknowledge that our memory would benefit from clarification and corroboration. But what we generally call "memory" could never be clarified and corroborated by "the Scriptures," faith statements, or anything else totally alien to the initial empirical experience. John, however,

---

John's "Paraclete Sayings"

JOHN 14:15–17	[Jesus said,] [15]"If you love me, you will keep my commandments. [16]And I will ask the Father, and he will give you another paraclete, so that he would be with you forever: [17]the Spirit of Truth, which the world is not able to receive because it does not see nor know it [the Spirit]. But you know it, because it remains with you and will be in you."
JOHN 14:26	[Jesus said,] [26]"But the Paraclete—the Holy Spirit, whom the Father will send in my name—that one will teach you everything and will remind you of everything that I said to you."
JOHN 15:26–27	[Jesus said,] [26]"When the Paraclete comes, whom I will send to you from the Father—the Spirit of Truth, who goes out from the Father—that one will testify about me. [27]And you will testify, because you were with me from the beginning."
JOHN 16:7–11	[Jesus said,] [7]"But I tell you the truth, it will be better for you should I go away. For unless I go away, the Paraclete will not come to you. But should I depart, I will send him to you. [8]And when that one comes, he will convict the world about sin and about righteousness and about judgment—[9]about sin, because they do not believe in me; [10]about righteousness, because I am going to the Father and you will no longer see me; [11]about judgment, because the ruler of this world has been judged."
JOHN 16:12–14	[Jesus said,] [12]"I have yet many more things to say to you, but you are not able to bear them now. [13]But when that one comes, the Spirit of Truth, he will guide you into all truth. For he will not speak from himself, but rather he will say whatever he hears and he will tell you the things to come. [14]That one will glorify me, because he will take from me and tell it to you."

apparently oblivious to this problem, consistently postures his images of Jesus as someone's direct "witness," yet makes these recollections contingent upon a subsequent faith in Jesus' resurrection and the Christian interpretation of the Hebrew Bible. Arthur Dewey has therefore defined the term "witness" in the Johannine literature as "a revision through memory," an image of the past that combines recollections of Jesus with "both the Gospel story [viewed from the perspective of its conclusion] and the resources of Jewish scripture."[6]

JOHN ON THE PERSISTENCE OF MEMORY

It is perhaps not surprising that the memory of Jesus is stamped with faith in the Fourth Gospel, for John portrays memory as a gift of the Holy Spirit to all believers after Jesus' death and glorification (John 7:37–39; 20:22). According to John, Jesus made a number of specific promises to the disciples shortly before his arrest concerning the coming of the Paraclete (παράκλητος), a title for the Holy Spirit that is unique to the Johannine literature and may be variously translated "Helper," "Comforter," "Counselor," or "Advocate."[7]

It is clear from these "Paraclete Sayings," preserved now in the Fourth Gospel's farewell address (John 13–17), that John understood the Holy Spirit to be an extension of Jesus' living presence in the church. At John 14:16–17, Jesus tells the disciples that he will send them "another counselor" (ἄλλον παράκλητον; cf. 1 John 2:1) who will "remain with you and be in you" (unlike Jesus, who is about to leave them; 16:7). While commentators are divided on the relationship between the coming of this Counselor and the reference to Jesus' own "coming" at v. 18,[8] almost all agree that Jesus' subsequent statements indicate that the Spirit will function in the Christian community "as remembrancer and interpreter."[9] The Paraclete will "teach you all things and remind you of all things that I said to you" (John 14:26), "guiding" the disciples "into all truth" by speaking "only what he hears" from Jesus (John 16:13–14). As Schnackenburg suggests, John 16:13–14 should be taken to mean that the Spirit "simply continues Jesus' revelation, not by providing new teachings," but only by enhancing and clarifying his words, thus fulfilling the ministry of "a commemorative deepening of that revelation."[10] Notably, this revelatory memory and the comfort it affords are the only "gifts" that the Johannine Holy Spirit gives to the church, a presentation strikingly different from the pneumatology of Paul (see Rom. 12:6–8; 1 Cor. 12:28–31).

For John, then, the Spirit is the archive of the community's Jesus tradition, preserving both the content of his memory and the correct interpretation of that data. The implications of this doctrine for the present study are evident in 1 John 2:20–27, a passage that clearly indicates that the Johannine Christians did not feel an inherent need for a written Gospel to store information about Jesus.

The Anointing (1 John 2:20–27)

²⁰And you have an anointing from the Holy One, and all of you know. ²¹I have not written to you because you do not know the truth, but because you do know it, and [you know] that every lie is not from the truth. ²²Who is the liar, if not the one who denies that Jesus is the Christ? This is the Antichrist, the one who denies the Father and the Son. ²³Everyone who denies the Son also does not have the Father; the one confessing the Son has the Father also. ²⁴Let what you heard from the beginning remain in you. If what you heard from the beginning remains in you, you will also remain in the Son and in the Father. ²⁵And this is the promise that he promised us, eternal life. ²⁶I have written these things to you about the people who are deceiving you. ²⁷And the anointing that you received from him remains in you, and you have no need for anyone to teach you; but rather, as his anointing teaches you about everything and is true and is not a lie, remain in him, just as it has taught you.

In this controversial passage, the author of 1 John, who seems to be "the Elder" of 2 John and 3 John, urges his readers to guard themselves against the heretical teachings of the "many Antichrists" who have invaded the world and the church (2:18–19). Genuine believers (i.e., those who accept the Elder's interpretation of the situation) will be protected from this blasphemous doctrine by an "anointing [χρῖσμα] from the Holy One," an anointing that seals them in the truth and in fact makes it unnecessary for anyone to teach them what is true (2:20–21, 27). For centuries, debate has raged over the specific identity of the "anointing" in question. Is the Elder referring here to the community's tradition and/or orthodox teaching about Jesus, the doctrine "which you have heard from the beginning" (v. 24) that reveals the falsehood of those who deny that "Jesus is the Christ" (v. 22)—that is, of those people who remember Jesus in a different way? Or is the "anointing" the Holy Spirit, who, as noted above, lives in believers and provides a constant witness to the truth about Jesus?[11]

While reasonable arguments may be offered for either position, from the perspective of the present study both answer the wrong question. Since, in John's view, the content, continuity, and veracity of the orthodox tradition are all guaranteed by the work of the Paraclete, it seems a moot point whether the Elder has the tradition or the Spirit in mind when he refers to the anointing— these two entities are functionally synonymous, because the tradition is the ongoing work of the Spirit. Based on John's view of memory, 1 John 2:20–27 most likely encompasses both realities: the anointing that believers enjoy is the ability to combine memory, faith, and Scripture under the impulse of the Spirit, producing a "true" image of Jesus.

But whether the anointing at 1 John 2 is the Spirit, the tradition, or both, it is important here to note what it is *not*. The anointing is certainly *not* the written text of the Gospel of John, nor a primitive Signs Gospel, nor the Elder's autographed copy of Luke, nor anything else that the audience of 1 John might pick up and read about Jesus. Christians do not "know" these things about Jesus because they have read, or could read, them in a book somewhere, and they do not remember the truth about Jesus because it has been written down. The Elder does not, in other words, refer to some written document as the special, definitive resource for the community's memory, and does not seem to regret his inability to do so. In his view, the genuine witness to Jesus persists adequately in the form of traditional teaching, sustained and verified by the ongoing influence of the Holy Spirit. The Spirit and the tradition are themselves the archive of memory, a repository that both supports and is supported by the community's theological creeds and that refutes the claims of the Antichrists (see 1 John 4:1–6).

MEMORY, AMBIGUITY, GOSPELS

The passages surveyed above highlight three facets of the Johannine theory of memory that are relevant to the question, Why did John write a Gospel? First, John does not reduce recall to a mechanical, neurological process; as a result, his view of memory contrasts sharply with popular modern conceptions of the workings of "memory" and "tradition." As noted in chapter 2, "the classic [modern] theory of memory, after a study of the acquisition of memories, studies their preservation [in the brain] before giving an account of their recall," an approach that assumes that "memories as psychic states subsist in the [individual's] mind in an unconscious state, and that they become conscious again when recollected."[12] In other words, in today's common parlance, "memory" is a comprehensive term for all the sensory and intellectual processes by which the brain receives data, stores data, and later recalls data for review. For John, however, the memory of Jesus is not a simple act of storage and recall, but rather a complex reconfiguration of past experience in light of faith and Scripture.

John's perspective might have led to a thoroughly existential approach to the past, were it not for the second aspect of his theory: memory is a spiritual gift, not a cognitive process. The memory of Jesus is preserved and enriched by the Paraclete, and this doctrine supports a key literary theme in the Fourth Gospel:

misunderstanding. The Johannine Jesus is incomprehensible to everyone who encounters him, no matter how clear his words and actions seem to be, because, for John, memory is not reducible to the sum total of the sensory impressions that the associates of the historical Jesus stored in their brains. While memory begins with witness, it ends with Scripture, Spirit, and faith, so that unaided recall could never truly recreate the total person of Jesus or even individual moments from his life. For this reason, the Jews who watched the historical Jesus drive animal vendors from the temple could never "remember" that incident, even though they witnessed his deeds and words. In fact, because they are unable to receive the Spirit (John 14:17) and therefore do not enjoy the Paraclete's "guidance into all truth," the Jews' most detailed accounts of that event would simply be wrong. This would be the case even if the Jews could compile an infinite list of eyewitnesses, and even if their reconstruction of the scene were historically "accurate" in the modern sense of the word. For John, recall is a work of the Paraclete, memory is a product of faith, orthodoxy is a gift of the Spirit, and "history" is the sum of these values.

The third implication of John's theory of memory is the most significant to the present study: because John views memory as a spiritual community experience rather than a personal mental hard drive, it seems unlikely that he

---

Summary: John's Theory of Memory

JOHN'S THEOREM	IMPLICATION
1. Memory is a complex reconfiguration of past experience in light of faith and Scripture.	blurs the modern distinction between "memory" and "tradition" as analytical categories
2. Recall and the interpretation of the past are guided by the Paraclete, a special anointing given only to true believers.	all true memories of Jesus will be uniform, because there is only one Spirit of Truth: uniform from one generation to the next and in every church everywhere
	people who do not have the Spirit cannot remember Jesus, even if they had personal empirical experiences of him
3. Written texts are not necessary to preserve the memory of Jesus for posterity.	**the Gospel of John was not written to archive information about Jesus for future reference**

would feel compelled to produce a written Gospel primarily in order to archive traditional information about Jesus. So long as the Paraclete continues to work in the church (and John does not seem to foresee a time when such work would cease), pneumatic memory will continue to preserve the community's Jesus tradition for future generations. As such, there would be no need for a book about Jesus to function as an *aide mémoire*, the primary assumption of the archival approach to the Gospels.

Why, then, did John write a Gospel? If John did not see his text as an aid to memory, what did he hope to achieve by producing a book about Jesus? The next chapter will suggest that a definitive answer to this question lies within the media culture in which the Fourth Gospel was produced.

4

Writing as Rhetoric:
The Fourth Gospel in John's
Media Culture

The Johannine theory of memory weighs against the view that the Gospel of John was written primarily as an archive of traditional Jesus material, although it has certainly fulfilled that role for the past nineteen centuries. But if John believed that the Holy Spirit would preserve and enrich the memory of Jesus in the church, why did he bother to write a Gospel?

Viewed from the angle of his own beliefs and social context, John wrote a Gospel not just to preserve Jesus tradition, but rather to capitalize on a second major function of writing. Rosalind Thomas has noted that written texts can play "monumental" or "symbolic" roles, giving them social values "which take us beyond the message merely contained in the written content of the document."[1] From the perspective of authorial intention, this phenomenon may be labeled the "symbolic" or "rhetorical" function of writing, the production of documents in cultures where the written word carries special weight or authority. In these cases, the very existence of a document is of greater social significance than the actual contents of that text, as when we appeal to a sales receipt when negotiating with a store manager, or remind our roommates that "the lease says somewhere" that they have to pay part of the electric bill. For purposes of the present study, while the archive function

> ### Two Reasons to Write Something
>
> **1.** "Archive Function"—Written documents help people remember things they might forget.
>
> **2.** "Rhetorical Function"—Information seems more valuable and more credible when it's put down in writing. If it's worth preserving and distributing, it must be important.

stresses the value of the information contained in a written Gospel, the rhetorical function stresses the symbolic force of the very fact of a Gospel's existence.

Obviously the archive and rhetorical functions of writing are compatible, and most history books are produced under the influence of both concerns. Both functions of writing are, for example, evident in the introduction to the very first Western "history" book, Herodotus's *Histories*.

Herodotus on "Why Write a History Book?"

What Herodotus the Halicarnassian has learnt by inquiry is here set forth: in order so that the memory of the past may not be blotted out from among men by time [ὡς μήτε τὰ γενόμενα ἐξ ἀνθρώπων τῷ χρόνῳ ἐξίτηλα γένηται] and that the great and marvelous deeds done by Greeks and foreigners and especially the reason why they warred against each other may not lack renown [ἀκλεᾶ γένηται].[2]

Herodotus's opening remarks reveal a twofold purpose. First, his book will protect the deeds of the past from the decaying effects of time. Despite the translation in the box above (from the Loeb edition), the word "memory" does not appear in the original. The Greek text simply acknowledges that the "things that were done by men may be undone by time" and claims that a written account will prevent this from happening. Writing is thus an archive for memory, and historical investigation and the writing of history books serves as a preservative interface between the past and the future. But at the same time, Herodotus hopes that his written record will maintain the luster of renown with which these events are endowed in popular memory, preventing great deeds from becoming ἀκλεής, "fameless." Writing preserves information, but in the process it glorifies what it preserves by stamping it as uniquely worthy to be saved from the ravages of passing years, giving the history book a special aura that living memories cannot possess.

The symbolic value of writing and the power of appeal to written texts are especially relevant to the historical context of the Fourth Gospel for two reasons. First, John lived in a culture where the majority of people could not read but where documents played a key role in social organization, political administration, and legal process. When written texts pervade a society's infrastructure but most people in that society do not have direct personal access to them (either because they are illiterate or because they are forbidden to handle them), documents wear a halo of authority that transcends what they actually say. Such was the case in John's world.

Second, within the larger Greco-Roman world, Jews in particular attached special symbolic significance to written texts, and for at least half a century now the majority of Johannine scholars have argued that the Fourth Gospel should be understood against the backdrop of ancient Judaism.[3] John, as a Jew living in the Roman Empire, must have been aware (at least intuitively) that a written Gospel would not only preserve memory but would also pack a greater rhetorical punch than the mere sum of its contents.

WRITING WITHOUT READING: THE POWER OF THE PEN IN THE GRECO-ROMAN WORLD

One might object that physical evidence disproves the first claim above—that John lived in an illiterate culture—for at first glance it seems obvious that most people in the Greco-Roman world must have been able to read. A casual perusal of the Loeb Classical series on the shelves of any library will give the impression that many intellectual Greeks and Romans read, cherished, and preserved books on a wide range of topics. At a more popular level, the much-publicized proliferation of public and private letters in Roman Egypt and Britain suggests a relatively high literacy rate in those regions, and one could argue that similar evidence from other parts of the empire has simply been lost through physical decay due to atmospheric conditions.

But the fact that written texts exist in a given culture is not evidence that most people in that culture could read them, as William V. Harris has demonstrated in his landmark study, *Ancient Literacy*. Rather than focusing on the mass of extant manuscripts and inscriptions, Harris highlights what is *absent* from the ancient evidence: the social structures necessary to produce widespread literacy. Appealing to recent anthropological data, Harris notes that mass literacy is closely linked to other cultural factors. These include a society's level of urbanization (cities foster literacy), its ability to produce and distribute inexpensive reading and writing materials, and the complexity of its economic system (more complex economies require higher levels of documentation and a larger semiliterate workforce).[4] Above all else, mass literacy depends heavily on the existence of an extensive educational system that covers both urban and rural areas and includes all social classes; indeed, subsidized education has been "an essential instrument" in "every single early-modern or modern country which has achieved majority literacy."[5] After examining each of these preconditions for reading, Harris concludes that "the classical world, even at its most advanced, was so lacking in the characteristics which produce extensive literacy that we must suppose that the majority of people were always illiterate." He specifies this "majority" as "above 90%" and even "far above 50%" in the most educated Greek cities.[6]

There is no evidence to suggest that Harris's statistics would not apply to the Diaspora Jews who lived in these Greek cities, and Roman Palestine, possibly John's homeland, would certainly be no exception to the rule—its economy was largely agrarian, its social patterns were largely traditional, its labor force was largely unskilled, and its theological scholarship was driven by oral traditions. For these reasons, Meir Bar-Ilan has suggested that "the total literacy rate in the Land of Israel" during the period of Roman occupation "was probably less than 3%."[7] Even if some Jewish boys did receive enough rudimentary training to pronounce Hebrew words from a section of the Torah, in John's day reading was not an everyday feature of private Jewish life.

Ancient (Il)literacy

"[T]he classical world, even at its most advanced, was so lacking in the characteristics which produce extensive literacy that we must suppose that the majority of people were always illiterate."

—William Harris, *Ancient Literacy*, 13

"[T]he total literacy rate in the Land of Israel [in Roman times] . . . was probably less than 3%."

—Meir Bar–Ilan, "Illiteracy in the Land of Israel in the First Centuries C.E.," 55

If John were a Jew—or at least, a member of a church heavily influenced by the Jewish religious tradition—and if most ancient Jews were illiterate, why would he write a Gospel? While most of them could not read, Greco-Roman Jews clearly recognized the symbolic value of written documents. In fact, Jews may have been more sensitive to the rhetorical power of texts than members of other groups, due to the pervasive presence of the Hebrew Bible in Jewish thought and life. As Goodman notes, "no ancient society was more blatantly dominated by a written text than that of the Jews in the Roman period."[8] Josephus's exaggerated claim that Jews could "repeat [the Laws] all more readily than [their] own name" (*Against Apion* 2.178) is particularly striking if, as Harris and others have suggested, 50–97 percent of all Jews had no direct personal access to the Bible.[9] Sacred writings formed the core of Jewish life in the late Second Temple period, whether or not individual Jews could read them and whether or not specific Jewish customs were actually based on their contents.

The prestige of written revelation was regularly reinforced for first-century Jews through the public reading of the Hebrew Bible in weekly Sabbath celebrations. The earliest material evidence for a Judean synagogue, the Theodotos Inscription (a first-century CE dedication plaque discovered in a Jerusalem well), commemorates the establishment of the building "for the reading of the Torah and studying the commandments."[10] The Gospel of

Luke portrays Jesus' first public message as a synagogue sermon in Nazareth of Galilee based on a reading from Isaiah 61 (Luke 4:17–19). Philo (ca. 20 BCE–50 CE) says that training in the Scriptures was also a primary feature of weekly synagogue meetings in Egypt, and claims that Jews were taught "even from the cradle, by parents and tutors and instructors and by the far higher authority of the sacred laws and also the unwritten customs, to acknowledge [only] one God" (*Embassy to Gaius* 115, 156–157; *Life of Moses* 2.215–216).[11] The Alexandrian Jews' dedication to written revelation is particularly notable in Philo's description of a festival held each year on the island of Pharos, the traditional site of the translation of the Septuagint (the Greek version of the Hebrew Bible). Through this celebration of translation, Philo says, "the laws are shown to be desirable and precious in the eyes of all, ordinary citizens and rulers alike" (*Life of Moses* 2.41–43).[12] Closer to John's geographical context, a similar picture of Diaspora Judaism is offered at Acts 13:15, which shows the apostle Paul preaching a Sabbath sermon in a synagogue in Pisidian Antioch "after the reading from the Law and the Prophets" sometime in the mid-40s CE. Based on the evidence, one can scarcely doubt James's claim that "Moses has been preached in every city and read in the synagogues on every Sabbath from the earliest times" (Acts 15:21).

Of course, one might argue that examples such as this do not apply to the present study, on the grounds that Josephus, Philo, Luke, and many Diaspora Jews in major cities were literate. Jews who could read the Bible and other documents would of course attach special value to those texts. But the Hebrew Scriptures clearly carried great symbolic value for illiterate Jews as well, a fact that may be illustrated by two passages from Josephus's *Jewish War*, both relating to events in Roman Palestine in the time period under consideration here.

Soon after Cumanus took office as procurator of Judea (48 CE), a group of Jewish bandits attacked an imperial slave on the road to Bethhoron. Cumanus retaliated by rounding up the residents of several nearby villages and reprimanding them for harboring brigands. During the mass arrest, a Roman soldier confiscated a copy of the Jewish Scriptures, which he publicly mutilated and burned. "At that," Josephus says, "the Jews were roused as though it were their whole country which had been consumed in the flames." An enraged mob appeared before Cumanus in Caesarea, demanding restitution. Faced with a potential riot, the procurator, in a rare Roman acknowledgment of Jewish sensitivities, paraded the offending soldier before the Jews and had him publicly executed (*War* 2.228–231).[13] In this instance, even after a Roman show of force, the illiterate Jews could not tolerate a direct affront to the Scriptures, because these texts inherently symbolized their core social values and identity.

The second telling incident appears as a minor detail in Josephus's account of Titus's victory parade in Rome after the suppression of the first Jewish revolt. Among the spoils of Palestine were various sacred items from the ruined Jerusalem temple, including the table of showbread and a golden menorah. "After these, and last of all the spoils, was carried a copy of the Jewish Law" (*War* 7.150). In the absence of idols, even a Roman mob understood that the presence of the vanquished Jewish god was most clearly represented by the written word. Written revelation was the symbolic glue that bound literate and illiterate Jews together as a distinct community.

The pervasive influence of the sacred Scriptures disposed ancient Jews to view written texts as the final authority in matters of faith and conduct, and this seems to have enhanced their appreciation for the prestige of secular documents as well. For example, the Zenon Papyri, a private file of records and correspondence kept by a Ptolemaic bureaucrat in Egypt, include Zenon's correspondence with Toubias, a Jewish tax collector in Palestine. Zenon visited Toubias in 259 BCE and returned home with a number of new documents, suggesting that Toubias also maintained a similar file of important personal papers and that the two sometimes shared copies.[14]

While Zenon lived long before John, a contemporary example may be found in the three private archives discovered in the Cave of Letters at Nahal Hever, west of the Dead Sea. All three sets of documents were hidden there in the final year of Bar Kokhba's rebellion against Rome (135 CE), the ancient Jews' last major attempt to achieve independence. One stash included the much-publicized letters from the rebel leader Bar Kokhba himself to two of his leading aides, who apparently preserved them for personal legal protection because the documents "backed up various confiscatory actions."[15] The second stash, the Babatha archive, was stored in a leather purse and included thirty-five documents written sometime between 94 and 132 CE, the same period in which the Gospel of John was most likely written. Babatha, a Jewish woman who fled to the cave to escape the advancing Roman army, preserved a variety of legal papers dealing with "matters of property and with the law suits instituted by her or against her." The fact that Babatha chose to save these documents, carefully arranged by subject matter, underscores her sense of their significance, yet is seems unlikely that she could read all or even most of them—some are in Greek, some Aramaic, some Nabatean.[16] The third cache of documents discovered in the Cave of Letters includes six leases and deeds relating to properties acquired by one Eliezer b. Samuel of Engedi.[17] The preservation of these papers by private individuals in the face of a complete breakdown of the social order indicates the value that ancient Jews attributed to written texts, even when they could not read them.[18]

What social conditions prevail in a culture that is 90 percent illiterate, yet saturated with sacred and secular documents? How would members of such a society respond to written texts, and what value would they attribute to them? Specifically, what force would written Gospels carry for John, a Christian Jew who saw no need to write down memories in order to preserve them? Such questions are difficult to answer if writing is viewed solely as a tool for preserving the content of speech, the medicine of memory. But writing can play other roles, roles that transcend the contents of documents themselves. For this reason, "the character of a religious system can still be fundamentally determined by writing and by a 'literate mentality,' even in situations where very few of the practitioners of that religion are themselves literate."[19] The evidence suggests that a "literate mentality" of this kind prevailed in Second Temple Judaism, even though less than half of John's Jewish contemporaries, and perhaps as few as 10 percent, could read beyond a bare functional minimum. Even illiterate Jews from Palestine, the homeland of John's Beloved Disciple, recognized the role of writing in the systems of political and religious power that dominated their lives. John could not have been ignorant of this fact as he contemplated writing a Gospel.

LUKE THE HISTORIAN, JOHN THE EVANGELIST

As a Jewish person immersed in an oral media culture, John may have felt that a written version of his gospel message would carry more weight in debates over the correct understanding of Jesus. The Fourth Gospel would thus both preserve John's memory of Jesus and, more important, add authority to that memory. John's awareness of the potential rhetorical force of a book about Jesus is evident in two key passages, John 20:30–31 and 21:25. The implications of these verses are underscored when John's approach is compared with that of Luke. While Luke and John each took advantage of both functions of writing, Luke's stated purposes for writing a Gospel emphasize the archive function, while John's stated purposes emphasize the rhetorical function.

Luke on "Why Write a History Book?" (Luke 1:1–4)

[1]Whereas many have taken it to hand to compile an account of the events that have come to fulfillment among us, [2]just as those who were eyewitnesses from the beginning and the servants of the word passed [these things] down to us, [3]it seemed good to me also, having investigated everything carefully from the beginning, to write them in an orderly way for you, Most Excellent Theophilus, [4]so that you may know the certainty of the words you have been taught.

Among the canonical Gospels, only Luke and John directly indicate the reasons for which their respective books were written. The Prologue to Luke–Acts (Luke 1:1–4) acknowledges that other accounts of Jesus' life, based on the testimony of eyewitnesses (αὐτόπται), were already in existence. Luke, however, posturing himself as the first historical Jesus scholar, has carefully reviewed these texts against his own field notes, and is now prepared to preserve in writing a definitive version of Jesus' life and teachings.

The verb κατηχέω ("have been taught," v. 4), whatever its technical nuances, indicates Luke's awareness of the significance of the move from orality to literacy. Theophilus was "taught" these things about Jesus by mouth, but Luke now writes to preserve a more permanent and "orderly" (ἀκριβῶς) record of this information. By reviewing the data contained in this treatise, Theophilus may "know the certainty" (ἐπιγνῷς . . . τὴν ἀσφάλειαν) of what he has heard. The text will become, as it were, a surrogate memory for Theophilus, allowing him to recall information about Jesus from the manuscript in much the same way that the original witnesses could recall information about Jesus from their brains. That Luke does not see a qualitative difference between the content of his history book and the teaching Theophilus has already received orally is evident from the facts that (a) he claims his story has been compiled from information that was passed down by eyewitnesses, presumably the same type of tradition that informed Theophilus's teachers, and (b) he thinks that the contents of his Gospel are essentially synonymous with the contents of the oral catechism, so that reading his book will only affirm Theophilus's prior religious training. The Gospel of Luke will thus complement Theophilus's education mainly by helping him remember what he already knows.

But Luke clearly does not intend to simply archive trivial bits of information about Jesus. While Theophilus has already heard much or most of this information before, Luke assumes that a written Gospel will be more rhetorically effective in communicating his own highly nuanced view of the subject. Theophilus's "certainty" will, then, derive not so much from the content of Luke's book (much of which he must already know) as from the fact of the book's existence and from certain inherent differences between oral teaching and written texts as media of presentation. Luke, then, is clearly aware of the inherent symbolic force of written texts, but weights the balance of his objectives toward the archival function of writing.

In John's case, however, the scale is tipped in the opposite direction. While John is also aware that books can preserve memories, he seems indifferent to this fact and instead emphasizes the symbolic value of written versions of the gospel in support of Christian faith. In a passage universally recognized as the purpose statement of the Fourth Gospel, John admits that his account contains only a small percentage of the available information about Jesus, a fact that

John on "Why Write a History Book?"

JOHN 20:30–31	JOHN 21:24–25
30But then also Jesus did many other signs in the presence of his disciples that are not written in this book. 31But these things have been written so that you may believe that Jesus is the Christ the Son of God, and so that by believing you may have life in his name.	24This is the disciple [the Beloved Disciple] who testifies about these things and who wrote these things, and we know that his testimony is true. 25But there are also many other things that Jesus did; should they each be written down, I do not think the world itself could hold the books that had been written.

would presumably be obvious to his original readers. "Jesus did many other signs in the presence of his disciples," he says, "that are not written in this book" (20:30). The similar remark in the last verse of the book, John 21:25, excuses this selective approach on the basis of space limitations: "there are also many other things that Jesus did; should they each be written down, I do not think the world itself could hold the books that had been written." Further, contra Luke 1, neither of these passages claims that the small amount of material John has chosen to present is necessarily the most valuable data from the church's store of memories. Whether books like this have already been written by other people, what they might contain, and whether their presentation is more or less "careful" than that of the Fourth Gospel—such things are of no concern to John, who simply wants his reader to understand that his book does not even begin to exhaust what he could have said about Jesus, a strange fact indeed if John intended to provide a permanent record of tradition for later reference.

At the same time, however, both passages above indicate that the Fourth Gospel was produced in service of specific rhetorical objectives. "These things have been written so that you would believe that Jesus is the Christ" (John 20:31), clearly a rhetorical purpose for writing, whether one understands the "you" in the second-person verb πιστεύσητε to be a believing or nonbelieving reader. Somehow, then, the fact that John has committed this information to writing will help the reader achieve faith in Jesus. The sidebar at 21:24, whether by the same author or a later editor, indicates an even narrower aim. According to this verse, at least some portion of the Gospel of John is intended to demonstrate that the Beloved Disciple's witness to Jesus is accurate, perhaps over against claims to the contrary. Thus, John alludes to the archival dimension of his Gospel mainly to warn readers that his efforts are not intended to preserve the whole memory of Jesus, and appeals to the prestige of written texts to add authority to his version of the Beloved Disciple's testimony.

Luke and John, then, differ at three key points in their answers to the question, Why write a Gospel? First, Luke, presents his book as an archive of carefully selected Jesus material, culled from eyewitness reports and produced in dialogue with other written accounts. John says that he has written a few things about Jesus to generate faith, faith in Jesus and also (perhaps mainly) in the Beloved Disciple's special witness to Jesus. Second, Luke emphasizes the value of what he has included over against what has been left out. His remarks can be taken to imply that other accounts of Jesus' life are less ἀκριβῶς—less "orderly," "accurate," or "careful"—and therefore necessarily less valid, than his own.[20] The reader therefore has the impression that Luke is serving up the best of the tradition. John, however, makes no such promises. The Fourth Gospel contains whatever information is most likely to produce faith, with an understanding that a great deal more of the same type of thing might have been said. Third, Luke feels that a perusal of his book will place the reader in a position similar to that of the first disciples, a position of recalling objective information. The contents of his written Gospel and the testimony of the eyewitnesses are essentially synonymous; the book and the tradition will therefore function as dual witnesses, allowing Theophilus to "know the certainty" of what he has been taught orally. In John's view, however, Theophilus should already know the truth, because he has "an anointing from the Holy One" and does not need anyone to teach him about Jesus (1 John 2:20, 27). If Eusebius is correct that the Gospels were written to preserve the early Christians' memories of Jesus, Luke's comments make perfect sense, but the Gospel of John has no reason to exist.

PROBLEM TEXTS IN PERSPECTIVE: JOHN 19:35, 21:24

Against this backdrop, John 19:35 and 21:24—the two verses that might be cited to support the idea that the Fourth Gospel was written primarily to preserve John's Jesus tradition for posterity—come into sharper focus.

John 19:35	John 21:24
[35]And the one who saw this has testified, and his testimony is true, and that one knows that he speaks the truth, so that you also may believe.	[24]This is the disciple who testifies about these things and who wrote them, and we know that his testimony is true.

POINT ←→ COUNTERPOINT:
MEMORY, TRADITION, AND GOSPELS

Tonight's Topic:
Luke and John on "How to Write about Jesus"

Luke	*John*
• "Posture your study as the result of careful research about Jesus based on the best written and oral sources."	• "Record a few of your best stories about Jesus."
• "Emphasize the value of what you have included and imply that what was omitted is less relevant. Then insinuate that your version is better than what other people have already said."	• "Tell people upfront that you've left out a ton of the same thing, and let other people cover that stuff if they want to. Like this: 'Hey, I could write five hundred books about Jesus. Who's got the time?'"
• "Try to put your reader in the position of the eyewitnesses, so that she can remember facts about Jesus. She's already heard this stuff before. You just want to make her feel as if she knows the story firsthand, so she'll believe what she's been told."	• "Try to get people to think about Jesus the way that you do. Real Christians don't need books to 'remember' anything about Jesus. They need books to tell them what to believe about Jesus. By which I mean, they need to believe what the Beloved Disciple says, and forget about all that other junk."

"Is the mic off? Are we off? Listen, you know, people just aren't going to take you seriously with that kind of attitude."

"Listen at Thucydides over here. Hey, Clio, not all of us get paid to do this, you know."

While both of these verses insist that the written account supports and is supported by the testimony of the Beloved Disciple, both also clearly indicate that this testimony has not been recorded primarily for purposes of preservation. John is reporting the Beloved Disciple's recollection of the piercing of Jesus' side "so that you also may believe" (19:35). The text seeks, in other words, not only to present the reader with the Beloved Disciple's memory of Jesus, but also to instill in the reader the Beloved Disciple's faith in Christ. This faith will, in turn, lead the reader into her own genuine memory of Jesus under the guidance of the Paraclete, at which point she will no longer need to read the Fourth Gospel. In this sense, the Gospel of John is designed to make itself obsolete. Similarly, while John 21:24 suggests that the Beloved Disciple's witness will live on in the form of "the things that have been written," emphasis is clearly placed on the claim in the latter half of the verse: "We know that his testimony is true." As was noted in chapter 2, John 21:20–24 is driven by a desire to establish the validity of the Beloved Disciple's witness in the face of evidence that might raise doubts about his memory of Jesus. In both of these passages, then, the memory of Jesus is preserved by the text, but it is preserved for the purpose of establishing the validity of John's claims. The symbolic function of writing—the possibility of appealing to written testimony that cannot be easily forgotten or ignored, and the rhetorical force of the very existence of the Fourth Gospel—remains at the forefront of both passages.

It seems likely, then, that John wrote a Gospel primarily to capitalize on the potential symbolic value of writing. As such, the Fourth Gospel is not merely a record of John's response to his situation, but an aspect of John's response to his situation, one of several strategies he adopted to defend his unique witness to Jesus. If this is the case, two questions remain. First, what circumstances made John feel that this response was relevant? If John believed that the Spirit would preserve the memory of Jesus, what aspects of his situation would make a written version of that memory rhetorically effective? Second, what aspects of the shift from orality to literacy, from memory to Gospel, would be especially useful to John's purposes in such a situation? How would a written history book meet John's needs? The first question touches on the historical circumstances in which the Gospel of John was written, while the second raises the broader issue of why anyone would choose to convert living memories into a history book.

The chapters in part 3 will address both issues. The first question above may be approached through an analysis of John's conflict with the Antichrists, a group within the church that refused to accept his version of Jesus as final and authoritative. This conflict was the social context in which the inherent differences between memories and history books become relevant to the present study, differences that would have made a written Gospel especially useful to John in his debates with the Antichrists.

The Fourth Gospel is not merely a record of John's response to his situation, but an aspect of John's response to his situation, a strategy he used to confront the problems that faced him.

PART 3

The Memory Wars:
Bent Frameworks, Countermemories,
AntiChristianity

Even at the moment
that it is evolving,
society returns
to its past.
(Halbwachs, *On Collective Memory*, 86)

5

John's Memory Framework

As discussed earlier, the Johannine literature evidences a highly nuanced understanding of "memory," at least of the disciples' memories of Jesus. Defying today's conventional paradigms, John presents the memory of Jesus as a complex composite of recall, Scripture, and faith, all melted together by the dynamic heat of the Holy Spirit. Consistent with this approach, John does not portray his written version of such memories—familiar to us now as the Fourth Gospel—as a permanent record of the past or an archive of tradition. Instead, his book plays on the symbolic significance of writing, the prestige that written texts add to their contents in oral cultures. In many respects, then, John's approach runs counter to contemporary understandings of the composition history of Gospels, or at least counter to typical answers to the question, Why did they write Gospels?

The remainder of this book will explore the circumstances in which John developed his unique perspective and the aspects of written texts that would make a written version of the gospel especially useful to his purposes. Memories and theories of memory do not develop in a vacuum, and John's approach must have been a response to some aspect(s) of his situation. This chapter will outline those aspects of John's context that might have motivated him to write a Gospel despite his belief that the Paraclete would preserve the memory of Jesus. As such, the discussion below will attempt to reconfigure standard discussions of the background of the Johannine literature to answer the guiding questions of this book.

MY PAST IS YOUR PAST:
THE PUBLIC FRAMEWORKS OF PRIVATE MEMORIES

I turned five years old on March 23, 1972. I was an only child then, and between that date and September 15, the day I started kindergarten, I spent weekdays under the care of my grandmother in her big house on Sherwood Lane in Norwood, Ohio. My mother was working as a secretary at American Laundry Machinery (once the world's largest manufacturer of industrial washers and dryers, it recently went out of business), and she was pregnant with my brother Greg, who was born in early August. That experience nearly killed both of them and left my mother in the hospital for a long while under the immense weight of a rare blood disease (more accurately, a rare dysfunction of the spleen that caused her body to destroy its own blood). For much of that early August of 1972, my tiny newborn sibling—taken three months premature by C-section in an effort to save his life and our mother's—lived with me and my grandparents, while my father divided most of his time between his two jobs and the hospital.

I mention these details, some of which may not be entirely accurate but all of which characterize my thinking about that early period in my life, only to contextualize the following memory, which I believe originated somewhere in that time frame. My grandparents' house was located at the end of a cul-de-sac immediately adjacent to a church, and one wall of the church building was separated from the fence in my grandparents' backyard only by the width of a narrow concrete walkway. One weekday morning I was playing alone outside, digging in the dirt with a spoon and some rusty Tonka trucks while my grandmother was occupied in the house. For some reason my attention was drawn to a narrow stained-glass window set in the nearest wall of the church only a few feet above the ground.

I cannot reconstruct the exact sequence of logic that led to the next scene, but for some reason I went to the fence and began throwing rocks at this window. Of course, I was still too young to have bad feelings toward that or any other church. As is so often the case with children, even my most destructive and violent acts were driven not by malice but rather by a genuine interest in cause-effect sequences. In any case, this activity went on for some time, as my awkward aim and lack of strength made it difficult for me to do any damage. Suddenly, however, my rock located a weak spot in one of the smaller panes, which shattered and collapsed. I stared at the smashed glass for a moment (I believe it was a pale yellow piece of the pattern), looked around carefully, realized that no living thing had witnessed my crime, and then ran into the house and turned on *Sesame Street*.

My memory now shifts suddenly to another episode later that same day (or perhaps the next), in which my grandmother is approaching me in her living room and asking if I had noticed that the church window was broken. No, I had not noticed that, so we went to the yard together to investigate. After surveying the damage, I informed her, with much regret, that I could provide no information about this unfortunate situation. My next image in this sequence must have taken place shortly after the initial incident, in which I can recall seeing, from the perspective of the top of the slide on my grandparents' swing set, the church window temporarily repaired with masking tape. As I think about it, that tape seemed to stay there for a long time. Stained glass must be hard to replace.

My grandmother often teased me about this episode, but I never confessed and she had no witnesses and no ultimate proof. Fortunately, no one thought to take fingerprints from the rock. And the case is now closed forever because my grandmother died while I was writing this book.

This story, and many others that I could tell, might suggest that memory is a private phenomenon. Memories seem especially private when the individual is alone at the moment of the experience. I, and I only, saw the rock break the window of Zion Church, and therefore I alone am capable of recalling and relating that incident. No conflicting testimony has come forward, or ever could come forward, to challenge my claims, nor to correct the details of my recollections. You remain entirely at the mercy of my report.

In a general sense, one might refer to memories of this type as "personal" or "autobiographical," images of the past that claim to capture and freeze moments of individual experience. Such recollections would be different from "historical" memories, memories that claim to represent an objective past that is relevant to all people in a group or society.[1] Under this paradigm, if I refer to the Zion Church rock incident as a "personal memory," I mean that the experience behind that memory is of special significance to me, and on the basis of that significance I claim some special authority over this image of the past. At the same time, I admit that the contents of this personal image of the past may not be particularly relevant to anyone else, so that the incident would not be recorded in, say, a history of Norwood or even in a biography of my own life.

Yet the nature of memories is not necessarily synonymous with the nature of the events to which they refer. Specifically here, the simple fact that I was alone when certain events occurred does not make my memory of those events "personal" or "autobiographical," even if my autobiography might include them. For while the Zion Church rock incident was an utterly private moment, a scene with only one actor, in order to call my story a "personal memory" I must choose to ignore everything around me at the time the event occurred and every resource I must now draw upon to make this image of the past coherent to you. Even though the rock incident was a private experience, my memory of that experience and, especially, my account of that experience above are both thoroughly public. In proper theoretical terms, even my most personal memories are always "social memories."

Personal memories are "social," ultimately public in nature, in at least two respects. Maurice Halbwachs argues that "there must exist in collective mem-

---

The Public Private Past

 All "personal" memories are "social" memories in at least two respects:

- At the moment of the initial experience, we interpret and categorize sensory data according to group language, logic, and norms;

- At the moment of remembrance, we package and present our past experiences in group language to make our past sensible to others.

---

ory two systems of conventions which ordinarily impose themselves on people and even reinforce each other through association, but which can also manifest themselves separately."[2] These two systems of conventions are (1) the system of encoding personal experiences in group language and (2) the system of connecting oneself to a group when we talk about our experiences later on. The system of encoding allows me to name the people, things, and situations I am remembering, and to organize those remembered elements around meaningful themes and narrative structures. The system of connections reflects my ability to think of myself as a member of a group and to link my individual thoughts into larger, more complex systems that reflect my culture's order of values. Memories are thus "social," both in the sense that we have to use group language to think about the past and in the sense that we are always members of some group whenever we think about and/or talk about the past.

Halbwachs's dual emphasis may be smoothly applied to my example above. First, even though I was the sole witness to, and actor in, the Zion Church rock incident, I was nevertheless deeply embedded in a larger society at the moment that incident occurred. As Halbwachs points out, our perception of the nature and significance of our experiences is always influenced by the world around us, so that other members of society are present even in our most private moments. The force of their influence is often enhanced simply by the fact that it is indirect, which is to say that these social influences often touch us most deeply when we are least conscious of them.[3]

Second, whenever I recall a personal experience or an event from general history, I must shape my image of the past so as to make it comprehensible to others. If I want to talk about the past, even my most private moments must become sensible to people who have not had similar experiences, which means that my unique experience must be forced into the common idiom of my culture. Realizing this fact, I have attempted to communicate my rock incident in a way that will be comprehensible and meaningful to you; in a very real sense, then, you were a silent partner with me in the production of this memory. All memories are ultimately social memories, both at the point of reception (the initial experience) and at the point of recall (thinking about and telling the story). This principle—that even my personal memories are doubly social—is so critical to the theoretical orientation of this book that I need to briefly unpack its implications before moving on.

Reception: My Public Private Life

Memories are "social" first in the sense that remembered information is conditioned by social forces even before it is stored in our brains. For example, as a child I participated in a number of intersecting social groups, most notably my family and my local community, and my role and identity as derived from these groups conditioned my initial reception of the sensory data of the Zion Church rock incident.[4] To begin at the most basic level, the physical context of this private experience was entirely a product of social norms and realities: the layout of my grandparents' house and yard; the architecture of American church buildings; the location of such buildings relative to private properties; the use of building materials such as stained glass that can be destroyed by small projectiles. Whatever I might have done on that occasion, my options were limited to actions that could occur within such an arena, but obviously that arena was built by hands other than mine. As such, even my private deeds depended on public realities, and my memory of those deeds was thereby imprinted with the shape of the physical space in which they occurred.

But much more significant to both the rock incident and to my initial memory of that incident were the many social myths and cultural notions that shaped the experience even as it unfolded. My initial empirical impressions of that episode, the raw sensory data, were conditioned from the moment they entered my childish head by cultural ideas about the things little boys might do when alone and ways they could escape getting caught and cultural ideas about "Grandma's house" and about the standards of conduct at such a place. Such notions intersected with archetypal narratives that I, as a young child, could never outline but followed intuitively: narratives in which young boys could be sent out to play in the yard alone, narratives in which it would not be inherently suspicious for a child to suddenly burst into the house and turn on *Sesame Street*, narratives in which grandmothers can mete out only the mildest punishment for flagrant crimes. These narratives became the script for my memory even at the moment of reception, providing the mental categories that would make it possible for me to retain this image of the past while millions of others have been forgotten.

So while the Zion Church rock incident was "private" in the sense that no one else was there when it happened, my memory of that event was, from the very beginning, public. The data stored in my brain were already inscribed with cultural forces that transcended me, forces that in fact served as boundaries both for what it was possible for me to do on that occasion and for the shape of all my subsequent thoughts about those actions.

Recall: My Public Private Memory

Memories are, then, "social" in the sense that each person's private life is embedded in public realities, so that, even at the point of initial perception, our memories are already shaped by social forces. But memories are also social at a deeper level, one much more significant to the present discussion. All my memories, regardless of the nature of the events they describe, become thoroughly—indeed, purely—social at the moment I relate them to others. In other words, while it might be possible to argue that some experiences are truly "private," any account I may I give of those experiences must be inherently public.

The very fact that I can recount the Zion Church rock incident in a sensible form in a book such as this illustrates how thoroughly public all memories must be. Memories are not experiences; rather, they are *texts about experiences*. As such, memories, like all other texts, are dialogic, developed in the context of communication with other people. "If we examine a little more closely how we recollect things, we will surely realize that the greatest number of memories come back to us when our parents, friends, or other persons recall them to us"—which is to say, we normally produce memories in dialogue with other people or to meet the practical needs of some situation that might potentially involve other people.[5] This is obviously true when we swap detailed stories about the past over lunch or in books like this one, but it is also true even in

> "But individual memory is nevertheless a part or an aspect of group memory, since each impression and each fact, even if it apparently concerns a particular person exclusively, leaves a lasting impression only to the extent that one has thought it over—to the extent that it is connected with the thoughts that come to us from the social milieu."
>
> —Halbwachs, *On Collective Memory*, 53

more mundane instances of recall when we are not consciously thinking about other people.

For example, from time to time I go into the garage, get my lawnmower, and cut the grass in my yard. Obviously, the lawnmower is a complex machine, and I must recall certain information in order to operate it: where to put the fuel and oil, what kind of fuel and oil to use, how to clean the excess grass off the blades, how to set the throttle and pull the cord so as to make it start, and so on. I am generally alone when I recall all this information. But at the same time I am aware that someone at some point in the past spoke to me about lawnmowers and taught me how to start them—possibly my father or grandfather, more likely my mother. I've also read portions of operating manuals for lawnmowers from time to time, although I couldn't name any specific document of that genre or when I may have read it. These manuals were, however, written by human beings who sought to impart the knowledge of lawnmowers to me in a culturally relevant way. As such, all the information that I now recall to start the lawnmower was received in dialogue with other people, and that dialogue is still somewhere present in my mind at the moment I call it forth to cut my grass. Further, I remember this information because my yard is adjacent to my neighbor's yard, and I must mow my lawn in order to avoid her criticism for having a messy yard. So I find that even my memory of how to start my lawnmower and the reasons I would need to recall that information are deeply embedded in a variety of social contexts, past and present.

As another example, I recall the requirements for the Cincinnati Christian University Master of Arts degree so that I can advise a student on what courses to take. As we speak about his schedule, he relates a humorous incident from his college days in a way that he hopes will amuse me. Here both of us recall the past in order to relate it to another person, even though our discussion functions at the mechanical level of advising sessions. Similarly, when I am depressed and seeking help from my colleagues in the counseling department, I reduce my most private experiences to terms that will admit of a quick diagnosis, and their prescribed remedies reflect the standardized wisdom of their field. My memories never cease to be personal, because they are always connected to my life experience; but my memories never cease to be social, because my life experiences are always connected to the world around me and are meaningful only in the context of that world. Should I become unable to make these meaningful connections, I would be diagnosed with catatonic schizophrenia and quietly consigned to a mental hospital because, in my culture, disconnected memory is viewed as a form of madness.

Yet the social dimension of memory goes beyond the simple observation that most of our memories are recalled in dialogue (or in anticipation of dialogue) with other people. At a deeper level, memories are "social" in the sense that the pressure of the group's legacy and lifeways is always formative when one of its members attempts to describe something from the past. This is the case, again, simply because all memories are texts, and as texts memories are structured and limited by group language systems.[6] We can recall the past and think about it only through the signs systems available from our culture, signs systems ranging from basic schematic images of objects to complex human languages. "Language" here includes lexicon and grammar, but also the larger motifs, themes, genres, and narrative schemes by which members of a group structure stories.[7] The fact that all members of a group share a common set of signs forces all individuals in the group to construct even the most personal memories in the terms of a common idiom. No matter how dear to us, all the memories of our private past are built from words that may be found on the lips of other people, and follow plot lines drawn from stories we've heard and movies we've seen.

Halbwachs refers to the totality of these social influences on memory—including the individual's network of relationships, the norms that operate within these groups, and the language and themes that members of these groups use to communicate with one another—as the "frameworks" of memory. Every act of recall is shaped by these frameworks, even when the individual is not conscious of their influence.

It appears, then, that my very personal memory of the Zion Church rock incident of August 1972 is not quite so "private" as I once thought. Of course, now that I've told the story in a book like this, it's public information in the sense that anyone can read about it. But it was already public information, even when I was the only person who knew the details. My initial impressions of the incident were framed by the social setting of my life at that time, and my recollection of that event is entirely dependent on the memory frameworks available to me from the groups in which I participate today. The fact that I have related this private experience in the English language, in the genre of "illustrations for academic books," against an unwritten code of what it is appropriate to reveal about oneself in a venue such as this, against broader cultural stereotypes about little boys and things they do at Grandma's house, against a set of expectations about what I should or must do both as a member of my family and as a member of the academic community—all these facts reveal the extent to which this memory is a dialogue that belongs to you just as much as it belongs to me. As we speak about the past, I stand with you and view my childish self and actions in the third person, across the great gulf of a life now infinitely distant from the life of that solitary boy who carelessly threw rocks at a church window in the summer of 1972.

THE JOHANNINE MEMORY FRAMEWORK

Once we acknowledge that recall is a thoroughly social phenomenon, it becomes clear that discussions of "the background of the Johannine literature" are actually plat maps of the Johannine framework of memory, the intersecting social contexts in which John shaped his image of the past. In textbooks for New Testament introduction courses these memory frameworks appear in the guise of topics relating to John's historical circumstances ("provenance," "place," "date"), the nature and situation of his churches ("John's audience," "the Johannine community"), and his relationships with members of other groups ("the world," "the Jews"). Explorations of these topics essentially map out the social matrix in which John formed his memories of Jesus and eventually converted that memory to a written Gospel.

A thorough investigation of the frameworks of John's memory is beyond the scope of this study, but two factors seem especially significant to the development of John's views of memory and writing: John's relationship to people outside the church, and the emergence within John's churches of the "Antichrists," a group specifically opposed to John's image of Jesus. The Antichrists—or, at least, the way of thinking about Jesus that they promoted (and by "way" I mean not just the content of their thinking, but how they actually went about constructing images of Christ)—represent the challenge that motivated John to commit his memory of Jesus to writing. The Johannine churches, with the baggage of their experiences, were the arena in which that struggle was played out.

The first readers of the Fourth Gospel seem to have been members of a group of house churches with local independent leaders, several of whom are mentioned in the Johannine Epistles (see 3 John 1, 9–10; 2 John 1?). At least some of these leaders looked to an individual who called himself "the Elder" as their spiritual patron (2 John 1; 3 John 1). The Elder's system of administration was similar to Paul's: he managed his network through a group of itinerant disciples, including Demetrius and "the brethren" mentioned at 3 John 5–6, 12. For purposes of the present study, it may be assumed that John was a member the Elder's network (if not the same person) and that their views about Jesus were in substantial agreement. From ancient times, scholars have situated these Johannine churches in western Asia Minor, with John's headquarters in Ephesus.[8] Regardless of the specific geographical location, it is everywhere plain that life had been very difficult for the Johannine Christians, who faced both external and internal threats to their faith and unity.

The Johannine literature is characterized by a dualistic approach to reality, an approach that has populated the Fourth Gospel and the Johannine Epistles with archetypal heroes and villains. The heroes—those on the side of God, Light, and, of course, John—are the "children of God," people who have been "born again" and redeemed from the clutches of darkness through their faith in Christ (John 1:12; 3:3–5; 1 John 4:7; 5:1–5). Logically, the villains should be billed as "children of the devil," but the Elder and John instead refer categorically to those who oppose Jesus as "the world." God loves the world (John 3:16), but his love is unrequited, for the world hates Jesus and rejoices over his death (John 7:7; 16:20). Believers, unfortunately, catch the ricochet of this conflict, for the world hates the disciples just as it hated Jesus (John 15:18–19; 17:14–16). Jesus, however, conquered the world (although John does not say exactly how he did this; see John 16:33), and Christians will also conquer if they hold fast their faith in him (1 John 5:4–5).

It should be stressed that the terms "love" and "hate" as used above are drawn directly from the text of the Johannine literature, and reflect the intensity of John's feelings and the absence of a gray zone in his thought. In John's view, every person in "the world"—everyone who does not share his belief in Christ—operates in willful rejection of, and open hostility toward, all that Jesus represents. While it is impossible to know for certain why John felt this way about "the world," most scholars conclude that he must have experienced persecution of some kind from nonbelievers, leading him to think of all people who did not accept his gospel as enemies of Christ and the church. It may therefore be argued that a sense of widespread opposition and hostility from outsiders was a core element of the Johannine memory framework, a fact that explains many unique aspects of John's presentation of Jesus, the disciples, and nonbelievers.

The key to this sense of suffering, and to the dark lines John draws because of this perception, may lie in another dualistic label that appears frequently in the Fourth Gospel, "the Jews." Regardless of the specific group to which this label refers, it must be stressed that John does not use the word "Jews" in the way that term would be used today. Specifically, John's "Jews" are not a distinct group of people with a common ethnic or religious background. For example, at John 5:15, the lame man whom Jesus heals at Bethesda "told the Jews that it was Jesus who made him well," despite the fact that the lame man is himself Jewish. Similarly, at 13:33 Jesus says to his disciples, "As I told the Jews, so I tell you now: Where I am going, you cannot come." This statement seems to suggest that the disciples are not "Jews," although they are obviously Jewish by both race and religion. Following this logic, John sees no inconsistency in the fact that Jesus several times reminds "the Jews" about things written in "your law" (John 8:17; 10:34) even though Jesus is Jewish and, as God Incarnate (1:1–18), presumably the author of the Hebrew Scriptures in some sense.

Whatever their specific identity, it is clear that John sees "the Jews" as a subset of "the world." Hence, while the disciples are "born of God" (John 1:12–13; 1 John 3:1; 4:7), "the Jews" are children of the devil, who is a "liar" and "murderer" (John 8:44). Not surprisingly, "the Jews" constantly do the devil's work of harassing those who accept Jesus (John 9:22; 19:38–39). It is therefore reasonable to conclude that John uses the word "Jews" to refer

> The AntiChrists presented the challenge that motivated John to commit his memory of Jesus to writing; the Johannine churches, with the baggage of all their experiences, were the field of contest.

to Jewish people who reject Jesus and, more specifically, who might abuse Johannine Christians. Whether such abuse had actually occurred at the time the Fourth Gospel was written, and what forms that abuse would have taken, are difficult to determine. Following J. Louis Martyn's groundbreaking *History and Theology in the Fourth Gospel* (1968; 1979), many scholars have argued that some Jewish Johannine Christians had been excommunicated by the local synagogue authorities. Jesus warns his disciples that they will be outcasts from the synagogue at John 16:1–4 (see 9:22), and it is reasonable to assume that this event had already happened by the time the Fourth Gospel and the epistles were written. Removed from the relative safety of the Jewish community, the Johannine Christians would be left to face a hostile and unbelieving world on their own, without the rights and privileges granted to Jews in the Roman Empire. It is difficult to tell, however, whether John 9 and 16 are speaking about events that have already occurred, or about things that John thinks will happen to Jewish Christians if they attempt to fully participate in synagogue life. In either case, one may argue that a feeling of opposition from non-Christian Jews was a key component of John's memory framework, and that John's experiences with and/or attitudes toward the Jewish authorities significantly shaped his memory of Jesus' relationship with nonbelieving Jews.

Alongside these dangers from the world, and probably after their excommunication from the synagogue, the Johannine churches were threatened with internal divisions over an emerging group whom the Elder (the author of the Johannine Epistles) calls "Antichrists." The Antichrists were clearly well known to the original readers of the Johannine literature, and perhaps for this reason the Elder and John provide almost no specific information about them. The Antichrists are first mentioned at 1 John 2:18, where the Elder warns his "children" that "just as you have heard that Antichrist is coming, even now many antichrists have come." Despite its popularity in modern religious jargon, the label "antichrist" was apparently unique in John's day. As David Rensberger notes, "the notion of *antichrist* . . . is not found at all in Jewish literature, nor in Christian literature except where it is dependent on 1 and 2 John."[9] Of course, the Hebrew Bible and other ancient Jewish writings sometimes anticipate the appearance of eschatological figures who epitomize evil, but these characters are always pictured in opposition to God, not the Messiah (i.e., "anti-God," not "antichrist").[10] The term "antichrist" therefore seems to reflect a uniquely Johannine theological theme, one that unfortunately cannot be fully reconstructed on the basis of the slim evidence now available.

Whatever the Elder thought "the Antichrist" was, and whether he coined the term or borrowed it from somewhere else, his use of this word to label his opponents highlights his primary point of contention with them. The Greek prefix ἀντι- technically means "in place of," and the Elder's opponents are "antichrists" in the sense that they promote a different version of the gospel, a different memory of Jesus "in place of" the Elder's understanding. In other words, the Antichrists did not necessarily oppose the concept of a messiah, but they did disagree with orthodox Johannine teaching about Jesus and his divine identity. Despite these disagreements, they presumably thought of themselves as Christians. The Elder's admission that "they went out from us" (1 John 2:19) indicates that even he considered them Christian at one time, and Diotrephes, the leader of a Johannine church, apparently prefers their doctrine (3 John 9–10). The Antichrists were probably former disciples of the Elder, Christian teachers who departed from his theological position. Because they were known to, and accepted by, members of Johannine churches, it was easy for them to secure a following. For these reasons, the term ἀντίχριστοι is best translated "Anti*Christs*," the capital "C" indicating that they specifically opposed the traditional Johannine view that Jesus was the Christ come in flesh (1 John 2:22; 4:3–4).

Some readers may be surprised to see that I have mentioned the AntiChrists as an aspect of John's memory framework. Most Johannine scholars—actually, almost all of them, it seems—assume that the Gospel of John was written before the Johannine Epistles, and also before the emergence of the AntiChrist crisis. For this reason, studies of the background of the Fourth Gospel have focused primarily on John's negative views toward "the world" and "the Jews," while leaving the AntiChrists for commentaries on the Johannine Epistles. I should confess at the outset that I do not find this model persuasive, and also explain why I do not think that this issue would substantially impact the main thrust of my argument either way (i.e., why I think my points would be valid even if the Fourth Gospel came before the epistles).

In the first place, it is my personal belief that the Johannine Epistles were written before the Fourth Gospel was written. There are a number of reasons for this conclusion, but most of them fall outside the scope of this book. The short version would be that, in my view, the way that the Elder makes his case

The "Antichrist Sayings"

1 JOHN 2:18–26

[18]Children, it is the last hour, and just as you heard that "Antichrist is coming," even now many AntiChrists have come—thus we know that it is the last hour. [19]They went out from us, but they were not "from us" [="one of us"]. For if they were "from us," they would have remained with us. But [they went out] so that it should be manifest that they are not all "from us." [20]And you have an anointing from the Holy One, and all of you know. [21]I have not written to you because you do not know the truth, but because you do know it and because you know that every lie is not from the truth. [22]Who is the liar, if not the one who denies that Jesus is the Christ? This is the Antichrist, the one who denies the Father and the Son. [23]Everyone who denies the Son does not have the Father, either; the one who confesses the Son also has the Father. [24]What you heard from the beginning, let that remain in you. For if what you heard from the beginning remains in you, you will also remain in the Son and in the Father. [25]And this is the promise that He made to us: eternal life. [26]I have written these things to you about those who are deceiving you.

1 JOHN 4:1–6

[1]Beloved, do not believe every spirit, but rather test the spirits as to whether they are from God, because many false prophets have gone out into the world. [2]This is how you know the Spirit of God: every spirit that confesses, "Jesus Christ has come in the flesh," is from God; [3]and every spirit that does not confess Jesus is not from God—this is the spirit of the Antichrist. You have heard that it is coming, and now it is in the world already. [4]You are from God, children, and you have conquered them, because the One who is in you is greater than the one who is in the world. [5]They are from the world, and because of this they speak from the world and the world listens to them. [6]We are from God—the one who knows God listens to us; the one who is not from God does not listen to us. This is how we know [the difference between] the Spirit of Truth and the spirit of deceit.

for Christ would more logically precede the way that John makes his case for Christ. Specifically, the Elder seems content to stake his claims on a general appeal to the reader's loyalty and to community creeds that he assumes that everyone knows and holds dear. This strategy apparently failed, and John, as

1 JOHN 5:5–10

⁵Who is the one who conquers the world, if not the person who believes that Jesus is the Son of God? ⁶This is the one who comes through water and blood: Jesus Christ—not in the water only, but rather in the water and in the blood. And the Spirit is the witness, because the Spirit is the truth. ⁷For there are three who testify—⁸the Spirit and the water and the blood—and the three are in agreement. ⁹If we accept the testimony of human beings, the testimony of God is greater—because this is the testimony that God testified about his Son [i.e., that the Son came in water and blood]. ¹⁰The one who believes in the Son of God has the testimony in himself [about the Son coming in water and blood]; the one who does not believe in [the testimony of] God [about the water and blood] makes him out to be a liar, because she has not believed in the testimony that God testified about his Son.

2 JOHN 7–11

⁷Because many deceivers have gone out into the world, those who do not confess, "Jesus is the Christ coming in flesh"—this is the deceiver and the Antichrist. ⁸Watch yourselves, so that you do not destroy what we worked for rather than receiving a full reward. ⁹Everyone who runs ahead and does not remain in the teaching of Christ does not have God; the one who remains in the teaching has the Father and the Son. ¹⁰If anyone comes to you and does not bring this teaching [that Jesus is the Christ in flesh], do not receive him into the house and do not say, "Welcome," to him. ¹¹For the one who says, "Welcome," to him shares in his wicked work.

3 JOHN 9–11

⁹I wrote something to the church, but Diotrephes, the one who loves to be first among them, does not receive us [i.e., will not let people see my letter]. ¹⁰Because of this, when I come I will remind [the believers] of his deeds that he does, slandering us with wicked words. And not being content with this, he also does not receive the brothers [i.e., will not let the Elder's liaisons come to his church], and he forbids those who want [to talk to the Elder's liaisons] and throws them out of the church. ¹¹Beloved, do not imitate the evil, but rather the good. The one who does good is from God; the one who does evil has not seen God.

The Shape of John's Memory: A Love-Hate Triangle

John's memory of Jesus was significantly shaped by three major frameworks:

1. A general feeling of hostility from all nonbelievers, people of "the world"

2. A specific feeling of hostility and persecution from Jews who did not agree with him about Jesus

3. A need to counter and oppose the claims of the AntiChrists (or at least, of their way of remembering Jesus)

I will proceed to argue, wrote a Gospel to make up for the deficiencies of this approach. For our present purposes, however, please note that I will show no fear in assuming that at the time that the Fourth Gospel was written the AntiChrists were a real and coherent threat, a group that John specifically sought to refute by writing his book about Jesus.

But even if you do not agree with me that the epistles were written before the Fourth Gospel, and/or if you feel that the AntiChrists were not yet a distinct movement at the time that John wrote his book about Jesus, I do not think that our differences on this issue would necessarily invalidate my argument here. As will be seen, I am not so much interested in the AntiChrists' specific beliefs about Christ as in the way that they went about constructing their beliefs about Christ, the approach to the issues that they adopted. I am concerned, in other words, not with the *content* of the AntiChristian memory of Jesus, but rather with the *means* by which the AntiChrists created their memories of Jesus, what we might call the "generative grammar" of their Christology. In my view, the approach that the AntiChrists advocated would have been a problem for John, the Elder, and others in their camp long before the AntiChrists actually left the Johannine churches, and I see John reacting against this approach in general more than against this group of people in particular.

In support of this claim, I would note that John Painter—who firmly believes that the Fourth Gospel preceded the epistles—has argued quite some time ago now that John 17 was written in anticipation of the challenge that the AntiChrists would later present. According to Painter, Jesus' prayer for unity at John 17 was written in reaction to an influx of Gentile believers who "no longer had a direct link with the Jesus tradition" and instead tended "to think of the revelation of new truth through the Spirit of Truth." These charismatic Gentiles, Painter argues, began "to interpret the activity of the Spirit in terms of 'ecstatic utterance,' " leading them to develop and promote innovative ideas that threatened to divide John's congregations. In Painter's view, John's warnings about this problem in his Gospel were ineffective, and the schism gradually grew into the AntiChrist situation reflected in 1 John.[11] I think it reasonable to argue, then, that the Fourth Gospel interacts with the AntiChrists' approach to Jesus tradition, either by anticipating that approach at the early stages of the conflict (à la Painter) or by attacking that approach after a formal split had occurred. As noted, I personally lean toward the latter option, but would again stress that my discussion focuses on a spectrum of options for thinking about Jesus that existed within the Johannine community around the time that the Fourth Gospel was written. Regardless of the precise chronological relationship, John's Gospel would fall on one end of this spectrum, the AntiChrists' preaching would fall on the other, and the differences between these perspectives will provide crucial clues to the question, Why did John write a Gospel?

The Johannine memory framework, then, was characterized by conflict and controversy. John's memory of Jesus was shaped in dialogue with Christians who felt persecuted and who faced significant doctrinal divisions. Within that framework, he sought to construct a vision of the past that would unify his churches on the basis of a common image of Jesus. But in doing so, he encountered an obstacle that made a written Gospel especially useful to his purposes. That obstacle was his own theory of charismatic memory and its inherent limitations when applied to the management and use of Jesus tradition. The specific contours of this problem are the subject of the next several chapters.

6

One Way Back to Two Places:
AntiChristian Countermemory

John's memory of Jesus was driven by the Spirit and shaped to meet the needs of churches alienated from the world and threatened by the AntiChrists (or, again, threatened at least by the kind of thinking that would later evolve into AntiChristianity). This social context may be thought of as the framework of Johannine memory, the mold in which John's image of Jesus was constantly shaped and reshaped. The Fourth Gospel's unique presentation of Jesus, the disciples, and their antagonists reveals the extent to which John's memory framework differed from those that guided Matthew, Mark, Luke, and other early Christian authors.

In many respects, John's charismatic approach to memory would be a powerful tool for persuading suffering Christians to maintain their faith against challenges from outsiders. For John, genuine memory recalls events from Jesus' life but reconfigures these recollections through Scripture and Christian faith under the Spirit's guidance. It is therefore impossible for faithless people who do not possess the Spirit to accurately interpret Jesus' words and actions. Appealing to this rule, the Johannine Jesus can confidently assert that his contemporaries do not understand him simply because they, lacking faith, are unable to hear what he says (John 8:43–45). In the broader context of the Fourth Gospel, this means that "the Jews" of Jesus' day could not, and could not possibly, grasp the true significance of what he was doing, because they refused to accept that he "came from the Father" and was on his way back to heaven (16:28–29).

John could easily extend Jesus' principle to demonstrate that "the world" and "the Jews" of his own time also knew nothing about Christ. No one outside the

John's Memory Bubble: Strengths and Weaknesses

Strength

People who don't have the Spirit can't challenge what John says about Jesus; "the world" and "the Jews" can't oppose him because they can't remember Jesus correctly.

"So you want to tell me that this bastard from Nazareth was, what, a god or something? He wasn't even a good Jew, for Pete's sake. Look what he said about the temple. So if he's God, why is your life such a stinking mess? Explain that to me."

a man of the "the world"

"Ignore him. He's just some godless fool. You hear that over there? I said a *'godless fool.'*"

??????

John

a confused Christian

Weakness

Anyone who does have the Spirit can challenge what John says about Jesus; the AntiChrists can claim that the Spirit is guiding their memory of Jesus and their interpretation of that memory, just like John's.

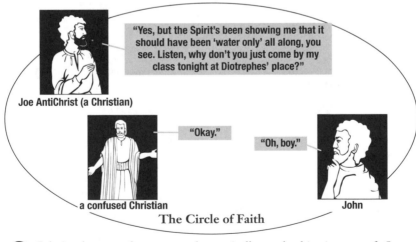

Joe AntiChrist (a Christian)

"Yes, but the Spirit's been showing me that it should have been 'water only' all along, you see. Listen, why don't you just come by my class tonight at Diotrephes' place?"

"Okay."

a confused Christian

"Oh, boy."

John

The Circle of Faith

John's theory of memory hermetically seals his image of Jesus: Nothing outside can be pushed in—BUT—nothing inside can be pushed out, either.

church—no person who "walks in darkness" and refuses to confess that Jesus is the Christ come in flesh (1 John 1:6; 2:23)—could seriously challenge John's claims about Jesus, because such people do not possess the Spirit and are therefore categorically unable to understand what Jesus said and did. Put another way, John's charismatic outlook insulated his memory of Christ from outside forces to such an extent that it would be impossible for any nonbeliever to seriously threaten the authority of his claims about Jesus. Since the world does not know Jesus (1 John 3:1), there's not much point for a Christian to listen to anything that worldly people have to say about him.

But while John's theory of memory made it impossible for outsiders to threaten his claims, it left him especially vulnerable to internal challenges. In a Christian context where the memory of Jesus was viewed as an operation of the Spirit, anyone who claimed to possess the Spirit could also claim that her memory of Jesus was authoritative, even in instances where that memory differed substantially from John's memory. As Rensberger notes, if "opponents claimed that their ideas were inspired by the Spirit . . . they would not hesitate to offer *new* concepts built up from their basic interpretation of the tradition," "new" in the sense that these concepts might not necessarily coincide with previous orthodox teaching.[1] Specifically, it seems that the AntiChrists, as an internal threat to John's authority, were able to challenge his position by creating a charismatic "countermemory," an alternate way of thinking about who Jesus was and what he did.

JOHN VS. THE ANTICHRISTS: A THEOLOGICAL DEBATE?

Traditionally, the conflict between John and the AntiChrists has been postured as the first of the many great theological debates that would eventually underlie the rulings of the church councils. Following this model, one may utilize traditional christological categories to picture John encamped on one hill and the AntiChrists on another. In the valley below lay their field of conflict: the incarnation, specifically the relationship between the human and divine aspects of Jesus' nature. John insists that the divine Christ was fully incarnate in the human Jesus (John 1:14), but the AntiChrists hold that the human Jesus and the divine Christ should be kept separate, with primary emphasis being placed on his deity (see 1 John 5:6–8). The AntiChrists would therefore dispute John's claims that "[the historical] Jesus is the [divine] Christ" and that "Jesus [is the] Christ come in flesh" (see 1 John 2:22; 4:3; 2 John 7). In modern terms, one might say that the AntiChrists' Christology was "too high," an unbalanced equation in which Jesus' humanity was swallowed up by his divinity.

A theological approach to the John vs. AntiChrists conflict carries with it certain assumptions about the Johannine memory of Jesus, assumptions that need not be articulated in most studies but are critical to the present inquiry. Specifically, the theological approach assumes that John and the AntiChrists must have developed their thinking under the impetus of different memory frameworks, and that they probably also utilized different memory databases to construct their images of Jesus. This conclusion would be seen as self-evident in view of the fact that their respective conclusions about Christ were so different; such radically different Christologies could not have grown from the same root. In other words, since John and the AntiChrists seem to fall into very different theological camps, their ideas must have come from very different places.

As noted in the last chapter, John's database and his memory frameworks, at least the parts of them that are relevant to the theological approach, may be reconstructed from the Fourth Gospel and the Johannine Epistles. But since the AntiChrists left no literary remains, one can only speculate about the frameworks and database that may have informed their position. In general, this gap in the evidence has been filled by the assumption that the AntiChrists adopted an "invention of tradition" approach. Invented traditions are fabricated versions of history, often complete with new rituals and commemorative rites, that combine bits of the true past with a large measure of present ideas. People invent traditions to create a sense of continuity between "now" and "then" in service of some political or economic agenda, borrowing the prestige of yesterday to add authority to something totally new.[2] Following this model, one may easily argue that the AntiChrists achieved their theological objectives mainly by importing alien elements into the sterilized Johannine outlook, attaching fabricated memories to orthodox tradition in service of their contemporary philosophical theories.

The notion that the AntiChrists invented tradition follows easily from the general tendency, becoming less common lately, to associate them with some branch of quasi/incipient/proto-Gnosticism, and the correlating view that Gnostics were seedpickers who simply conflated canonical Christian materials with Jewish and Hellenistic philosophical ideas.[3] This interpretation of the Johannine situation is very ancient, and in fact emerged within decades of the Fourth Gospel's publication. Irenaeus (ca. 180 CE) records an encounter in a bathhouse between the apostle John and Cerinthus, an early gnostic teacher who argued that "the Christ," a spiritual being, descended on the human Jesus at his baptism and inhabited his body during his public ministry, departing just before his helpless host's agonizing death on the cross (*Against Heresies* 1.26.1; 3.3.4). One can easily imagine that the AntiChrists, who refused to accept that Jesus came "in the water and *in the blood*" (1 John 5:6), subscribed to the opinions of this individual. Or perhaps the AntiChrists were actually Docetists, an early heretical group that believed that "the Christ" was a spiritual being who only "seemed" (Greek δοκέω) to have a human body, making Jesus a sort of phantom illusion and casting those who doubted his deity in the skeptical role of Velma in a cosmic Scooby Doo mystery ("there's no such thing as ghosts"). The writings of Ignatius (ca. 115 CE) suggest that docetic ideas were circulating in western Asia Minor soon after the Johannine literature was produced (*Trallians* 9–10; *Smyrneans* 2–7). As proto-Gnostic inventors of tradition, the AntiChrists imported so much foreign material into John's orthodox database that they essentially created a whole new Jesus tradition. And when that invented tradition was pushed through the AntiChrists' distinct memory framework, it naturally produced an elevated image of Jesus that looked quite different from John's image.

Viewed within the paradigm of a great theological debate, one might refer to the AntiChrists' christological position as a "countermemory," in the general sense that they disagreed with John about what Jesus did in the past.[4] John's theological outlook generated one christological image, one distinct memory of Jesus; the AntiChrists' theological outlook generated another image, a countermemory. And because the Johannine Epistles describe the interaction between these two positions in terms of a cosmic conflict between truth and falsehood, it is reasonable to suggest that the AntiChrists presented their memory of Jesus as a counter to John's memory in hostile opposition to his theological position. At the very least, this approach to the background of the Johannine literature has produced some interesting exegesis in the nineteen centuries since it was first postulated.

A GENEALOGY OF CONFLICT:
THE ANTICHRISTIAN COUNTERMEMORY

It is possible, then, to coherently portray John's conflict with the AntiChrists—or, again, with the AntiChristian way of thinking about Jesus— as a theological debate, the opening volley in a war that would wage fifty years later between the great Gnostic teachers of the second century and the orthodox bishops who claimed John as their ecclesial father. Such an approach is amenable to the present discussion in that these theological differences can be explained in terms of alternate Jesus traditions, different memory frameworks, and countermemories: John was coming from one place; the AntiChrists were coming from somewhere else. In view of the archetypal patterns that would later emerge in the history of Christian doctrine, it seems logical to modern readers to model the skirmish between John and the AntiChrists after the titanic struggles between Augustine and Pelagius, Calvin and Arminius, Luther and everyone.

Yet here again, the difficulty lies not so much in the nuances of the "theological debate" model as in its incompatibility with the Elder's understanding of the AntiChrist situation. The theological approach tends to assume that the AntiChrists were working with a traditional database and a memory framework inherently different from John's database and framework—different enough, at least, to justify treating them as an outside group, one obviously distinct from John, the Elder, and other orthodox believers. Schnackenburg, typical of those who follow this model, interprets 2 John 9 to mean that the AntiChrists "aspire to higher insights in a manner typical of gnostic behavior," "higher" in the sense that they include ideas alien to "the teaching given by Christ himself."[5] Some scholars have even suggested that the AntiChrists were Gentiles who entered the Johannine community after the Johannine Jesus tradition had already taken shape and then reinterpreted this tradition in light of pagan religious and philosophical concepts, a view that reflects the invented tradition approach in its purest form.[6] But this sharp distinction between John and the AntiChrists was apparently not quite so obvious to the early Johannine Christians. The Elder does not accuse the AntiChrists of inventing tradition, or of bringing alien, gnostic elements into the church's pure memory of Jesus. He admits, in fact, that the AntiChrists "went out from us," meaning that they were once (possibly very recently) members of his community (1 John 2:19). Further, despite the general Johannine obsession with "the world" and "the Jews," the Elder does not accuse the AntiChrists of importing ideas from outside the sphere of Christian thought. He simply says that they have "run ahead" (προάγω) of the orthodox teaching, a term that seems to imply that they had developed traditional Johannine thinking beyond the safe boundaries of community creeds.[7] Some Christians, even leaders like Diotrephes, saw this as a positive development, and refused to entertain teachers who reflected John's more antiquated perspective (3 John 10). The very name the Elder gives his opponents, "Anti*Christs*," implies that their vision was attractive to believers (and therefore dangerous to John) because they were preaching "a gospel," a message of "Christ"—albeit not the same message that John preached. In fact, even the term "opponents" should be used cautiously in this discussion, with the understanding that this label may not reflect the AntiChrists' own feelings about their relationship to John. They may have viewed their own teachings as a logical extension of John's position.

The AntiChrists were apparently a group of Christians who thought of themselves as orthodox and who appealed to other Christians who thought of themselves as orthodox (if the term "orthodox" is at all meaningful for the time period that we are discussing here). And in view of their origin within the

Johannine community, their image of Jesus was presumably generated in a memory framework very similar to John's, and built up from a traditional database similar (or identical) to the one that John was using. It seems, then, that the conflict between John and the AntiChrists is best conceived as an internal dispute between two theological positions generated from the same community framework and against the backdrop of the same basic set of experiences. In other words, rather than assuming that the AntiChrists were outsiders who developed their theology by importing gnostic, Hellenistic, and/or heterodox Jewish ideas into the true Christian faith, it will be more fruitful to assume that their views were developed from basically the same substance, and in essentially the same context, as John's views.

But if this were the case, *how did the AntiChrists come to such a radically different perspective? And on what basis were they able to seriously challenge the older, established understanding of Jesus?* The answer to these questions lies in a fuller

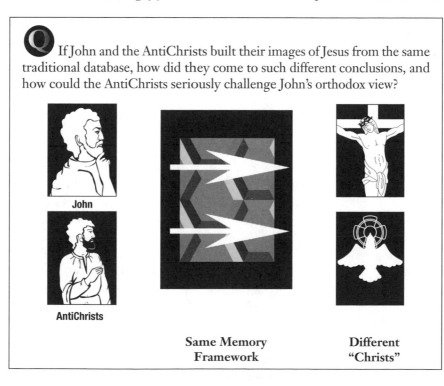

Q If John and the AntiChrists built their images of Jesus from the same traditional database, how did they come to such different conclusions, and how could the AntiChrists seriously challenge John's orthodox view?

John

AntiChrists

Same Memory Framework

Different "Christs"

consideration of how countermemories—images of the past that oppose and compete with mainstream views—develop and function.

As noted above, the AntiChrists' vision of Jesus might be labeled a countermemory in the general sense that their thinking about Jesus was different from John's thinking. But the term "countermemory," coined by the French sociologist Michel Foucault, carries a deeper implication that relates more directly to the actual circumstances of the conflict. Specifically, in Foucault's conception a countermemory is not simply a different idea about the past—"you say X happened, I say Y happened"—but rather an alternate means of constructing the past, a different *way* of remembering. Countermemories do not necessarily dispute facts about the past; they reconfigure those facts by realigning the very frameworks on which memories are built.

Foucault used the term "countermemory" to describe the product of a Nietzschean, "genealogical" approach to history. Nietzsche argued that history books generally seek to identify a distinct point of origin for things and institutions, the moment when "historic" people and events burst suddenly onto the scene of human affairs. A genealogical history, by contrast, would treat all events and social institutions as products of a complex interplay of

 A true "countermemory" reconfigures not only the content of the past, but also the frameworks of the past. It may simply reorganize and repackage the contents of the mainstream view—same pieces, different puzzle.

social forces, and would attempt to trace their development (their "genealogy") by identifying these forces. From this perspective, major social movements and figures emerge gradually in the ongoing conflict of power relations and perspectives that drive a society. As such, a genealogical approach to history "will cultivate the details and accidents that accompany every beginning" by focusing on "the minute deviations . . . the errors, the false appraisals, and the faulty calculations that gave birth to those things that continue to exist and have value for us."[8] Nietzsche referred to this genealogical approach to the past as *wirkliche Historie*, "effective history" or, better, a "history of effects," the "effects" being the observable products of this interplay of social forces—the famous events, institutions, and people that fill the pages of most history books. Essentially, a "history of effects" is not so much concerned with "what happened" as with why certain things that happened have come to be viewed as "historical moments" of special importance.

Obviously, such an approach is not typical of the Western historical tradition, a fact of which both Nietzsche and Foucault were well aware. Foucault notes that a history of effects will specifically oppose mainstream ideas about "history" at several key points. At each of these points, it is clear that Foucault is thinking of history books as a form of cultural memory, a way that societies shape and preserve their image of the past. Thus, his genealogical approach "opposes the theme of history as reminiscence or recognition," resisting the idea that history books are simply archives of information that objectively preserve and describe events for later reference and review. It also "opposes history given as continuity or representative of a tradition," defying the way that history books suggest events naturally occur in logical, cause-effect sequences. As a corollary, the genealogical mode opposes "history as knowledge" by insisting that historical inquiry could never produce a purely objective memory of the past "as it really was." Because this approach differs so radically from most fundamental assumptions about historiography, Foucault calls genealogical histories a "counter-memory," an entirely different way of talking about the past. Specifically, a "history of effects" "severs its [history's] connection to memory [= simple recall of the past], its metaphysical and anthropological model, and constructs a counter-memory—a transformation of history into a totally different form of time."[9] Essentially, then, in Foucault's conception a countermemory is not simply a different version of the past, but rather *a different way of creating a version of the past.*

This aspect of Foucault's concept of countermemory has been emphasized by sociologists such as Ann Burlein. In her recent study of the rhetoric of the Ku Klux Klan, *Lift High the Cross*, Burlein uses a countermemory model to analyze Klan speeches that appeal to traditional religious values and the Bible in service of white supremacist politics. Obviously, the content of such speeches would differ at many points from the way that most Americans think about, or remember, their nation's past. But this fact alone does not make the Klan message a countermemory—that is, it is not a countermemory just because the majority of people disagree with it. In fact, most of the "evidence" thrown from the Klan soapbox is drawn from the database of basic historical "facts" that most Americans would accept as true, the same database that supplies material to mainstream ways of thinking. The difference, then, lies not in the content of the Klan's memory, but rather in the way that their memory of U.S. history is structured. The Klan speech becomes a true countermemory at the point where it appeals to "religion as an alternative way of remembering history and empowering people."[10] By reorganizing events from the common database of the American past within a religious framework, the Klan is able to present an "alternative history," a story that functions as a countermemory not simply because most Americans disagree with the Klan's version of the past but, and at a much deeper level, because that image of the past is built on an entirely different framework of values. "Such memories are counter-, not because they are foreign to the mainstream, but because they draw on mainstream currents in order to redirect their flow."[11] As such, countermemories are actually best understood as undercurrents within the orthodox way of thinking about the past.

Foucault's notion of a countermemory, especially as developed by scholars such as Burlein, echoes Maurice Halbwachs's earlier comments about the ways groups gradually or suddenly change their collective memories. "When society becomes too different from what it had been in the past and from the conditions in which the traditions had arisen, it will no longer find within itself the elements necessary to reconstruct, consolidate, and repair these traditions." At this point, it will become essential to rethink the past so as to make the events of yesterday comprehensible in the context of present experience. But this process of reimaging memory must be closely regulated in order to maintain a sense of continuity between past and present, lest a society lose its sense of heritage and orientation. For this reason, "it is within the framework of these old notions and under the pretext of traditional ideas, that a new order of values would become slowly elaborated."[12] In other words, new versions of the past, countermemories, will be most successful when they explicitly build on the older versions of the past that they seek to replace.

Halbwachs illustrates this principle by discussing Christian origins. In general, new religious beliefs are formulated in opposition to old beliefs, and

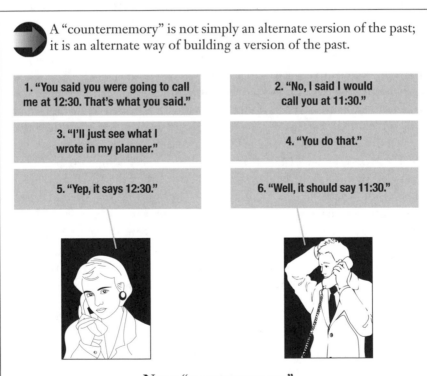

A "countermemory" is not simply an alternate version of the past; it is an alternate way of building a version of the past.

1. "You said you were going to call me at 12:30. That's what you said."

2. "No, I said I would call you at 11:30."

3. "I'll just see what I wrote in my planner."

4. "You do that."

5. "Yep, it says 12:30."

6. "Well, it should say 11:30."

Not a "countermemory"
(same ideas about time, appointments, and planners; dispute about *which* time was discussed, the facts of the case)

innovative religious thought tends to demonstrate the superiority of the new way of thinking by evoking old ideas and then specifically rejecting them. By building on and/or destroying the old theology, the new religious movement becomes comprehensible to society and, indeed, comprehensible to its own members through a process of comparison and contrast. Following this rule, the founders of Christianity expressed their new religious ideals by opposing them to the older ideals of Judaism, evoked in the form of concepts and prophecies from the Hebrew Bible. "Through terms borrowed from the Old Testament, and through an interpretation of the prophecies that the Jews understood only in the literal sense but that the new religion permeates with its spirit, Christianity is defined." Paul's reading of the Psalms and Prophets was thus "new" in that it projected Christ backward into the ancient text, but Paul's reading was "old" in that it still appealed to the Hebrew Bible to make Jesus sensible to, and compatible with, established patterns of religious thinking. By this means the early believers forged a distinctly Christian countermemory simply by reconfiguring key elements of Judaism around a new framework, Jesus, making it possible for the church to find a place in the Roman Empire as an extension of the ancient Hebrew faith. This process illustrates the way in which every countermemory "enframes the new elements that it pushes to the forefront in a totality of [established] remembrances, traditions, and familiar ideas."[13]

Applying these principles to the problem at hand, it seems that the AntiChrists were a threat to John, not simply because they disagreed with his theological position, but because they were able to create a coherent and appealing Christian countermemory of Jesus. Of course, technically speaking, the AntiChrists were not consciously engaged in a Nietzschean genealogical project. But their arguments must have gone beyond a simple disagreement

 The AntiChrists did not just promote a different memory of Jesus; they promoted a countermemory, an image built on John's image of Jesus and calculated to improve it.

with John about whether Jesus did or did not do and say certain things—that is, beyond the arena of, "You [John] say that Jesus healed a man at Bethesda (John 5:1–9); we [AntiChrists] haven't been able to document exactly where that place was, so we think he probably actually healed this man somewhere else, and it probably didn't really happen on a Sabbath, either, because Jesus would not likely have . . ."—a debate over documentation and the correct facts. There is, in fact, no clear evidence that the AntiChrists rejected John's traditional database or doubted that Jesus did most of what John claims that he did.

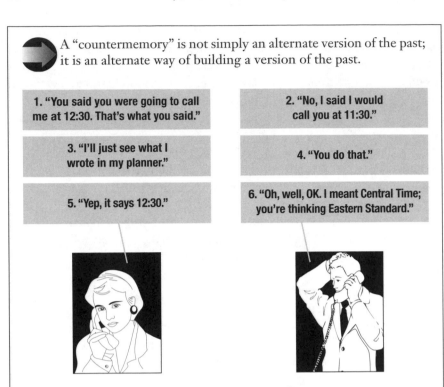

»A "countermemory"«
(no dispute about *which* time; dispute about what *kind* of time—which time zone? same data, different framework)

Nor is it clear that the AntiChrists developed their vision by importing alien, gnostic elements into the orthodox Johannine framework; certainly, there is no evidence to suggest that they thought they were doing this or intended to do so. The AntiChrists' position represents a true countermemory in the sense that their image of Christ was forged in the same context as John's on the basis of the same traditional database, yet with the elements of that common memory organized in a new and different way.

Chapters 7 and 8 below will analyze the specific means by which the AntiChrists developed their Christian countermemory in opposition to John's thinking about Jesus. While John clearly believed that the memory of Jesus was charismatic, preserved and guided by the Spirit, the AntiChrists seem to have interpreted this doctrine under what Maurice Halbwachs calls a "mystical" paradigm, one that departed significantly from John's "dogmatic" model. This mystical memory framework allowed the AntiChrists to build a Christian countermemory that challenged John's version of Jesus and, consequently, challenged his authority over the community's beliefs. Part 4 will show that John's decision to write a Gospel was a logical response to this challenge.

 "[E]very idea of the secessionists [AntiChrists] . . . can be plausibly explained as derivative from the Johannine tradition as preserved for us in GJohn [the Gospel of John]."

–Raymond Brown, *The Epistles of John*, 72

7

Jesus Now and Then: John's Dogmatic Memory

John's memory of Jesus was shaped in a framework of perceived danger. These dangers included the threat of persecution from outside forces—the unbelieving "world" and "the Jews"—and internal doctrinal threats from the AntiChrists. As bad as the world might be, the AntiChrists must have posed the greatest immediate risk to John's position. While "the Jews" could do no worse than deny John's claims, the AntiChrists, as (former) members of John's own community, built their vision of Jesus from the same stuff as John's own understanding and, like John himself, could insist that their memory was driven and guided by the Holy Spirit. John's decision to write a Gospel was one aspect of a larger response to this threat, and the tactical advantages of a written text are set in bold relief when the conflict is analyzed in terms of the tension between "dogma" and "mysticism" in religious memory.

THE LOOK OF JESUS IN THE LIMINAL ZONE

Any consideration of the AntiChrists' theological position must answer two questions: Why did the AntiChrists "run ahead" of the traditional Johannine way of thinking about Jesus? How did the AntiChrists manage to develop a countermemory of Jesus that would appeal to Christians like Diotrephes (3 John 9)? Both questions are subheadings under a larger problem that is relevant to any serious discussion of the way that memory works. A theory of memory must explain two phenomena: the persistence of coherent views of the past over time and the discontinuity of views of the past over time. A theory of memory must, in other words, explain both remembering and forgetting, and

Two key questions:

1. Why did the AntiChrists "run ahead" of John's way of thinking and develop a countermemory of Jesus?

2. How did the AntiChrists develop a countermemory of Jesus that was appealing to some Christians?

the factors that lead an individual or a group to retain some pieces of the past while discarding the rest. For the current study, this means that it is necessary to explain *how* the AntiChrists, as members of John's religious community, were able to create a countermemory that retained some elements of the conventional Johannine perspective while ignoring or forgetting other elements, and also to explain *why* they felt compelled to do this.

Why Reinvent Jesus?

To answer the question, *Why* did the AntiChrists develop a countermemory of Jesus? it will be necessary to consider why any religious group would change the way they think about the past, especially the way they think about the founding figures of their movement. This problem is perhaps more complicated than first appears, for the memory of religious groups is inherently conservative, at least more conservative than the memories of most other groups. Religious memory is "conservative" in the sense that it explicitly attempts to explain present social realities in terms of the period of origins, making the problems of today fit the teachings of the founders of the faith. Indeed, "what is peculiar to the memory of religious groups is that, while the memories of other groups permeate each other mutually and tend to correspond, the memory of religious groups claims to be fixed once and for all. It [religious memory] either obliges others to adapt themselves to its dominant representations, or it systematically ignores them." Religious groups attempt to remain in close contact with the period of origins through rituals, creeds, traditions, and sacred texts that preserve the image of that past. The founders of the faith are canonized through this constant rehearsal of their words and deeds, making the memory frameworks of the first generation a default value for the thinking of all later believers, one that seems to transcend the petty concerns of today.[1] One may therefore say that religious memories, the images of the past preserved by members of a religious group, are characterized by an acute sense of the distance between "now" and "then" and by an attempt to minimize that distance by interpreting the present through the frameworks of past ways of thinking.[2]

In the early days of a religious movement, the tension between the period of origins and present experience is minimal, simply because the community's current situation is similar to the situation of the founders. It is relatively easy for second-generation believers to align their thinking with that of their master because their social frameworks are very similar to the frameworks that informed the master's outlook on things. But as time goes by, the discrepancies between the founder's vision, anchored in a bygone age, and present social realities become more glaring. It becomes obvious that Jesus did not anticipate these new developments, and/or that his teachings (at least some of them) do not neatly align themselves with what is happening in the world today. And as Jesus' way of thinking becomes less and less relevant to modern life, the church, which must always make its own teachings comprehensible to people who think within the frameworks of contemporary secular society, runs the risk of losing its distinct identity. At this point, the religious group must develop a mechanism to create a sense of continuity between the founders of the faith and present experience, a continuity that will empower them to resist the overwhelming pressure to conform to worldly ways. The church must, in other words, reconfigure its memory of the formative period so that Christ can speak to current problems in a way that is relevant to, yet clearly distinct from, contemporary voices.[3]

John seems to have been one of the first Christians to feel this tension between "then there" and "now here." Jesus moved and thought within the confines of Palestinian Judaism; even though his views were radical, he found, as a Jew, a coherent identity and place in the world. The same may be said of Paul, a self-professed Roman citizen whose catalog of woes in 2 Corinthians 11 reveals that the Diaspora community continued to see him as a perplexing wayward son, a Jew whose views were exacerbating but still comprehensible within the frameworks of the ancient faith and contemporary culture. But

---

Two key questions:

 1. Why did the AntiChrists "run ahead" of John's way of thinking and develop a countermemory of Jesus?

 Because they, like John, sensed a need to make Jesus relevant to contemporary society.

John's experiences, or at least perceptions, of persecution and excommunication left him and his churches in a vague, liminal zone between Judaism and mainstream Greco-Roman culture, forcing him to operate within memory frameworks quite foreign to those that drove the thinking of Jesus. Further, most scholars today support (often simply for convenience) the traditional theory that the Johannine literature was written in western Asia Minor (Ephesus), a social context obviously very different from Jesus' old stomping grounds in Roman Palestine. As the Johannine Christians "became distanced from this [Jesus'] milieu, [their] Christian society had to establish its dogmas and cult and contrast these to the beliefs and practices of secular society, which represented another time [the present] and [therefore] obeyed impulses different from" those that animated the teachings of Jesus.[4] This situation forced the Johannine Christians to adopt a new hermeneutical strategy, one that would make traditional beliefs comprehensible in their new social context while keeping Christian thought distinct from secular thought.

Returning then to the question, Why did the AntiChrists create a countermemory of Jesus? it seems that they, as members of the Johannine community, felt the need to realign their memory of Jesus for the same reasons that John would have felt the need to realign his. Before they "went out" from John's churches (1 John 2:18–19) and probably still afterwards, the AntiChrists presumably experienced the same sense of alienation and persecution from "the world" and "the Jews" that John felt. They, like John, realized the growing distance between the historical Jesus and the world around them, forcing them to reinterpret the master's teaching so that Jesus could speak to contemporary concerns. But for reasons that cannot now be known, they were not content with John's reconfiguration of Jesus' memory, perhaps because they felt that John did not go far enough in updating the tradition. This would explain the Elder's complaint that the AntiChrists have "run ahead" ($\pi\rho o\acute{\alpha}\gamma\omega$) and not remained in the teaching about Christ (2 John 9)—like John, the AntiChrists needed to bridge the gap between the Jesus of yesterday and the world of today, but were unwilling to stop where John stopped.

The theological differences between John and the AntiChrists should not, then, be attributed to different motives for reimaging Jesus. Rather, the theological differences between these two groups were a byproduct of the fact that they adopted two different strategies in their attempts to make the memory of Jesus relevant to the same social setting. The AntiChrists were doing the same thing that John was doing and for the same reason, but in a different way and along a different trajectory.

How to Reinvent Jesus?

This returns us to the second "key question" that opened this section: *How* did the AntiChrists manage to develop a countermemory of Jesus that was appealing to Christians like Diotrephes (3 John 9)? How did their strategy for making Jesus relevant to contemporary society differ from John's strategy? And, ultimately, what aspects of their strategy would make a written Gospel especially helpful to John in his attempts to counter their teaching?

Halbwachs argues that a distinctly Christian identity, one that interprets current experience through the lens of the founders of the church, may be constructed through one of two modes of religious memory, the "dogmatic" mode and the "mystical" mode. Dogmatists "claim to possess and to preserve the meaning and understanding of Christian doctrine because they know how controversial terms, propositions, or symbols have been defined in the past, and also because they possess a general method for defining these today." The dogmatist, in other words, follows an orthodox hermeneutical model that allows her to continually reinterpret the ancient rites and teachings of the faith—rites and teachings that are in turn assumed to reflect the beliefs and practices of Jesus and the apostles—in ways that speak to contemporary life. Dogmatists are thus responsible for the church's academic theological tradition. "This is in contrast to mystics, who try by means of an interior light to recover the meaning of texts and ceremonies."[5] In general, the dogmatist meets current needs by reconfiguring Jesus' memory on the basis of established creeds, orthodox traditions, and accepted exegetical methods. The mystic, by contrast, meets current needs by appealing to an intensely personal vision of Christ that transcends conventional ways of thinking.

Following Halbwachs's paradigm, we can say that the debate between John and the AntiChrists took the form of a conflict between the dogmatic and mystical approaches to Christian tradition. At a point in time when the church was becoming acutely aware of the distance between Jesus' situation and its own situation, John adopted a dogmatic approach to the memory of Jesus, while the AntiChrists adopted a mystical approach.

JOHN'S DOGMATIC MEMORY

In a very real sense, Christian faith is obsessed with its own past. Indeed, "the entire substance of Christianity . . . consists in the remembrance of his [Jesus'] life and teachings," a claim verified by the fact that almost every component of the church's worship, creeds, confessions, and calendar "is essentially the commemoration of a period or an event of the life of Christ."[6] While Christian faith is energized by the example of charismatic founders like Jesus, Peter, and Paul, this backward focus always threatens to leave the church unable to address contemporary concerns. How, with its gaze fixed on yesterday, can the church "present itself as a permanent institution . . . [whose] truths can be both historical and eternal?"[7] In other words, how can the church claim that things Jesus did and said two thousand years ago are in any

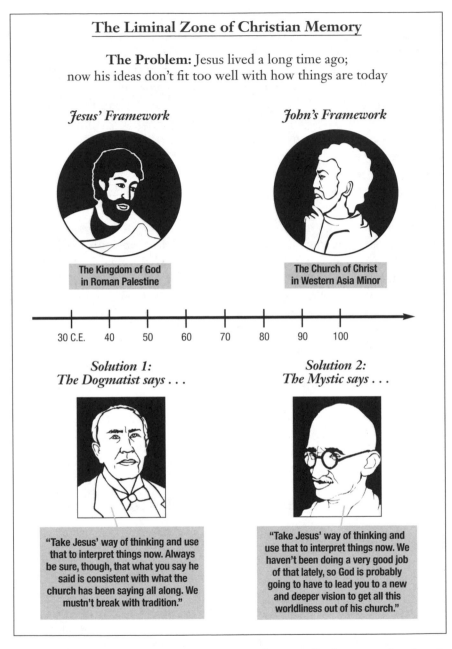

The Liminal Zone of Christian Memory

The Problem: Jesus lived a long time ago; now his ideas don't fit too well with how things are today

Jesus' Framework

The Kingdom of God in Roman Palestine

John's Framework

The Church of Christ in Western Asia Minor

30 C.E.   40   50   60   70   80   90   100

Solution 1: The Dogmatist says . . .

"Take Jesus' way of thinking and use that to interpret things now. Always be sure, though, that what you say he said is consistent with what the church has been saying all along. We mustn't break with tradition."

Solution 2: The Mystic says . . .

"Take Jesus' way of thinking and use that to interpret things now. We haven't been doing a very good job of that lately, so God is probably going to have to lead you to a new and deeper vision to get all this worldliness out of his church."

way relevant to the problems of today? And especially, how can the church make Jesus speak to today while maintaining even basic doctrinal continuity with past generations of believers and their own attempts to make Jesus speak to contemporary concerns?

Halbwachs argues that the church has achieved this continuity—continuity both with Jesus and with earlier generations of Christians—primarily through a "dogmatic" approach to tradition and doctrine. "Dogma" here refers not only to the doctrinal content of the church's faith, but also and primarily to the means by which orthodox doctrine has been developed and redeveloped over time. In each generation, clerics and scholars have interpreted the present in terms of the past, evoking the memory frameworks utilized by earlier generations of Christians to construct the doctrines of today. At any given moment, "orthodoxy" is the current official view of how today's society would look through the eyes of these bygone believers and, ultimately, through the eyes of Jesus. The basic continuity that one may observe in the history of Christian thought is a natural byproduct of the fact that each generation has attempted to apply the same basic memory framework—the framework of Jesus and the authors of the Bible—to its own situation. Any history of Christian doctrine thus traces the church's ability to develop new ideas using old forms and symbols, and to constantly reshape those old forms and symbols to make them meaningful for today.

When appealing to precedent, the dogmatist admits that "the past cannot be reborn," but insists that "we can fathom what it was like, and we are most successful if we have at our command well-established landmarks." These "landmarks" are primarily the texts of the Christian canon, which are believed to reflect the thought and memory frameworks of the first-generation believers, and the subsequent interpretations of these texts by canonized Christian scholars, whose conclusions may be cited as precedents to verify new interpretations. "There has been in effect a continuous existence of the group of clerics who in each period have taken up these same frameworks [of memory, encoded in canonical Christian documents] and then applied their [own] reflections anew to them, conforming to what tradition taught them in this respect."[8] Dogmatists thus bridge the gap between past and present by analyzing the Bible and trying to relate present social circumstances to the memory frameworks encoded in that book in a way consistent with their predecessors in the orthodox tradition of scholarship. In the process they forge the new generation's religious memory and doctrine, and the founders of the faith become, as it were, larger than life, so large that their memory frameworks can be imposed on every subsequent generation.

In Halbwachs's view, then, "dogma" is not so much a body of doctrinal content as an ongoing performance tradition, the ability of scholars in each generation to interpret present realities through past frameworks. This explains why some doctrines fade into obscurity over time and why the beliefs held to be orthodox in one generation are sometimes declared heretical by later generations. If the social situation has changed dramatically, the later generation may not be able to construct a dogma consistent with the earlier generation's view, making it necessary to reject those earlier constructions. When this happens, the church "resembles the case of a memory [group] that no longer calls up certain of its store of remembrances because the thought of contemporary people no longer has an interest in them. The Church can divert its attention from certain of its traditions if its doctrine remains intact as to its essentials, and if it does not lose too much force or substance while it gains greater freedom of movement."[9] The church can, in other words, gradually forget or ignore some of its memories to meet current needs, so long as there is still sufficient continuity between new images of the past and previous orthodox constructions.

At first glance, one might argue that John cannot be labeled a dogmatist in the sense outlined above. The Johannine Paraclete "anoints" each individual believer, helping her to remember things that Jesus said and guiding her in the application of those memories to present realities (1 John 2:20–24; John 14:26; 16:13). How could such an existential hermeneutic be associated with the church's later scholastic tradition, represented by great scholars like Origen, Augustine, and Thomas Aquinas? Further, those who believe that John was aware of the Synoptics, or at least the Synoptic Jesus tradition, might also point out that John shows an almost complete disregard for the conclusions of his predecessors and does not even follow Luke in a passing nod to their understandings of Jesus. How could one then suggest that John felt even slightly constrained to remain consistent with the opinions of earlier generations of believers?

> John's view of the Paraclete reveals just how dogmatic he is: everyone has the Holy Spirit, but the Spirit always points backward to the historical Jesus and always agrees with what the church has been teaching all along.

A closer examination, however, reveals that John's approach to tradition was thoroughly dogmatic, despite his emphasis on the Spirit's role in Christian experience. In fact, the dogmatic elements of John's thinking are most obvious in those passages that discuss the work of the Paraclete. For example, when John says that the Spirit will "guide you into all truth" (John 16:13), he clearly means that the Spirit will guide believers into the common past, back to the historical Jesus and the orthodox way of thinking about Jesus. Specifically, the Spirit will "remind you of everything *that I [Jesus] said to you*," "glorifying" Jesus by taking pieces of information from the traditional database of his words and deeds and bringing them to the attention of later believers (John 14:26; 16:14–15). The Spirit, in other words, can only point back to and affirm what Christians have already been taught ἀπ' ἀρχῆς, "from the beginning," making the Paraclete's work parallel to that of human beings like the Beloved Disciple in the preservation of the true witness (see 1 John 2:7, 24; 3:11; John

15:26–27). For John, the Spirit does *not* function as a direct interface between Christians and the world, helping believers make sense of their situation. Rather, the Spirit functions as an interface *between Christians and the historical Jesus*, who himself continues to abide in believers and in whom believers abide and find peace in their present circumstances (John 14:27; 15:1–10).

John's subjection of the charismatic impulse to conservative dogma parallels the odd blend of Spirit and creed in the Johannine Epistles. The Elder assures believers that the Paraclete will guide them to a place where they do not need anyone to teach them anything, but also warns them that the Spirit will never "run ahead" of what they already know and have been taught (cf. 1 John 2:20–24 and 2 John 9). The Elder sees no tension between Spirit and tradition, because, as noted in an earlier chapter, the two are essentially synonymous in his thinking. This theme underlies the enigmatic 1 John 4:1–6.

"Testing the Spirits" (1 John 4:1–6)

[1]Beloved, do not believe every spirit, but rather test the spirits as to whether they are from God, because many false prophets have gone out into the world. [2]This is how you know the Spirit of God: every spirit that confesses, "Jesus Christ has come in the flesh," is from God; [3]and every spirit that does not confess Jesus is not from God—this is the spirit of the Antichrist. You have heard that it is coming, and now it is in the world already. [4]You are from God, children, and you have conquered them, because the One who is in you is greater than the one who is in the world. [5]They are from the world, and because of this they speak from the world and the world listens to them. [6]We are from God—the one who knows God listens to us; the one who is not from God does not listen to us. This is how we know [the difference between] the Spirit of Truth and the spirit of deceit.

The Elder notes here that many people teach under a spiritual influence, but warns that not all "spirits" should receive our attention. How can the average believer distinguish between the genuine memories of Jesus that come from the Paraclete and false claims that originate elsewhere? By applying a simple doctrinal test: "Every spirit that confesses, 'Jesus Christ has come in the flesh,' is from God; and every spirit that does not confess Jesus is not from God" (1 John 4:2–3). Here as elsewhere, John limits charismatic experience to the boundaries of community creeds, creeds that explicitly look backward in time to the historical Jesus. The Spirit of Truth may be greater than the spirit of Antichrist (4:4), but that does not mean that the Spirit is great enough to reveal anything new about God.

In true dogmatic fashion, then, John limits the work of the Spirit to a memory of the founder of the faith, and measures the Spirit's present influence against the old, orthodox theological tradition. As a result, John's Paraclete doctrine is not a license for spiritual freedom, but rather a mechanism for doctrinal conformity. Because the same Spirit of Truth operates in all believers, John expects the Christian memory of Jesus to be doubly uniform: first, geographically uniform, in that all Christians in all churches should remember Jesus the same way; second, chronologically uniform, in that the image of Jesus should not change from one generation to the next. Because charismatic memory should be geographically uniform, the Elder attacks the itinerant AntiChrists and the leaders of the individual congregations that support them (3 John 9–10) for deviations from the majority position. The Spirit would not remind the Elder of one thing about Jesus and then tell Diotrephes something else, and since the Elder knows that his memory is true, Diotrephes' memory must be false. At the same time, because charismatic memory should be chronologically uniform, the Elder reminds his readers again and again that every new teaching about Jesus must be consistent with what "you have heard from the beginning" and, consequently, consistent with the community's established christological creeds. These creeds can function as doctrinal tests because they epitomize the Paraclete's mnemonic work, allowing believers to measure new recollections against old ones and thus giving tradition priority over personal spiritual experience (1 John 2:20–24; 4:1–6, 13–15; 5:6–12; 2 John 7–10).

John, then, responded to the gap between himself and Jesus by adopting a conservative, dogmatic approach to tradition. The Spirit works to point believers back to the founder of the faith and guides them into a deeper application of what they have already been taught. Because this process has been ongoing and uniform since Jesus' death—uniform because all believers in all times and places have been guided by the same Spirit—John feels a close continuity between his beliefs and the beliefs of earlier Christians, represented in his community's traditions and creeds. As a dogmatist, his image of Christ combined recollections of things that Jesus did with previous interpretations to create a figure who could speak to John's churches in their unique situation.

The AntiChrists opposed John's dogma not by rejecting his claims or adding new information to his database, but rather by refocusing the traditional view through the lens of mystical memory, a lens that magnified certain facets of Jesus' image while blurring other features that lay at the center of John's field of vision. Chapter 8 will explore the means by which they achieved this new focus to answer the second key question that opened this chapter, How did the AntiChrists develop a countermemory of Jesus that was appealing to some Christians?

8

AntiChristian Mystical Memory

As I've mentioned, I grew up in Norwood, Ohio, and the mystical impulse in religious memory may be conveniently illustrated by the recent Marian movement there, centered in the Our Lady of the Holy Spirit Center.[1] The center's history illustrates the uneasy, yet symbiotic, relationship that Maurice Halbwachs describes between dogmatism and mysticism as modes of religious memory.

Sometime in the late 1980s, the founder of the Our Lady of the Holy Spirit Center, one "Father Smith," traveled to Medjugorje—a small village in Bosnia-Herzegovina where Mary has been revealing herself to the faithful

Two key questions:

 1. Why did the AntiChrists "run ahead" of John's way of thinking and develop a countermemory of Jesus?

 2. How did the AntiChrists develop a countermemory of Jesus that was appealing to some Christians?

regularly since 1981—to experience the many miraculous goings-on there. After this visit, one of a dozen or so trips that he made to that sacred place, he formed a small prayer circle at his church in Northern Kentucky, which gradually grew to include more and more devoted Catholics who were interested in this same type of vision. At some point a lady named Sandy became involved

93

in this fellowship. Sandy drove in for the prayer meetings from Batavia, an Ohio farming town just outside the eastern loop of Cincinnati's circle freeway, known mainly for its church camps and large Chevrolet dealership. Sometime in the summer of 1992 the Blessed Virgin appeared to Sandy as "Our Lady of Light," and this incident began a series of mystical messages through the woman who came to be known, appropriately, as "Visionary Sandy" and/or "the Batavia Visionary." Mary instructed Sandy to build a grotto on a farm in nearby Falmouth, Kentucky, where the faithful were to meet every month for prayer. This farm is now home to a chapel, a healing spring, and several other sacred things that volunteers are glad to point out to visitors.

After her initial visitation, the Blessed Lady would appear to Sandy each year on August 31 for a substantial message. These meetings attracted large numbers of the faithful, along with a mixed multitude of curious onlookers and representatives of the media. The first several mass meetings took place at Father Smith's church in Cold Springs, Kentucky. But after a while Mary relocated to the campus of the old Mount St. Mary's of the West Seminary across the river in Norwood, Ohio, for her annual appearances, the last of which took place in 1999.

Mary's visits made quite a stir in my Catholic hometown, and even today a trip to any church or bar in Norwood can usually uncover direct testimony from someone who witnessed the amazing events at one of these meetings. Thousands of people would flock with their binoculars and lawnchairs to the tiny seminary campus to hear Visionary Sandy's play-by-play of the words of the Virgin and to witness the many miracles that confirmed her sacred presence: spots on the sun; silver crucifixes turning to gold in the hands of the faithful; shadowy visions of the Madonna in various trees, most of which you may still see standing today; mysterious bursts of light, much too bright to be from the flashes of cameras; sudden, inexplicable healings of chronic back pain and many other sore ailments; and so forth. An acquaintance of my wife made pilgrimage to Norwood one year and showed her a most remarkable photograph of two trails of airplane exhaust forming a giant cross in the summer sky. These and similar manifestations attended the annual advent of the Mother of God in Norwood, Ohio, at least as told to me by those who witnessed them.

The local bishops, both in northern Kentucky and Cincinnati, were understandably hesitant to endorse these proceedings, but Father Smith maintained his ordination and mass is still served with the bishop's blessing every day at the OLHS Center. This is the case because the Norwood prophecies, despite the unconventional circumstances of their delivery, actually gave the church hierarchy little cause for concern. When interviewed by *Share International* (a noteworthy publication in its own right), Father Smith explained that Mary had come simply to "get people back to Christ and Christian principles. . . .

She sees the darkness that she wants to bring the light of Christ into." Specifically, Christ's "message was a message of love of God and neighbor. We have forgotten that in our society. . . . She is trying to bring us back to Christ and a Christian way of life." When asked whether he thought that Mary's appearances suggest that the end of the world is nigh, Father Smith opined, "That's very possible because in most of the messages—from Medjugorje and elsewhere around the world—the message is: 'Time is short. Realize that there will be difficulties and problems, and that this is not the end of the world—but perhaps the end of an era.' "[2] One could scarcely disagree with any of these statements, a fact that no doubt explains why the archdiocese did not see Visionary Sandy as a more urgent threat.

The Norwood Marian movement is a good illustration of the workings of mystical religious memory. Christian mystics, like dogmatists, keenly sense the distance between their world and the world of Christ. But unlike dogmatists, mystics seek a more direct route back to the object of their devotion, a route that bypasses the church's academic traditions in favor of an intense personal vision of the founder of their faith. "Mysticism," Halbwachs notes, "responds to the desire for more intimate contact with the divine source than is possible within the group of believers"—specifically, a more intimate contact than conventional forms of piety will allow. At various points in church history, the dogmatic tradition has become so focused on maintaining continuity with the past that it could not communicate to contemporary believers in an adequate way. Doctrines and rites that were once relevant and meaningful thus "become immobilized into literary formulas and monotonous gestures whose efficacy declines." When this situation characterizes a large number of dogmas at a given moment in the church's life, a mystical impulse will arise to refocus the way the story of origins is remembered. In this respect, "we can, if we so desire, contrast mysticism with dogmatism as lived remembrance versus tradition more or less reduced to formulas."[3]

Viewed from this angle, it becomes clear that mysticism, despite its emphasis on the personal experience of the visionary and its preference for unconventional venues, is in fact a form of countermemory, a way of constructing alternate images of the past from a stock of common beliefs. This is evident both from the content of the mystical vision and from the broad parameters within which the mystical vision is articulated. In terms of content, mystical countermemory highlights aspects of the Bible and/or of Christian tradition that all believers would acknowledge but that have been ignored or marginalized by the church's official dogma. As such, "the role of the mystics was very often first of all to modify the picture of the early times of Christianity by enlarging it, and to attract the attention of believers to certain facts and persons in the Gospels that were initially neglected, poorly known, or little noticed." Indeed, the great Christian mystics have generally generated their visions through meditations on the Gospels, the sacraments, icons, and various devotional texts that were already officially endorsed by the church.[4] The mystical insight is thus "new" only in the sense that it centralizes things that were previously on the margins of mainstream memory, and is "personal" only in the sense that it represents the creative genius of a single individual rather than the collective wisdom of the academy or the church.

The case of the Norwood mystic follows this pattern. Visionary Sandy, in her private raptures, saw the Virgin Mary, a key figure in the New Testament and all subsequent Christian texts and iconography; she did not see some previously unknown mediatory figure. Further, Mary's "new" message—that Americans "need to get back to a Christian way of life" characterized by "love of God and love of neighbor"—could scarcely be considered innovative. Even her attendant signs and miracles involved objects and symbols of the ancient Christian faith: photographs of the Virgin where she appears to be Caucasian and is dressed in Western garb, typical of her representation on prayer cards and dollar-store prints; transformed crucifixes; healings that resemble the miracles of Christ; crosses in the sky. In these and other respects, while the mystical countermemory claims to transcend paralyzed dogma, it in fact borrows its visionary grammar entirely from the treasury of the church's dogmatic tradition.

The new mystical vision is a "countermemory," not only because it depends on the church's established traditions, but also because it relies on orthodox dogma to set appropriate boundaries for the mystical experience. "During his transports and his ecstasies the mystic hence maintains the continuous feeling that his particular experiences take place within a framework of notions that he has not invented, that have not been revealed to him alone, but that the Church preserves and has taught him."[5] The Christian mystic, in other words, rarely opposes dogma, but rather opposes either the inability of dogma to address contemporary issues or, in the opposite instance, the conflation of dogma with contemporary concerns to a point where it becomes difficult to identify a distinctly Christian perspective. In this way, Christian mystics remain distinctly "Christian," no matter how personal their visions may be. Those who entirely depart from the traditional dogmatic framework fall into another category, "heretics," whose memory cannot be integrated into mainline perspectives because it is not bounded by a familiar set of images and ideas.

Because of my background, career, and interests, I have had occasion to dialogue with charismatic Catholics, pentecostal evangelicals, and religious people of various denominations who claim that they have been abducted by aliens who revealed secret information to them. Analyzing such anecdotal data, I have noted that even the most radical mystical visions clearly reveal their traditional dogmatic frameworks as soon as they are compared with other visions that originated elsewhere. For example, the Blessed Virgin appears to Roman Catholic mystics but not to evangelical Pentecostals, who instead hear the voice of God in the form of prophecies and unknown tongues. Despite the structural similarity of these experiences, and despite the fact that both normally involve a call to repentance and a return to the old ways of the faith, I have yet to meet a pentecostal Protestant who accepts the legitimacy of Marian activity, and have encountered many who would in fact argue that Visionary Sandy was possessed by demons. This is the case because the Pentecostal's personal mystical experience is guided by a dogmatic framework quite different from that of the person who might make a pilgrimage to Lourdes, a Protestant framework that discourages any acknowledgment of Mary's mediatorial or revelatory role. The Pentecostal might even question the charismatic Catholic's basic spiritual integrity: How could anybody claim to be a Spirit-filled Christian when they still pray the rosary? To which the Catholic could only reply, How can you claim to be a Spirit-filled Christian when you don't?

An analysis of theological differences would, then, effectively plumb the depths to which the pentecostal Protestant and the charismatic Catholic remain married to their respective dogmatic traditions, despite their common claim to a unique and intense personal encounter with Christ. Such an analysis would also reveal points of similarity, areas where the differing dogmatic frameworks overlap. Benny Hinn (the popular televangelist famous for throwing balls of the Holy Spirit at people in his audiences) and Visionary Sandy would immediately join forces to oppose the revelations of the UFO enthusiast, on the basis that such teachings have no reference point in the Bible or the church's orthodox tradition (notwithstanding the fact that many abductees appeal to Christian theological categories to explain their experiences). Both would also refuse to join the Gnostic Ufologist on a pilgrimage to Roswell, New Mexico, because this location has not been a landmark for authentic Christian memories. But they would quickly part ways once again as soon as the discussion turned to the relative health benefits of visits to Fatima or the Pensacola revival. At the moment when Christ is encountered, the mystic is alone; yet at every moment the mystic "knows Christ [only] through [Christian] tradition; whenever he thinks about Christ, he remembers" what he has heard or read in his church library.[6] In this vein, it is relevant to note that Visionary Sandy's venue, the Our Lady of the Holy Spirit Center, was formerly a Roman Catholic seminary where priests were trained in the ancient academic and theological dogmas of the orthodox faith.

Mystical memory claims, then, to be personal, but in fact depends entirely on the database and dogmatic boundaries of mainstream religious thinking. It develops a countermemory, not by rejecting elements from the orthodox image of the past, but rather by reconfiguring those elements so that what has been forgotten or ignored is brought to the center of the church's field of vision. This fact explains the existence of the long-standing Christian mystical tradition, with clearly defined rules that allow each new visionary to be linked to predecessors who have done the same thing. The somewhat oxymoronic "mystical tradition" results from the fact that, once a new mystical vision has gained a following among Christians, the church will often highlight the points of continuity between this new perspective and old ways of thinking and simply absorb the new light into the developing dogmatic spectrum. The mystic will then be canonized, her biography reconfigured to fit the archetypal story of the heroes of the faith, and her disciples will be reintegrated into the mainstream community or their own new monastic order. Of course, the members of that order will continue to glamorize their founder by emphasizing his or her "unique" outlook, but the very existence of their group simply proves that this peculiar mystical vision was forged in the framework of what other Christian people believe.[7]

Halbwachs's approach to mystical Christian memory points to the answer to the second key question raised in the previous chapter, *How were the AntiChrists able to generate a convincing countermemory of Jesus?* The business of revising religious memory need not involve the invention of new traditions. Countermemories often challenge current perspectives simply by reorganizing the mainline perspective to highlight what has been marginalized or overlooked. Viewed from this angle, the AntiChrists appear to have been "mystics" who generated a countermemory of Jesus by emphasizing some aspects of the Johannine community's traditional database while marginalizing others. Specifically, they seem to have rejected John's dogmatic, creedal approach to the problem of the distance between Jesus and the church of today, and instead emphasized the work of the Spirit as the organizing principle for Christian memory. To support this mystical vision, they could point to traditional sayings such as those preserved in John 14:17–18, 26 and 16:7, which suggest that Jesus' human body was only a temporary abode for the Word of God, who now dwells within all believers. Of course, such an approach would allow them to significantly expand the database of "authentic sayings of Jesus," simply because they believed that Jesus was still actively speaking to the church on a regular basis.

The AntiChrists' mystical approach was particularly dangerous to John because it drew its energy and mandate from accepted dogma about the work of the Spirit. And because mystical religious memory operates within the confines of the church's dogmatic traditions, Johannine Christians could easily embrace the new AntiChristian vision and integrate that vision into the mainstream way of thinking. Second John and 3 John suggest that this process had already begun in the church in Diotrephes' home, where teachers who still advocated John's position were no longer welcome but where the AntiChrists could find safe haven (2 John 10; 3 John 7–10). The AntiChrists would, in turn, welcome invitations to share their message, because they thought of themselves as Christians and believed that their new vision was based on old information from and about Jesus. In the process, the Paraclete replaced dogma as the mechanism of doctrinal continuity, giving the AntiChrists' new mystical revelations equal authority with the community's orthodox creeds and the Beloved Disciple's "witness."

Two key questions:

 2. How did the AntiChrists develop a countermemory of Jesus that was appealing to some Christians?

 By refocusing the image of Jesus through one small piece of the church's accepted dogma: the Johannine Paraclete doctrine.

Alan Culpepper has rightly (in my view) characterized John's debate with the AntiChrists as an expression of "the tension . . . between the conservative principle and the liberal, the need to preserve and the need to adapt."[8] Both groups were confronted with the problem of Jesus' obsolescence, and both were forced to reconsider how his life and teachings could be relevant to the difficult situation of the Johannine churches. John, as a dogmatist, solved this problem by appealing to tradition and precedent, interpreting the work of the Spirit through the lens of community creeds. The AntiChrists, as mystics, found their answer by using the Spirit as an organizing principle for a new vision of Christ, one that bypassed the creeds and allowed Jesus to speak directly to the contemporary community at the expense of his historical ministry.

DOGMA AND WRITING:
JOHN'S BEST PLAN OF ATTACK

John wrote a Gospel as one tactical move in a broad campaign against the mystical claims of the AntiChrists. Specifically, he sensed that the symbolic value of a written text could be harnessed to suppress the AntiChristian countermemory, making his churches immune to this threat. As will be seen in part 4, a written Gospel would be especially useful to a dogmatist such as John in a debate with mystics over memory. Before proceeding to that discussion, it will be helpful to briefly highlight the inherent complexity of John's situation and the options available to him.

As noted earlier, the Johannine memory of Jesus was essentially personal, a product of the Spirit's work in individual Christians. This view of the Spirit could support both dogmatic and mystical approaches to the Johannine tradition. From John's dogmatic perspective, the Paraclete establishes a close connection between the historical Jesus and the risen Lord. Since the Paraclete is the presence of Jesus in the community, teachings that are inspired by the Spirit should closely resemble the teachings of the human Jesus; since the Spirit has been active ever since Jesus' death (John 7:37–39; 20:19–22), the beliefs of today should be consistent with the established creeds of yesterday. John's approach to Jesus tradition was thus conservative and minimalist, focused on the past and resisting expansions as dangerous innovations leading to error (1 John 4:1–6).

But it seems that the AntiChrists interpreted the community's traditional sayings about the Paraclete in a mystical way, one that allowed them to take a maximalist approach to dogma and tradition. If the resurrected Lord, through the Spirit, continues to speak and act in the church, the life and teachings of the human Jesus would be only of historical interest, the beginning of a story that is ongoing in the community's experience. From this perspective, there would be no point to stress that "Jesus [the man] was the [divine] Christ," for every believer possesses the divine Christ in the form of the Paraclete. As a natural consequence, the AntiChrists were more concerned with Christ's immediate presence and guidance than with the community's creeds about Jesus, and were also naturally less interested in his "blood" (1 John 5:6)—in the life and teachings of the historical Jesus as a reference point for current experience. This mystical outlook would quickly solve the problem of the growing distance between Jesus' social framework and the church's framework—it would, in fact, reduce that distance to zero by pulling Jesus out of Palestine and into the church's own liminal zone. Viewed from the AntiChrists' angle, John's dogmatic approach would appear not so much wrong as simply obsolete, too rigid in its database and unable to respond quickly enough to the needs of today.

Clearly John could not ignore this threat, and his best possible response to the AntiChrists seems obvious: seek and destroy the foundational premise of their countermemory. Specifically, John could have rejected the AntiChrists' emphasis on the Spirit as the organizing principle of Christian memory, either by denying that the Spirit works to preserve the memory of Jesus or by revising the community's dogma so as to invalidate the AntiChrists' claims. As an added bonus, this tactic would make it unnecessary to address the specific nuances of the AntiChrists' theological position—if the organizing principle is wrong, it goes without saying that a Christology built on that principle must also be wrong. In other words, John could have simply attacked the AntiChrists' understanding of the Spirit, dismantling the framework they were using to reconfigure the Johannine tradition and thereby automatically refuting any innovative christological ideas generated from that framework.

But the Fourth Gospel shows that John did not follow this tactic, and instead continued to emphasize the Paraclete's role in Christian memory. In fact, the Johannine Jesus makes a number of statements that would lend direct support to the AntiChrists' charismatic view (see John 14:26; 15:26–27; 16:12–14). While it may have been the most obvious response, John could not afford to reject the AntiChrists' emphasis on the Spirit for at least two practical reasons.

First, John could not attack the AntiChrists' foundational principle simply because that principle was derived directly from the church's established dogma. The AntiChrists did not invent the doctrine of "anointed memory"; they simply elevated that notion to a point where it refocused the traditional image of Christ. As such, the pressure of the past would weigh against John's efforts, following Schwartz's rule that "the earliest construction of an historical object limits the range of things subsequent generations can do with it."[9] Johannine Christians had believed "from the beginning" that their memories of Jesus were guarded by the Paraclete, and this belief was supported by the testimony of the Beloved Disciple and by a number of traditional sayings that originated with Jesus himself. Since Jesus, the Beloved Disciple, and earlier generations of Christians had advocated the same view of memory that the AntiChrists were now highlighting, John could scarcely oppose it, even if he wanted to. This problem would be compounded by the fact that the Johannine community's memory was maintained through oral tradition and therefore still somewhat fluid. No single, authorized version of the church's Paraclete doctrine existed that could be addressed and definitively refuted—John could not simply burn or ban the books that advocated the AntiChristian viewpoint. Thus, even if John could suppress his own dogmatic tendencies long enough to attack the established traditions on which the AntiChrists had built their position, it would have been practically impossible to achieve ultimate victory through this tactic.

Second, even if John were willing to tackle the monumental task of suppressing or revising his community's dogma about the Spirit, the side effects of his efforts would have outweighed the benefits. As noted earlier, John's memory of Jesus was shaped under pressure from two sources, the AntiChrists within the church and "the world" and "the Jews" without. While the doctrine of pneumatic memory made John vulnerable to the AntiChrists, it also made him immune to challenges from "the world" and "the Jews," people who do not know God and whose opinions need not be taken seriously because they come from the devil rather than the Spirit (see John 8:31–56). The belief that the Paraclete is foundational to an accurate understanding of Jesus was thus a key weapon in John's rhetorical arsenal, one that he could not afford to lose in his ongoing war with forces outside the church.

John, then, found himself in a difficult place, and the quickest way out was pitted with unavoidable traps and snares. He could not afford to suppress his

---

The Obvious Question

Q "So, if John wanted to get rid of these AntiChrists, why didn't he just attack their foundational belief that the Spirit guides Christian memory? Wouldn't that be the easiest way to deal with the problem?"

A good question; but the answer is no for two reasons:

1. Because this belief had long been part of the church's dogmatic tradition, it would be nearly impossible to get rid of it, even if John wished to do so.

2. He didn't wish to do so, because he could use this doctrine to argue that "the world" doesn't know anything about Jesus because they don't have the Spirit.

---

community's belief that the authentic memory of Jesus is preserved by the Spirit, but also he could not ignore the fact that the AntiChrists' counter-memory was built on this very doctrine. He needed to emphasize the Spirit's influence while limiting the scope of that influence, and found the key to the puzzle in the production of the Fourth Gospel. A written text could affirm the Spirit's role in Christian memory while confining that memory to the boundaries of traditional christological creeds. Part 4 will show why this was the case by comparing and contrasting memories and history books, a comparison that will provide an obvious answer to the question, Why did John write a Gospel?

PART 4

The Answer—Memory and History

The Medicine of Memory: A Tale of Egypt

by Socrates

"At Naucratis, in Egypt, was one of the ancient gods of that country, the one whose sacred bird is called the ibis, and the name of the god himself was Theuth. He it was who invented numbers and arithmetic and geometry and astronomy, and also draughts [checkers] and dice, and, most important of all, letters [= writing].

"Now the king of all Egypt at that time was the god Thamus, who lived in the great city of the upper region, which the Greeks call the Egyptian Thebes, and they call the god himself Ammon. To him came Theuth to show his inventions, saying that they ought to be imparted to the other Egyptians. But Thamus asked what use there was in each, and as Theuth enumerated their uses, expressed praise or blame, according as he approved or disapproved.

"The story goes that Thamus said many things to Theuth in praise or blame of the various arts, which it would take too long to repeat; but when they came to the [written] letters, 'This invention, O King,' said Theuth, 'will make the Egyptians wise and improve their memories; for it is an elixir of memory and wisdom [μνήμης τε γὰρ καὶ σοφίας φάρμακον] that I have found.'

"But Thamus replied, 'Most ingenious Theuth, one man has the ability to beget arts, but the ability to judge of their usefulness or harmfulness to their users belongs to another; and now you, who are the father of letters, have been led by your affection to ascribe to them a power the opposite of that which they really possess.

"'For this invention will produce forgetfulness in the minds of those who learn to use it, because they will not practice their memory. Their trust in writing, produced by external characters which are no part of themselves, will discourage the use of their own memory within them. You have invented an elixir not of memory, but of reminding; and you offer your pupils the appearance of wisdom, not true wisdom, for they will read many things without instruction and will therefore seem to know many things, when they are for the most part ignorant and hard to get along with, since they are not wise but only appear to be wise.'"

—Plato, *Phaedrus* 274–75

9

"Everything That Rises Must Converge": The Private Past in Memory

As I said way back in chapter 1, this book is an attempt to answer the question, Why did John write a Gospel? By now you may be feeling like it's actually a study in delayed gratification, since the question only has six words and I still haven't offered a definitive solution after a hundred pages. The three chapters in this final section (especially the last chapter—your patience is appreciated one last time) will, at last, address the issue directly. Everything we've looked at so far is preparatory to this discussion. Here's a summary of my argument to this point:

- Most people have assumed that John wrote a Gospel mainly to preserve his community's Jesus tradition for posterity. This theory emphasizes the archive function of documents, the use of written texts to preserve information that might otherwise be forgotten.
- John, however, believed that the Holy Spirit would preserve the memory of Jesus indefinitely for his community. This would make a written Gospel unnecessary, in the sense that you wouldn't need one to avoid forgetting things about Jesus.

These first two points just sharpen my guiding question, or at least highlight it. If you live in a culture where most people can't read, and if you believe that you don't need to read books about Jesus anyway, because the Spirit will remind you of everything you need to know about him, what's the point of writing a Gospel?

- People don't just write books to help them remember things about the past. In many cultures, including John's culture, documents carry a symbolic value that transcends their actual contents. So the very fact that John could appeal to a written Gospel would carry a certain rhetorical force, even if he didn't need one to help him recall facts about Jesus.

This point answers the question, Why did John write a Gospel? at the most basic level. Even if John didn't need a written Gospel to help people remember things about Jesus, he still might want to appeal to the symbolic force of a written history book from time to time. But this of course begs another question: Why did John feel the need to appeal to the symbolic power of a written history book about Jesus? What could a written Gospel do that a Spirit–driven memory of Jesus couldn't do?

- At the time the Fourth Gospel was written, John was facing pressure from a heretical Christian group whom he calls "AntiChrists." The AntiChrists emphasized the Spirit's role in Christian memory, making the experience of the Spirit the primary organizing principle for the Johannine Jesus tradition. Thus they could expand and reconfigure the community's traditional database, reducing the significance of the historical Jesus and producing an image of Christ quite different from the image John advocated.
- John could have attacked the AntiChrists' foundational premise and denied that the Spirit works in this way. But this would have been impractical, because (a) the idea of charismatic memory had been a part of the Johannine tradition all along, and as a dogmatist John would generally want to preserve the traditional way of thinking, and (b) John needed that doctrine himself to refute the claims of "the world" and "the Jews," people who can't say anything intelligent about Jesus because they don't have the Spirit in them.
- All this being the case, John needed somehow to maintain the doctrine of charismatic memory while limiting the scope of the Spirit's mnemonic work. He needed, in other words, to assert that you need the Spirit to have a correct memory of Jesus, but he also needed to make it clear that the Spirit would not say what the AntiChrists say Jesus says.

It remains, then, to explore the reasons why the symbolic value of a written Gospel would be especially useful to John in his conflict with the AntiChrists. Put another way, I still need to describe how living memories and traditions are somehow different from history books in the way that they conceptualize and package the past, and to show how John could exploit these differences for his own purposes. These last three chapters (9, 10, and 11) will attempt to show that a written Gospel was the best possible solution to John's problem, the perfect way to freeze the memory of Jesus in a form that would complement the Spirit's ongoing work while negating the AntiChrists' claims.

This chapter will discuss three key features of the past as preserved in memory, features that would characterize the Johannine tradition at the moment when John decided to write a Gospel. Each of these features of the remembered past could be harnessed by the AntiChrists in service of their countermemory, especially when magnified by a mystical interpretation of the Johannine Paraclete doctrine. Because the available data are so limited, the word "could" should be emphasized here—the AntiChrists may or may not have been conscious of any or all of these features of memory, and certainly would have discussed the

---

The Past in Memory

The Remembered Past . . .

> **1.** is a social contract, not a content
>
> **2.** can be conflated for convenience
>
> **3.** seeks a sympathetic audience

---

issue in terms of the Spirit's influence rather than in the psychological and sociological jargon used here. Nevertheless, the discussion below will describe what John would view as the liabilities of memory, aspects of images of the past that were ripe for the AntiChrists' purposes. The specific means by which written history books counter these aspects of living memory will be discussed in chapter 10. Chapter 11 will then apply these data to the Johannine context to provide a final answer to the question, Why did John write a Gospel?

THE PAST IS A CONTRACT

As noted in an earlier chapter, memory is a social phenomenon. This is true not only of events that affect many people in a society, but also of the ways that individuals recall and reflect upon private experiences. I have done many things that no one else witnessed; as a result, I and I alone can "remember" these things. Yet even my personal recollection of these very private acts is a social phenomenon in two respects: (a) because these things occurred in the broader context of my past life, a life that was always already intertwined with the lives of other people, and (b) because, as I now think about my private past, I am forced to conceptualize and express what has happened through the framework of terms and values drawn from my society of today. I was a member of a group when these things happened, and I recall them now as a member of a group—other people are always present in my memories, even when they are not at the forefront of my consciousness.

What sociologists call the "collective memory" of a group is therefore *not* simply the sum total of all the discrete memories of every individual in the group, all of my memories plus all of yours plus all of everyone else's. Rather, a group's "social memory" is the capacity that every member of the group possesses to relate stories about the past in a meaningful way, "meaningful" because they are molded by memory frameworks that other people share. In this respect, memory is not a *content*, a fixed body of data about the past, but rather a *social contract*, an agreement about how the past should be conceptualized and discussed.

The social contract of memory is illustrated by A. J. Hill's *Under Pressure*, the story of the U.S. submarine *S-5*.[1] The *S-5* sank on a test voyage in 1920 when a crew member forgot to close one of the exhaust valves before a dive—a serious faux pas when traveling in an underwater vessel. Like most books of this kind, Hill's volume tells the tale of the wreck and the heroic rescue of the crew. But *Under Pressure* departs from the standard format of naval disaster stories in many respects. Hill writes in an informal, novelistic style, moving suddenly back and forth between the different sections of the ship to narrate simultaneous events involving isolated groups of sailors. Each chapter has several divisions that describe what was happening at the same moment in various submerged compartments, reflecting the varying perspectives of the trapped seamen. This makes for a very interesting read, and at the end of the book the author explains that this unique format was possible because twenty of the survivors wrote personal testimonies shortly after their rescue. *Under Pressure* is thus a composite image of the *S-5* disaster as seen through the eyes of these survivors, a mosaic of the recollections of twenty witnesses.

In one sense, Hill's book might be called a "collective memory" of the *S-5* submarine rescue. By breaking from a conventional linear narrative, by changing scenes and perspectives, by giving character sketches and biographical flashbacks to contextualize individuals and their actions, by telling the story through the eyes of many people at once—in these and other ways, Hill draws the reader into the presence of the crew of the *S-5*, allowing her to share vicariously their image of the past. *Under Pressure* might therefore be thought of as a "collective memory" in the sense that it weaves together many recollections of a common experience into a master narrative. This composite narrative tells the story as remembered by the whole group, a story that includes the experiences and reflections of each individual crew member but ultimately transcends the personal recollections of any one of them.

But at a deeper level—the level at which the social dimension of memory becomes helpful for actually understanding what people do with the past—it becomes clear that twenty eyewitness accounts of a submarine wreck, even when conveniently sorted and collated into a single story, do not constitute a "collective memory" of that event. As Halbwachs notes, "the collective memory [of a group] . . . encompasses the individual memories while remaining dis-

---

The Past in Memory

The Remembered Past . . .

    1. is a social contract, not a content

    2. can be conflated for convenience

    3. seeks a sympathetic audience

---

tinct from them," and in the process "any individual remembrances that may penetrate are transformed within a totality having no personal consciousness."[2] In other words, group memories are not "collective" in the sense that they include many tiny pieces of the larger puzzle of the total past; memories are "collective" in the sense that the people remembering use a common framework to recreate the past. In mathematical terms, the memory equation is never additive—a collective memory is more than the sum of all the individual memories of the members of a group.[3] In fact, any effort to describe the framework of a group's collective memory is a subtraction, the remainder after the recollections of specific individuals are removed from the common image of the past, leaving only the symbolic logic of the equation through which each person was able to think about what happened.

Returning to Hill's book: the "collective memory" of the crew members of the ill-fated *S-5* submarine would represent everything that would remain if the specific recollections of the individual sailors were subtracted from the text of *Under Pressure*. The result would be zero in terms of specific content, but a rich possibility of creating memory texts about the disaster over beers at the Veterans' Club ten years later. The collective memory would be the intangible, the equation itself rather than the sum. Hence, there is no substantial loss of collective memory in the fact that only twenty crew members, rather than thirty, left accounts of the tragedy. The number of testimonies does not alter the equation or expand the framework, even though more eyewitness reports might make *Under Pressure* a longer book and perhaps more historically accurate.

The remembered past is a potential rather than a fixed content, the potential to create images of yesterday that are relevant to current social realities. Translating this principle into the jargon of biblical scholarship, it is relevant to distinguish between the *content* of a tradition and the *tradition* itself, the

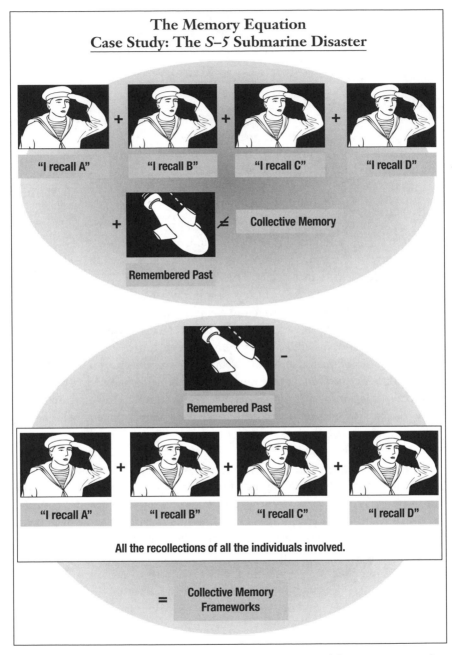

The Memory Equation
Case Study: The *S–5* Submarine Disaster

"I recall A" + "I recall B" + "I recall C" + "I recall D"

+ Remembered Past ≠ Collective Memory

Remembered Past −

"I recall A" + "I recall B" + "I recall C" + "I recall D"

All the recollections of all the individuals involved.

= Collective Memory Frameworks

"tradition" being the capacity to rehearse the content of the past in ways that are relevant and meaningful to the group today. In fact, a tradition is nothing more than a community's ability to talk about the past in a common idiom, and all traditions are collective in the sense that all members of the group may join in this conversation. Specifically here, the Johannine Jesus tradition, representing the sum total of the Johannine community's memories of Jesus, was not so much a body of data as a performance tradition, a social contract among the members of John's churches that specified how stories about the founder of the faith should be told. And because any member of John's churches could tell such stories as needed for teaching, evangelism, or personal reflection, one might refer to the Johannine Jesus tradition as a collective memory, a totality of recollections that transcended individual experiences and functioned as the community's common property.

Defining the Social Contract of Memory
Case in Point: Jewish Collective Memory

"The collective memories of the Jewish people were a function of the shared faith, cohesiveness, and will of the group itself, transmitting and recreating its past through an entire complex of interlocking social and religious institutions that functioned organically to achieve this. The decline of Jewish collective memory in modern times is only a symptom of the unraveling of that common network of belief and praxis through whose mechanisms . . . the past was once made present."

—Yerushalmi, *Zakhor: Jewish History and Jewish Memory*, 94

The social dimension of memory—the fact that a tradition is a social contract about how stories of the past should be told—would complicate John's situation by facilitating the AntiChrists' agenda. Because memory is a potential rather than a content, the database of memory cannot be closed and fixed; "it is stable, rather, [only] at the level of shared meanings and remembered images."[4] New things can be added so long as they fit the formula; old things can be forgotten or, just as significantly, rearranged into new patterns. Since the remembered past exists only at the moment that people talk about it, the content of that past is always subject to the needs of the present. This aspect of memory would be magnified in John's social context, where the memory of Jesus was seen as an ongoing operation of the Spirit. A sense of the Paraclete's presence would give the AntiChrists almost unlimited freedom to expand and reconfigure the database of the community's Jesus tradition. Rensberger's quote on this point, cited earlier, bears repeating: "If the [Elder's/John's] opponents claimed that their ideas were inspired by the Spirit . . . they would not hesitate to offer *new* concepts built up from their basic interpretation of the tradition."[5] So long as the AntiChrists' new revelations followed the basic terms of the memory contract, it would be extremely difficult for John to definitively counter their claims.

THE BLUR FACTOR:
THE ORGANIZED PAST IN MEMORY

The remembered past is "social" in the sense that all members of a group must express their thoughts about what has happened in common terms. As such, collective memory is not so much the total content of what people think has happened as the potential to tell stories about what has happened. This leaves the database of memory somewhat unstable, at least when compared to images of the past encoded, say, in photographs, DVDs, or history books—a living memory can be rearranged much more easily than words on a printed page. John's situation was characterized by an attempt to rearrange the memory of Jesus, and he needed a solution that would fix and freeze his community's memory once and for all. To highlight how a written Gospel might do this, it will be helpful to consider a key aspect of the memory contract: the means by which memory groups organize and order the past.

The Order of the Past

On December 29, 1890, about 350 men, women, and children of the Miniconjou and Hunkpapa Sioux (Lakota) Native American tribes were killed at Wounded Knee Creek in the Badlands of southwestern South Dakota. Chief Bigfoot and his people were overtaken by the U.S. Seventh Cavalry while fleeing to asylum at the Pine Ridge Reservation, and were forced to stop by the frozen stream for interrogation due to their suspected involvement in the millenarian Ghost Dance movement. The soldiers surrounded the Sioux tents, and as they were attempting to disarm their captives, a shot was fired somewhere in the camp—possibly the accidental discharge of a weapon as it was forcibly taken from a deaf man who could not understand instructions. The Americans responded by pouring gunfire—including payload from four Hotchkiss cannons, each capable of firing 100 explosive shells per minute—into the crowd. Many women and children were shot in the back as they fled up the bed of the small creek. After the "battle," as it was then called, the soldiers withdrew to tend to their wounded, leaving the injured Sioux to starve among the corpses in freezing temperatures and blowing snow. The U.S. government responded by awarding members of the Seventh Cavalry—incidentally (though perhaps not coincidentally) the regiment earlier led by General George Custer into Little Bighorn—an unprecedented number of Congressional Medals of Honor.

My wife Becky and I visited Wounded Knee several years ago, and since then I have investigated the circumstances surrounding the massacre in some detail. My initial researches were informal, motivated by a desire to learn more about this remarkable place and the tragedy that happened there. Later, however, I made a much more thorough study while writing an article for *JAAR* on apocalyptic rhetoric, which included a section on the 1890 Ghost Dance of the American Plains Indians. In the course of this research, I read all the available contemporary accounts of the massacre and also a number of secondary sources on U.S.-Sioux relations in that time period. Yet even after this extensive study, I still encounter an obstacle whenever I try to remember what happened at Wounded Knee: I find it impossible to relate the massacre accurately to other events in American history. Specifically, even though I am at this moment conscious that the massacre occurred on December 29, 1890, my memory wants to push the incident backward to a much earlier point in time, generally somewhere in the 1820s or 1830s, at least half a century before it actually happened. My memory, in other words, stubbornly resists what I know to be the historical chronology of the event. Why is this the case?

In his study of commemorative rituals, *How Societies Remember*, Paul Connerton notes the special challenges of field research in oral history. When gathering stories, field workers often meet an impasse when they ask their subjects for a chronological narration of personal experience. Connerton argues that this happens because such an approach "imports into the material [the individual's memory] a type of narrative shape, and with that a pattern of remembering, that is alien to that material." In fact, "when oral historians listen carefully to what their informants have to say they discover a perception of time that is not linear but cyclical. The life of the interviewee is not a curriculum vitae but a series of cycles" revolving around the recurring events of days, weeks, months, seasons, years, and generations.[6]

At first glance, Westerners might agree that Connerton's remarks are probably true of the way people think in oral traditional cultures, but believe that they do not apply to our modern literate societies—societies where people presumably think in a more logical and linear fashion. But the universal applicability of his observations has been confirmed by an extensive 1994 telephone survey that sought to identify popular uses of memory in the United States. In the introduction to the published results, the leaders of the survey team note that respondents' accounts of the personal past did not follow "conventional historical narratives and frameworks," in the sense that people seldom oriented their memories around the major public events that typically attract the attention of journalists and historians. Instead, the respondents "assembled isolated experiences into patterns," patterns that did not necessarily take the form of fixed plots with "inevitable endings." The survey also highlighted the utility of memory: people evoke these patterns of association not to preserve the past for its own sake but to "project what might happen next," allowing them to discriminate among the many choices they encounter in daily experience.[7]

As these results illustrate, the organization of the past in memory "is not necessarily linear, logical, or rational."[8] This is not to say that memories are organized in an illogical way, only that "memory retrieval is seldom sequential; we locate recalled events by association rather than by working methodically forward or backward through time."[9] In other words, individuals and groups do not memorize tight historical narratives and then store factoids about the past somewhere on these timelines (except maybe when cramming for history exams). Instead, memory orders images of the past through a continual process of comparison and contrast, analyzing events and people in terms of their similarities to, and differences from, both other past events and present conditions. This mental sorting and sifting makes it possible to assign memories to categories within the group's worldview and, in the process, to attribute socially appropriate meaning and value to them.[10] The ordering of memories is, in other words, one aspect of the broader social contract that guides the way members of a group think and talk about the past.

The fact that my memory is organized according to an order of values and a set of categories derived from my broader culture explains my difficulty in locating the Wounded Knee Massacre on the chronological timeline of American history. Wounded Knee is more than an event that occurred on December 29, 1890; Wounded Knee is symbol, a sort of summary statement, of U.S.-Indian relations. In my thinking, this symbolic event falls into the broader category of "minority relations," the way that European Americans have interacted with all minority groups and people. As such, whenever I think about Wounded Knee, I conceptualize that event through the framework of my thinking about the experiences of all American minority groups, a set of values about the history of my country that I have derived from my society of today. This memory category reflects the social contract of modern American memory (at least one such social contract), the way that stories about the minority experience are supposed to be told. And my inability to situate the Wounded Knee Massacre chronologically reflects the fact that the actual historical date of that incident violates the terms of this social contract.

In my mental organization of the past, certain events stand out as significant moments in the history of U.S. minority relations. Wounded Knee is one such event; the Civil War, including Lincoln's Emancipation Proclamation, is another; the women's suffrage movement is another; Dr. Martin Luther King Jr.'s March on Washington is another. Many Americans, including myself, tend to picture the Civil War as a major turning point in U.S. minority relations, a moment in time when our nation resolved that minority groups cannot be denied certain inalienable rights. Of course, this impression is not entirely accurate—any history book will tell you that the causes of the American Civil War were much more complicated than the benevolent desire of

Northern white people to free slaves. I am referring here, however, to popular conceptions of the Civil War that associate that conflict with more recent events like the civil rights movement, associations that make the popular 1960s folk song "Abraham, Martin, and John" sensible to modern Americans even though we know that it was not historically possible for Abraham Lincoln, Martin Luther King Jr., and John F. Kennedy to take a walk over a hill together. So while I can, as a member of the academic community, distinguish as necessary between historical fact and popular myth, I can also, as a person raised in a white, lower-class, American neighborhood in the 1970s, relate very well to the way that most Americans think about the Civil War as a sort of precursor to the civil rights crusade, and also to their surprise and disappointment whenever they discover that it really was not.

Abraham Lincoln resolved at Gettysburg that "these dead shall not have died in vain," and popular American memory takes this to mean that the lives lost in the Civil War to establish "liberty and justice for all" were not wasted. But the blood of these men does seem to have been wasted if, in fact, the Wounded Knee Massacre took place twenty-seven years after Lincoln spoke these words, for it is hard to identify a more flagrant single act of injustice against a minority group in all of American history. According to my social contract of memory, the massacre at Wounded Knee contrasts with the spirit of the Civil War so sharply that the two cannot be held together in the same category—the problem that Wounded Knee represents must have been resolved long before 1890. My memory therefore tends to shift Wounded Knee backward into an earlier time period, a time before the Civil War, when white American men must have been less conscious of their crimes against Native and African Americans.

I realize, of course, that what I am saying about my memory is not "logical," in the sense that it violates what I know to be the actual chronology of history. But this simply illustrates the fact that memory does not order the past in a logical, chronological sequence. Instead, it ties events together in an associative matrix, one that attributes value to past events and people by comparison to other past events and people, all viewed against the backdrop of present social realities. In my memory, all past events are essentially contemporary and are weighted in terms of my current values, and any narrative of the past that my memory constructs will significantly reflect these values. My stories about "what happened" will, in other words, reflect the social frameworks of values that guide my memories, completely apart from the issue of whether the things I am telling you are historically true. And even if I were to say, as I would say, that it is important to order remembered images of the past in correct chronological sequence as much as possible—even this assertion would reflect an American cultural value about how the past should be conceptualized and presented.

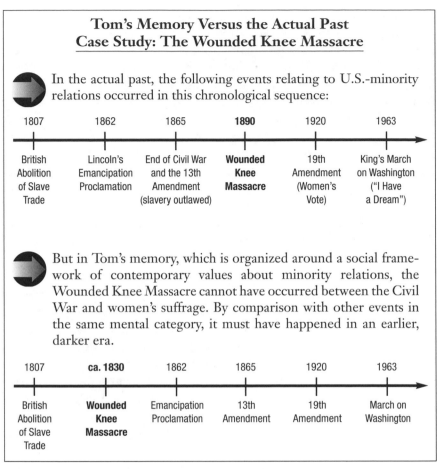

Tom's Memory Versus the Actual Past
Case Study: The Wounded Knee Massacre

In the actual past, the following events relating to U.S.-minority relations occurred in this chronological sequence:

1807	1862	1865	**1890**	1920	1963
British Abolition of Slave Trade	Lincoln's Emancipation Proclamation	End of Civil War and the 13th Amendment (slavery outlawed)	**Wounded Knee Massacre**	19th Amendment (Women's Vote)	King's March on Washington ("I Have a Dream")

But in Tom's memory, which is organized around a social framework of contemporary values about minority relations, the Wounded Knee Massacre cannot have occurred between the Civil War and women's suffrage. By comparison with other events in the same mental category, it must have happened in an earlier, darker era.

1807	**ca. 1830**	1862	1865	1920	1963
British Abolition of Slave Trade	**Wounded Knee Massacre**	Emancipation Proclamation	13th Amendment	19th Amendment	March on Washington

You may have detected that I am Caucasian, and perhaps for this reason my thinking about minority relations follows what Eviatar Zerubavel calls a "progress" narrative, a story line in which things are gradually getting better over time.[11] People of a different ethnic background may not share that same framework (I know several who do not), but it at least explains why I put Wounded Knee in the 1830s rather than the 1890s: it's hard to see that event as "better" than the abolition of slavery after the Civil War. This same progress narrative also frames and orders my memory of more recent events in American history. For example, I have to think for a minute whenever I try to remember whether Malcolm X (nee Little) was active at the same time as Martin Luther King Jr. In point of fact, the careers of these two men overlapped, but according to my memory framework Malcolm X must have come first and died before Dr. King's efforts really took off. My memory of the civil rights movement labels Malcolm X as the one who embraced violence as a form of political action, while Dr. King is the one who endorsed peaceful resistance. My progress narrative about minority relations leads me to think that violent solutions eventually give way to peaceful solutions, so it makes me feel good to think that Dr. King's superior vision won out. If I were writing a history book, I would need to be much more precise than that, but my memory contrasts these two men and orders their careers in a way that makes the chronological relationship null.

Because memory organizes information around systems of values, things that contrast more sharply with present experience are often felt to be more chronologically remote, while things that are more familiar feel more recent. The Wounded Knee Massacre occurred more than two decades after the end of the Civil War, but the Civil War feels closer to me because it represents values and attitudes that I perceive to be closer to my own values about diversity. For the same reason, Dr. King feels closer to me than Malcolm X, even though the two men lived and worked at the same time. Similarly, I can hardly believe that in the days when my own mother was a child running home after school to watch *American Bandstand*, she and my father had to enter their school building through separate doors, and neither of them was allowed to drink from the "colored" water fountain in the park. These values are so foreign to my experience that I cannot believe they characterized life in my own country so recently, even though I must accept these realities as historical facts that cannot be denied. In a similar way, dinosaurs and cave men can coexist in popular memory because both seem equally remote when compared to present experience.

Does this mean, then, that memory has no interest in history? Obviously not. As I said above, my faulty memory does not stop me from exploring the true relationships between past events and from attempting to develop an

---

The Past in Memory

The Remembered Past . . .

    1. is a social contract, not a content

    2. can be conflated for convenience

    3. seeks a sympathetic audience

---

accurate understanding of the actual past. I am well aware that Wounded Knee happened long after the Civil War and would tell the same to my children. And I would imagine that many anthropologists and paleontologists, who are quite well versed in the history of life on this planet, secretly enjoy reruns of *The Flintstones* in the privacy of their homes, and chuckle when Dino jumps on Fred and knocks him down as he comes through the door with his stone lunchbox. Memory does not necessarily deny the actual chronology of history; it simply does not depend on that chronology and therefore does not always order itself around the actual past. Instead, it organizes events from the actual past around a set of social values that reflect group logic, language, and experience. For this very reason, the way that we conceptualize the past may not make much sense to people outside our group.[12]

The Blur Factor: Memory Squeeze

Once a group labels memories, assigns them to ideological categories, and orders them, the items in each category tend to melt into larger conflated images that cluster around people, events, or situations that are deemed particularly significant.[13] Maurice Halbwachs, who discussed this phenomenon extensively, refers to these significant images as "landmarks" (*points de repère*) of memory. The Wounded Knee Massacre functions as a landmark in my memory of U.S.-minority relations, a symbolic event that gathers other similar incidents into itself and stands for all of them at once. "In collective memory," Halbwachs says,

> there are in general particular figures, dates, and periods of time that acquire an extraordinary salience. These attract to themselves other events and figures that happened at other moments. A whole period is concentrated, so to speak, in one year, just as a series of actions and events, about which one has forgotten its varying actors and diverse conditions, gathers together in one man and is attributed to him alone.[14]

The conflation of distinct people and events into archetypal landmarks is facilitated by a mental process that Fentress and Wickham call the "conceptualization of memory," "a tendency towards simplification and schematization" in recollections of the past.[15] This aspect of memory turns specific incidents and individuals into "generalizable markers about suffering, joy, commitment, and endurance."[16] Simplified schematic images are easier to remember and to organize, but necessarily make individual persons and events from the past appear less distinct. As a result, in many cases what seem to be discrete memories are actually composite images. Elements of several unique events crystallize like rock candy around the memory of a specific moment, and the traits exhibited by an individual over a period of time are brought together in a unified portrait of that person's character. This is especially the case when similar events recur many times with little variation or when we encounter the same people regularly in the course of typical activities. If, for example, we rode the same bus to school every day over a period of six years, specific things the driver did on different occasions will tend to merge into the larger conglomerate image of that person's character, making it impossible to distinguish them chronologically. For the same reason, we think of the apostle Thomas as the "doubter," even though "doubting Thomas" didn't doubt anything that we have heard about until the very end of Jesus' story, and even though his doubt immediately turned to faith (John 20:19–29). In popular Christian memory this momentary lapse in judgment becomes a persistent character trait, a sort of spiritual birthmark, much to the ongoing disgrace of poor Thomas.

Once memory puts things into the same category, they tend to bleed into one another, and once they get mixed up, it's hard to pull them apart again—somewhat like removing the chips from chocolate chip cookies after they've been baked. The process of conflation works alongside of, and entirely reflects, the social contract of memory, in the sense that the group determines which items can merge and which ones must be kept distinct for sake of meaningful communication about the past. And so long as memory exists solely in the form of oral traditions and personal recollections, it is almost impossible to control this process—even tagged events can be lost or put in the wrong order simply by removing the tags and attaching new ones.

This aspect of memory could be exploited by the AntiChrists in their production of a countermemory of Jesus. One could easily build a new image of Jesus from John's traditional database by applying new memory tags, setting up different landmarks, underlining some features of the orthodox image while forgetting others, blurring things that John wanted to keep distinct and distinguishing things his memory blurred, taking composite pictures apart and magnifying their individual elements to grotesque proportions—these and similar moves would quickly create a new Christ "in place of" the established image of the community's orthodox creeds. This would be especially true if the AntiChrists did indeed appeal to the Spirit's guidance to support their new vision. If Christ is continuing to speak to the church as the Paraclete, new revelations would naturally bleed into older memories of things that Jesus said and did in Galilee. These new composite images could then be rearranged and reordered around the axis of the Spirit. And so long as the Johannine community's Jesus tradition was preserved only in the form of creeds and oral teachings, it would be almost impossible for John to control this type of growth and expansion. John needed, again, something that would fix his Jesus tradition, something that would forever hold certain memories together while keeping others apart.

LISTENER SUPPORTED:
MEMORY'S SYMPATHETIC EAR

Memory organizes the past according to social contracts, in ways peculiar to the specific memory group that generates them. When individuals share recollections with other members of the memory group, they generally assume that the audience has some foreknowledge of the events under consideration, or at least that the audience could predict the outcome by appealing to the common frameworks by which that version of the past has been meaningfully arranged. If, for example, I am talking to my brother about a remarkable event that happened at the family dinner table in our house on Warren Avenue in 1979, I may assume that he will either recall the specific incident under consideration or will at least remember enough about family dinners in general to reconstruct the backdrop and cast of the scene quickly. I also assume that he will not challenge my memory to any significant degree, and that if he does challenge me, it will only be to enrich and deepen my portrait of the past.

Fentress and Wickham cite this phenomenon to explain some of the peculiar features of traditional folk stories. For example, it has long been noted that oral epics evidence a paratactic plot structure, with images and scenes strung together in rough sequences, one isolated event following another without strict narrative connections. While such stories often appear pedantic and awkward to literate audiences, and while their logic might baffle people from other cultures, the traditional poet assumes that he is simply reminding his listeners "of a story they already know." Audience foreknowledge also explains why traditional performers are less self-conscious than literate historians about information that might challenge the credibility of their presentation. For example, oral composers typically repeat scenes and events that they wish to emphasize, even when such repetition violates the chronological integrity of the story. Similarly, since the audience already remembers the idiosyncrasies of the traditional characters, the oral composer may reveal information about a character "before the events in the plot have made such an action appropriate," meaning that the character's actions may not make much sense to people outside the storyteller's group.[17]

Recently, my seven-year-old son and I were reading one of his library storybooks about Kwaku Anansi. Anansi, originally an African spider-god of some sort, appears as a character in a large number of African and Caribbean folk tales. In many of the children's books based on these tales, he isn't so much a god as a trickster, a lazy shyster who spends most of his time trying to con other animals out of their food or treasures. This particular book had something to do with Anansi stealing pineapples and bananas from other animals' houses while they went for walks in the jungle on a hot day. But because the story stayed close to the original Jamaican folk tale, many of Anansi's unethical behaviors were baffling to us and became sensible only when key information about his character was revealed on the last page. "Why is he stealing all those bananas?" Aaron kept asking. "A spider can't eat bananas." No, I concurred, he would more likely want to live in them. Aaron then pointed out that Anansi already had a large house, as illustrated on several pages. For my son, who comes from a narrative tradition where the main character in the story is almost always the good guy, the notion that the hero would be a conniving thief who steals from his own friends was beyond the range of comprehension. But I assume that a child from Jamaica or Ghana who is familiar with this and/or similar traditional stories about Anansi would not need to ask such questions, because she would already understand the nuances of his character and why he acts the way he does.

Memory, then, is a private phenomenon ("private" to the members of the memory group) that seeks a sympathetic ear, which is also to say that memory is ultimately subjective and inwardly focused. Even when things that I remember could be objectively documented, I generally do not feel a need to verify them and would probably be offended if you asked me to do so. We tend to give memory the benefit of the doubt, or at least we negotiate truth claims that are based on memory on different terms from other kinds of truth claims—say the truth claims in an academic textbook. Hence, if I say that Fentress and Wickham said X or Y about traditional folk tales on pages 55–57 of their book, you know that you could test my claim by looking up the reference, and you further assume that, because I know that you know this, I have been careful to reflect their views accurately. In other words, my citation of that source operates within a social contract that requires me to be careful about what I say, because you can easily test the veracity of my statements. But when I say that I remember a time when Aaron and I read a story about Anansi the Spider, you tend to agree with me just because it would be so hard (and so pointless) to prove or disprove my claims.

The sympathetic, subjective dimension of memory magnifies the first two aspects of memory described above. When telling a story from memory, we tend to assume that people will agree with what we're saying, and certainly assume that they could challenge us only by citing other information from their own memories that we could, in turn, counter and reject. As such, the data we select from the past and the way we package and present that data are negotiable in the context of a conversation, at least much more negotiable than data we might read in a book on the same subject. This is not to say, again, that memory is disinterested in the past or that we accept everything that people tell us from memory. But the social contract of memory becomes somewhat vague when it comes to the historicity clause, simply because memory asks to

---

The Past in Memory

The Remembered Past . . .

1. is a social contract, not a content

2. can be conflated for convenience

3. **seeks a sympathetic audience**

---

be accepted without comment and because it is hard to disprove people's claims about the past without documentation.

This dimension of memory would again be magnified in John's situation, where recall was viewed as an operation of the Spirit. John and the AntiChrists agree that Christ comes to the church in the form of the Spirit and helps Christians remember things about Jesus. The AntiChrists say that Jesus is reminding them of things that John has forgotten, is revealing new things to them, and is showing them new ways to think about things that the Johannine community has known all along. As a result of this mystical outlook, they have developed a vision of Jesus that differs significantly from John's view. Some Christians support John, while others, like Diotrephes, turn a sympathetic ear to the AntiChrists and do not require them to measure their new outlook against previous orthodox teachings. Also because he is sympathetic to this new vision, Diotrephes does not apply strenuous criteria of historicity to the AntiChrists' statements and seems to discourage other people from doing so as well. True, the AntiChrists could document their claims only by appealing to Spirit-guided memory, but John could do no more than this himself. How, then, could he respond to their challenge, and how could he stop these new memories from getting out of hand?

It is important to stress here that the discussion in this chapter remains relevant to John's situation regardless of one's estimate of the historicity of the Johannine Jesus tradition. I have argued that living memory has an inherently fluid quality that would allow the AntiChrists to reconfigure the image of Jesus by expanding and reordering John's traditional database of information. So long as the Johannine tradition existed only as a series of oral performances— as a potential to tell stories about Jesus whenever necessary—it would be subject to multiple renderings and multiple interpretations, regardless of whether all or some elements of that tradition were historically accurate. This is the case because the framework of a tradition—the social contract about how the past should be discussed—can to some degree shift and bend independently of the historical content of that tradition.

Obviously, any new revelations that the AntiChrists might generate would not be "historically accurate," in the sense that they did not originate with the historical Jesus. But whether or not specific pieces of information from John's database originated with the historical Jesus is beside the point here. So long as they exist only in the form of living memory and oral tradition, a thousand bits of authentic historical data will still be subject to compression, suppression, conflation, and reordering if the terms of the social memory contract change. Such historical facts, and past understandings of such facts, will to some degree limit the extent of their own reconfiguration, but very little movement is required to place new images of Jesus outside the strict boundaries of orthodox dogma. John was not faced with a need to prove the historicity of his own

---

The Past in Memory: John's Dilemma

The Remembered Past . . .

1. **Is a social contract, not a content**
   meaning that it builds its image of the past not on the basis of "what happened," but rather on the basis of the group's order of values. This is the case whether or not the content of a memory happens to be historically true.

2. **Can be conflated for convenience**
   meaning that items in memory are arranged by comparison and contrast against the backdrop of the issues and values of today, and that sometimes those values cause certain memories to blur together while others remain distinct.

3. **Seeks a sympathetic audience**
   meaning that memory is subjective, expecting the audience to accept its claims without extensive verification.

1 + 2 + 3 + John 14:26 + John 16:13 = big trouble for John

All these features of memory, magnified and complicated by the doctrine of charismatic recall, would characterize the Johannine Jesus tradition up to the moment in time when John decided to write a Gospel.

claims; he was faced with the need to disprove another memory of Jesus that was very appealing to some Christians in his churches.

While John could have adopted a number of different strategies to deal with this problem, a written Gospel would be the ideal response to the AntiChrists' mystical countermemory. Every liability of the remembered past discussed in this chapter would be eliminated by appeal to a history book about Jesus. This is the case because history books conceptualize and order the past in ways very different from living memory and oral traditions. Several of the most significant differences will be discussed in the next chapter.

10

Beyond the Scope of the Present Study: The Public Past in History Books

The production of the Fourth Gospel represented a conscious shift from a living memory of Jesus preserved in community tradition to a history of Jesus preserved on paper. Of course, history books are themselves a form of collective memory, one way that groups preserve images of the past. But history books differ significantly from living memory for two reasons: because they are *histories* and because they are *books*. In other words, history books diverge from collective memory in their conceptualization and presentation of the past, and then magnify these differences by committing the historical past to writing. These differences would make the composition of a written Gospel particularly appealing to John in his struggles with the AntiChrists.

The Past in History Books

The Written Past . . .

    1. is universal and unitary

    2. is broken into permanent periods

    3. loves ignorance

THE TOTAL OBJECTIVE PAST

Memories are generated for private audiences, either for personal reflection or for consideration by others who are members of the same memory group. History books, by contrast, are public documents, and as such they treat the past as an objective, universal phenomenon open to any reader's scrutiny.[1] This basic distinction—that memories treat the past as subjective private experiences while histories treat the past as objective public events—generates significant differences in the way that memories and history books conceptualize, organize, and present the past to their respective audiences. Specifically here, history books treat the past as an additive equation and require their readers/audiences to view the whole of the past and all of its parts from a third-person perspective. In the process, they establish themselves as the final authority in all discussions of "what has happened."

In mathematical terms, historiography—the business of writing history books and all the rules and regulations that guide that business—operates on an addition equation. Every individual moment of the past is treated as a single, distinct item, and all these items could theoretically be added into a sum that would represent the "total past."[2] Each history book is simply a subset of that larger whole and borrows its contents from the greater mass; "the historical world," Halbwachs observes, "is like an ocean fed by the many partial histories." One could therefore, if so inclined, scan all the history books that have ever been written and post their texts on a massive Web site, "the universal memory of the human species[.com],"[3] complete with a search engine that would allow anyone anywhere to discover anything that has ever happened, even if such information is of no immediate relevance to any living person or memory group.

Of course, reviews of this Web site would immediately point out that the database is incomplete, because it is impossible to record everything. But while this fact is a great comfort to students who are cramming for history exams, historians view it as a significant loss. In the universe of history, all people and events from the past are essentially equal and worthy of record, and items are excluded from a particular study not because they are not worth remembering but simply because time, space, and money-hungry publishers (who for some reason stubbornly refuse to print books that people will not read) do not permit them to receive the attention they deserve.[4]

Memory and history books, then, both try to preserve the past, but they do so in ways that reflect very different sets of priorities. For example, I noted earlier that A. J. Hill's book *Under Pressure*, when viewed as the collective memory of the crew members of the *S-5* submarine disaster, does not suffer from the fact that only twenty survivors left accounts of the event, rather than thirty. This is the case because collective memory is not so much a content as a contract, a way of thinking about the past that would enable all of the survivors to talk about the wreck in a meaningful way whenever they wished. As a social contract, this memory framework would specify which facts could be forgotten and which must be remembered, which images could be safely compressed or conflated and which should be differentiated and enlarged. But a naval historian could only wring his hands in dismay upon learning that fewer than half of the *S-5* crewmen left written accounts of their experience, because history always strives for 100 percent documentation and is loath to leave anything out. Even if certain facts are of no particular interest to readers today, who knows what future generations will think? Indeed, the historian of tomorrow might find valuable potsherds in the garbage heap of our memory. It is therefore imperative to keep everything distinct and objective—objective either in the positivistic sense or through rigorous application of an approved hermeneutical model with substantial footnotes—leaving the reader to decide what is important and how it is significant. If "memory" consists of both social frameworks and the contents of the past, it may be said that living memory highlights frameworks over content, while history books crave content and discard the frameworks. In fact, "historical objectivity" may be defined as a thorough attempt to liberate the contents of the past from the orders of values utilized by living memory groups.

Of course, history books are not quite so neutral as they claim to be, and closer examination reveals the extent to which they fix and order the past in service of particular rhetorical objectives. I shall elaborate on that issue in a moment, but first it is relevant to note a significant side effect of the quest for historical objectivity and/or scholarly distance that is magnified by the technology of writing.

History books attempt to extract images of the past from the memory frameworks of the groups that have experienced that past. The specific contents of these group memories are reduced to a set of distinct events and people, and these are then treated as a subset within the larger, total past, a total past that is ultimately neutral and objective, carrying no inherent value because it is not shaped by any group's memory framework. As a result, history

---

from *Halbwachs's Dictionary of Memory*

his·tor´i·cal (-ĭ·kăl) **ob´jec·tiv´i·ty** (ŏb´jĕk·tĭv´ĭ·tĭ)—
n. **1.** the content of the past as liberated from the memories of living groups. *adj.* **2.** a quality of representations of the past that claim to achieve #1, such as history books. *n.* **3.** the rhetorical posture of authors, especially historians, who claim that their works possess #2. **—total objectivity** *n.* the fiction that #2 is attainable in an absolute sense.

The Memory Recipe: Same Ingredients, Different Flavors

 According to FDA guidelines, all items classified and sold as "memory drinks" must exhibit the following chemical composition:

Memory = *social frameworks* + *content*
(group values) *(images of the past)*

Living Memory Cola
("The Flavor of Today")

History Book Blast
("The Taste You Can Trust")

Cola

Ingredients:
(content by weight)
frameworks—90%
content—10%

*may contain traces
of peanuts

Cola

Ingredients:
(content by weight)
frameworks—10%
content—90%

*includes artificial
flavors and coloring

books generate what Roland Barthes would call "degree zero" images of the past, texts where memories are detached from people and carry no inherent meaning or value.

Barthes developed the concept of "writing degree zero" in a discussion of contemporary art forms like surrealist painting and stream-of-consciousness novels, genres where the audience's perception of a piece is not guided by a strong sense of the author's intended meaning. The authors and artists of such texts claim that their work does not attempt to communicate a single, distinct "point" or message: the images in the painting and the words on the page are simply thrown out for the viewer's contemplation, disattached from anyone's personal agenda. As a result, such texts achieve "a state which is possible only in the dictionary or poetry—places where the noun can live without its article—and [are] reduced to a sort of zero degree, pregnant with all past and future specifications."[5] "Zero degree" is thus a measure of the author or artist's control over the meaning of a piece—they have no control over the meaning at all, so that the words and images are left to stand completely on their own before the audience's scrutiny. It is important to stress here that Barthes is not referring to a postmodern, reader-oriented interpretive posture, but rather to the type of text produced by an author who claims that personal interests have not guided her work. The surrealist painters and poets of the early twentieth century made such a claim; so do all historians. This is true not only of positivistic historians who assume a simple correlation between their texts and "what happened," but also, and equally, true of autobiographical and ideological historians, who must cram their material into rigid genres of scholarly discourse that are shaped by the rules of the academy and the house style sheets of university presses rather than by contracts of living memory. Because historians imply that their presentations are controlled by abstract laws of objectivity or the principles of a theoretical model, all history books in one sense operate in a zero degree—perhaps the reason they leave many readers with a cold feeling.

If you have been following my argument to this point, the paragraph above about "degree zero" historical memory may seem to contradict some things I've already said. In previous chapters I argued that recall is always a social phenomenon, in the sense that our memories are always shaped by the terms and values of the social groups in which we participate. Then, earlier in this very chapter, I said that "history books are themselves a form of collective memory, one way that groups preserve images of the past." Now I am saying that history books operate in a degree-zero environment where the content of memory can exist apart from the social frameworks of anyone's memory. How can all of these claims be true at once? In other words, if reading history books is a form of recall, and if history books call their readers to view the past from a degree-zero perspective, then history books must represent a special form of memory in which images of the past are not shaped by anyone's social frameworks. This being the case, it is possible to think of an objective species of memory, one that is not shaped by social frameworks and values. This is the specific sense in which historians would claim that their work is "objective": their books are neutral zones of memory, a place where the past roams free and unencumbered by the values and prejudices of popular society. But if such a neutral zone exists, then it must be theoretically possible for memories to exist and function free of frameworks, right?

This line of thinking would, indeed, threaten my overall argument, *if* it did not overlook one key fact. While history books do extract the contents of the past from the living frameworks of memory groups and preserve those contents outside the minds of human beings, *they do so by replacing the living frameworks of memory with themselves.* The history book becomes, in other words, a surrogate memory framework, asking the reader to evaluate the past from the perspective of its own internal order of values. As such, the history book does not deny that the past must be framed in order to be meaningful; it simply insists that everyone must view the past through its own myopic frame. The same would be true of other technologies that inscribe the past in order to preserve it—photographs, films, CDs, DVDs, and so forth. All these media remove images of the past from the living minds of people and preserve them in a mechanical format, turning organic memories into a series of inkspots or codified electrical impulses. In the process, the inscribed text itself—the book, the photo, the tape, the film—becomes a surrogate memory group for those who wish to review these data later on, always under the condition that all reviewers must operate on the text's own terms.

It is fair to say, then, that the technology of writing—the "book" part of history books—magnifies the notion of "historical/methodological objectivity" to a point where it takes the shape of nonnegotiability, to a point where any

---

The Past in History Books

The Written Past . . .

1. is universal and unitary

2. is broken into permanent periods

3. loves ignorance

---

dialogue about what may or may not have happened has to follow the rules of the history game. The past in history books is "public," not because it belongs to everyone but because it belongs to no one, and as a result it is accountable to no one's memory. So while the remembered past is negotiable within the social contract that guides the dialogue of individuals in a memory group, the inscribed past of history books is not negotiable on any terms. Readers can only agree or disagree, accept or reject; it either happened the way book says, or it didn't.

This being the case, it is also important to stress what historical documents—books, photos, paintings, and so forth—do *not* do: they do *not* evoke images of the past from living memory. Instead, such texts insert structured images of the past into their audience's present social context, and these new structures immediately become the organizing principle for the images in living memory. For example, in my mind right now, I arrange my childhood memories of the huge playground at Lunken Airport on the basis of the way that the place looks today and occasional discussions with my wife (who also played there) about how it used to look. My memory of that place is therefore fluid and negotiable. But if Becky and I were to look at a brochure for the Lunken Airport Playfield written in, say, 1977, our memories would be immediately

Memory and Writing: The Order of the Past

 In my living memory of the playground at Lunken Airport, images of the past are arranged on the basis of the way the place looks now and discussions with Becky about how it used to look

"The train used to be over by that tree, right? To the left of the tree?"

"It must have been, because remember how it . . ."

 But as soon as we look at a picture and description in an old brochure, the discussion is over.

"Hmmm. Well, this says there used to be two trees."

"Oh, yeah. Yeah. Remember how I was thinking that you used to go past the one tree to get to the boat? . . ."

The Lunken Express (1977)
Just past the slide, little engineers discover the Lunken Express, shaded by ancient elms.

rearranged and fixed on the basis of the images and descriptions in that document. The inscribed past is potent simply because it forces readers/viewers to think on its own terms, and this is the very reason why we appeal to pictures and books when we feel our memories failing and in need of support. Historical documents, then, do not help us to remember; they make it unnecessary for us to remember.

This aspect of the inscribed past—its ability to function as a surrogate memory framework—is enhanced in cultures where writing possesses an inherently symbolic quality. In societies such as the one I live in and the one John the evangelist lived in, the social contract of memory gives written versions of the past a special authority, one that elevates the value of their organizing principles. The image of the past in history books rises to a point where it stands in judgment of all living memories and threatens to label as "false" every scheme that does not comply with its terms. In these cultures, one scrap of paper can override the testimony of a dozen witnesses, and the organizing principles of a sacred text condemn to damnation every memory that does not follow their lead. Written texts do not acquire symbolic rhetorical force because a society views their contents as necessarily superior to the contents of living memory and oral traditions. Indeed, documents simply preserve in written form the same facts and figures that once inhabited, and in most cases still inhabit, someone's living memory. Instead, written texts carry symbolic rhetorical force when members of a society agree that documents organize and frame the past in an inherently superior fashion.

PERMANENT PERIODS, FROZEN TIME

Eviatar Zerubavel notes that it is impossible to think about the past—or, for that matter, to think about anything—without the aid of a guiding organizational scheme. There are simply too many things in the world to think about, and we can concentrate on individual items only by distinguishing them from the larger backdrop of things that are not getting our attention right now. "It is the fact that it is differentiated from other entities that provides an entity with a distinctive meaning as well as with a distinctive identity that sets it apart from everything else."[6] Things acquire value as we sort them into mental categories, and in the process they are defined both in terms of what they are and what they are not. Bananas are fruits, which means that they are not vegetables; vegetables are food items, which means that they are not a means of transportation; cars are a means of transportation, which means that they are not to be eaten but are useful for driving to the store to get more bananas. The meaning of things is thus "always a function of the particular mental compartment in which we place them."[7] Applied to a theory of memory, this means that images of the past are comprehensible only when they are discriminated, sorted, and arranged into meaningful patterns.

As noted in chapter 9, living memory organizes the past by sorting recollections into categories and patterns that reflect the group's value system, and for this reason the remembered past follows an internal logic that may not make sense to outsiders. Further, because they are dependent on group values, the frameworks of memory shift whenever these values shift, leading a group continually to reorganize its memories to reflect current realities. In the process, some clear images are blurred, some blurred images become clearer, composite pictures are broken apart, and broken pieces melt together. Continuity in memory is maintained not necessarily at the level of content, but rather through the persistence of the social contract that allows all members of the society to speak about the past in a meaningful way at any given moment.

History books, however, organize the past in ways very different from living memory, and then state their version of what happened in nonnegotiable terms. To highlight these differences, it will be helpful here to consider both the means by which history books order the past and the effect of writing on that organizational scheme.

Narrative Logic

Memories are comprehensible only when they are sorted and arranged in meaningful patterns. The most basic, yet perhaps most significant, means by which both memory and history books order the past involves the insertion of conceptual breaks into the mathematical flow of time, a process sometimes referred to as "periodization." "Periods" are distinct blocks of time that are bracketed by "watershed" moments, events and/or individuals whose appearance marks the beginning or end of an era. Eviatar Zerubavel, who has discussed this phenomenon extensively, notes that watersheds are significant because "they are collectively perceived as having involved significant identity transformations," moments when the life of the individual or group under consideration "took a turn" and began to move in a different direction. Once events and people are bracketed by watersheds and grouped together in a distinct period, it is generally assumed that they share certain characteristics that reflect the "spirit of the age." This spirit, of course, differs from the spirits that drove other eras (eras in the life of an individual or eras in the larger life of a society), a fact that helps us remember the relevant characteristics of people who lived at that time and understand the reasons they did the things that they did.

In the case of living memory, watersheds parallel the mental boundaries in a group's value system and function alongside those boundaries. The mental gaps between categories of concepts are superimposed onto the flow of time to project backward into the past the origin of these discontinuities, and of the group's overall way of thinking.[8] For example, Westerners typically see 1789, the opening year of the French Revolution, as a major turning point in world history, and treat that event as a watershed moment dividing two distinct eras. This mental move is possible because Westerners believe that the culture and values of post–Revolution France are irreconcilable with those of the monarchy, so that the France of 1788 and the France of 1790 cannot fit into the same mental category. In the same way, my tendency to situate the Wounded Knee Massacre in 1830, rather than the true date of 1890, reflects the fact that I view the Civil War as a turning point, or a watershed moment, in U.S.-minority relations, and under my paradigm Wounded Knee fits better with the spirit of the earlier age. My memory, in other words, arranges images of the past in ways that reflect my personal order of values, breaking time into distinct periods that reflect the way I interpret the things that happened in each era.

But as noted above, history books claim to transcend all value systems under the guise of objectivity, and therefore presume that events and people from the past are inherently neutral entities. Even contemporary, postmodern historians—feminists and post-colonialists, for example—who are acutely aware of the value systems inherent in all interpretations of the past, treat the actual events of the past as inert objects that can be viewed and reviewed from a variety of different angles. As a result, while living memory picks watersheds that reflect and reinforce the group's current system of beliefs, histories carve out periods of time on the basis of "the state of the [academic] field, the coherence of the argument, [and] the structure of the presentation."[9] In the Western tradition of historiography—the tradition whose conventions regulated John's production of a written Gospel—the "structure of the presentation" generally takes the form of a chronological narrative. Historical narratives organize the past by weaving the chaotic fabric of time into a coherent tapestry of causes and effects, creating a story that leads from a fixed beginning to a definitive end. The past is manageable in history narratives because effects are linked to causes in such a way that the relationship between the two cannot be negotiated—if things didn't happen this way, we can't get from the first page of the book to the last.[10] Other historians who disagree might suggest different causes or point out multiple side effects, but critical review of this kind only replaces one narrative with another and thereby affirms the overall logic of historiography, even when specific facts are debated.

Of course, one can write a chronological narrative only from a vantage point where the causes and effects come clearly into focus. The historian must therefore situate herself beyond the conclusion of the story, outside the plot rather than within it, so that she may view the past "as a whole from afar." For this reason, "hindsight as well as anachronism shapes historical interpretations."[11] Specifically, historians work backward, viewing every moment of the past through the lens of the end of the story and shaping every event to make it fit neatly between its precipitating causes and subsequent consequences—consequences that people living in the time period under consideration might have guessed but could not have known. Neither John F. Kennedy nor the mass of people gathered at Dealey Plaza in Dallas, Texas, on the morning of November 22, 1963, knew that the president would be dead by 1:00 p.m., but every biographer of Kennedy must know this information and must write the story of a life that could have ended at that fixed point. "In short, historical explanation surpasses any understanding available while events are still occurring. The past we reconstruct is more coherent than the past was when it happened."[12]

In order to squeeze the past into tight chronological sequences with clear beginnings and logical conclusions, historians must set precise boundaries for their data pools. Here again, periodization plays a key role. "In the process of transforming history into a story, the decision of where to begin and end the story defines what constitutes the relevant event and determines its meaning."[13] Eviatar Zerubavel refers to this phenomenon as "mnemonic decapitation" and notes that history narratives always operate on an ex nihilo principle, pretending that the story was preceded by a sort of historical void during which nothing really relevant was going on.[14] On the flip side, decapitation creates the impression that the events and people that fall within a history book's narrative boundaries must be important to the topic under consideration; otherwise, they wouldn't be included.[15]

The Digital Past

History books organize the past by removing people and events from living frameworks of memory and threading them together in cause-effect sequences with fixed beginnings and endings. Of course, memory often does the same thing. If I were to tell you some tales from my camping trip to the Rocky Mountains over a cup of coffee at Starbucks, all of them, though evoked from my memory and structured by my memory frameworks, would make my life experiences look like a string of causes and effects leading up to a punchline. But if we were talking in this way, you could ask me questions or make comments that would influence my presentation; my narrative would thus be guided by our contract of memory, so that your presence would add something unique to the shape of my stories. On the other hand, if I were to write these stories up in an autobiography, they would follow the rules of that literary genre and you would have no effect on them. We could discuss what I had written, and you might even influence my subsequent thinking about those events, but this would in no way change the words on the printed page. This is the case because history books, after they break the past into periods and arrange specific memories into sequences within those periods, fix their arrangements of the past in a mechanical medium that does not listen to arguments.

This point—the fact that history books do not invite dialogue the way that memories do—must be stressed, because it is critical to my understanding of the reasons why John (and probably Mark, Matthew, Luke, and Thomas as

---

The Past in History Books

The Written Past . . .

    1. is universal and unitary

    2. is broken into permanent periods

    3. loves ignorance

---

well) wrote a Gospel. Both memories and history books break up the past and arrange it into narratives, but once a historical narrative is committed to writing, its periodization system and overall scheme of arrangement obviously cannot change. Memory can gradually (or suddenly) readjust the boundaries of temporal periods to reflect evolving values and perspectives, forgetting some watersheds and elevating things that once seemed insignificant to the level of major turning points. But a history book can't do that; it sits unchanged on the shelf forever, proposing a specific division of time to every subsequent reader in every generation, even when its view of the past is radically obsolete from the perspective of current values. For this very reason, Plato tells us, wise Socrates warned Phaedrus not to write anything down: "So it is with written words; you might think they spoke as if they had intelligence, but if you question them, wishing to know about their sayings, they always say only one and the same thing."[16]

An illustration of this attribute of history books may be taken from Yael Zerubavel's excellent discussion of modern Israeli social memory. In *Recovered Roots*, Zerubavel describes changing Israeli perspectives on the deadly shootout between Jewish settlers and Palestinian Arabs at Tel Hai in March 1920. In the decades following the engagement, Zionist Hebrews viewed the events at Tel Hai as a major turning point in their group identity, a watershed moment in the struggle to reclaim the land of their ancient ancestors. Today, however, Tel Hai has lost much of its social significance and is in fact a frequent object of parody and satire. Zerubavel explains this shift in terms of a variety of social changes since the establishment of the state of Israel in 1948, and particularly since the debates over the settlement of occupied territories in the late 1970s. The diminished commemorative value of Tel Hai has resulted from diverse factors, ranging from shifting sentiments on Arab-Israeli relations to the simple fact that the site is too far away from major population centers for modern Hebrews to conveniently visit there on a regular basis.[17] For these and other reasons, the engagement at Tel Hai has gradually become a less significant watershed in popular national history.

Such has been the fate of Tel Hai in the shifting sands of Israeli social memory. Yet anyone who happened to pick up a Hebrew history book written in 1951 would quickly discover that that text still dares to affirm the commemorative values attributed to Tel Hai in the late 1940s. Further, such a book will continue to proclaim its obsolete version of the past until its pages dissolve into dust, just as astronomy books written in the early 1920s continue to assert that eight planets orbit our sun, and geography books written in 1971 still speak of countries called East Germany and Rhodesia, places that seem as old as Atlantis to people who never lived in such a world—people who might also assume that CCCP must be a new Internet domain. The old book on Tel Hai thus functions as a mnemonic time machine, bringing its readers into contact with the values and memories of sixty years ago, values and memories that may now appear alien and grotesque. And these values and this memory can be erased only by ignoring the book or destroying it, for the text is deaf to all protests and competing claims and refuses to rearrange the words on the page, even at its own author's request. The author might, of course, adjust the story to fit current values by releasing a second, revised edition. But this new edition is a new book, and the old one will still spew its story on anyone who haplessly picks up a decommissioned copy on the library's sale table.

When compared to living memories and oral traditions, history books exhibit what Eviatar Zerubavel calls a "digital" mode of thought. Zerubavel's analogy refers to the way that digital clocks, as opposed to analog clocks (i.e., clocks that have faces with hands that move in circles), present moments of time. A digital clock can display only one distinct moment at once because it tells time in the form of a written text—you see 8:08, then 8:09, then 8:10, one number after another with sharp breaks between them, breaks that are actually a little startling if you're staring at the clock intently and waiting for the minute to change. A digital clock can't show 8:08 and 12:27 at once, in contrast to an analog clock, where you can always see all the numbers even when the hands are not pointing to them. For this reason, there can be no debate about the time on a digital clock, unlike analog clocks, whose minute marks may blur together when viewed from a distance—"Does that say 8:26? Or is it 8:28? You can hardly tell from here." Digital clocks do a good job of making each individual minute clear and easy to see, but they create this clarity by hiding every other minute that might have been displayed.[18]

In a similar way, written history books present the past in a digital mode, one that displays every moment of time in distinction from every other moment and hides all those other moments to focus attention on what is happening right now in anticipation of what will happen next. From the viewpoint of the digital clock, when it's 5:35 you need to be looking at the numbers 5, 3, 5 in that sequence, and you should be getting ready to see a 6; your eye should not be wandering over to the 10. Similarly, from the viewpoint of a history book, you should be looking at the event that is under discussion right now and thinking about how that event followed from the last one and will lead into the next one; you should not be asking for more background details or information about facts that lie outside the scope of the present study.

The permanent periodization of the past in history books affects not only the readers of history books. Sometimes written history books influence the ways memory groups organize and divide the past by interacting with their living frameworks of memory. The very existence of a book can, in other words, sometimes rewrite the terms of the social contract of memory. At least two such influences are relevant to our discussion of John and the AntiChrists.

First, as noted above, the written past is "definitively closed." Because the contents of history books are permanent, their images of the past can be changed only by conscious acts of revision or destruction, giving them an "immunity to correction."[19] Unless the author of a history book chooses to revise the text, effectively creating a new volume, that text will forever proclaim a fixed vision of the past and its divisions. For this very reason, while history books cannot prevent the ongoing evolution of the past in collective memory, they can and sometimes do subvert popular ideas by preserving images of the past that are inconsistent with the latest version of memory. In this sense historians are often "the guardians of awkward facts, the skeletons in the cupboard of the social memory," preserving information that challenges current views of reality because it was not shaped in the context of today's perspectives.[20] There are many people from my high school days, and many things I did in that season of life, that I would prefer to forget, but the yearbook simply won't let me.

Second, while both history books and memories introduce artificial watersheds and periods into the natural flow of time, history books, unlike memories, can themselves function as watershed moments by distinguishing the period before their publication from the period after. The "prehistoric" or "aboriginal" era of any society's history refers to every facet of its existence before the moment when the members of the group began to document the past. Similarly, even people (like myself) who are unaware of the specific contents of the Magna Carta perceive that Western civilization turned a corner at the moment that document was produced, and understand that the publication of Thomas Paine's *Common Sense* marked the emergence in the colonies of a new spirit that would eventually lead to the American Revolution. One prominent theorist has even suggested that the very notion of historical periodization is supported by the technology of writing. "Indeed, it is our ability to envision the historical equivalents of the blank spaces we conventionally leave between the different chapters of a book or at the beginning of a new paragraph that enhances the perceived separateness of such [historical] 'periods.'"[21]

Written documents can impact the social contract of memory in at least two ways:

 By preserving obsolete facts and arrangements of the past that challenge contemporary ways of thinking because they do not reflect the frameworks of today's values;

 By functioning as watershed moments that mark significant steps in a society's evolution.

Of course, ancient books such as the Gospel of John did not utilize paragraphs, punctuation, or other modern publishing techniques. But the appearance of the Fourth Gospel in a community that had previously preserved Jesus' memory only by oral tradition—a community immersed in a culture where written documents carried high symbolic value even though most people could not read them—would signal a significant change in the way the past could be managed and discussed. This change would be obvious even to people who could not read John's book and who therefore did not know what it actually said.

THE VIRTUES OF VAGUENESS

Up to this point, you may have agreed with some of what I have been saying about the ways that history books arrange and freeze the past. But perhaps your mind has wandered back to earlier chapters, leading you to reflect once again on my claims that the vast majority of people in John's society could not read. What difference does a history book make to people who can't read history books? This question threatens to make everything I have said in this chapter irrelevant. If the Johannine Christians were largely illiterate, their charismatic memories would be insulated from the effects of writing, and the AntiChrists would be not so much threatened by John's Gospel as simply disinterested in it. Even if the Fourth Gospel, as a history book, bears all the characteristics of fixed memory outlined above, what difference would that make to Diotrephes or anyone else who couldn't read it, anyway?

These are good questions, but they reflect an assumption about the role of history books that I have already shown to be inapplicable to the Johannine context. Specifically, the fact that most Johannine Christians could not read

---

The Past in History Books

The Written Past . . .

1. is universal and unitary

2. is broken into permanent periods

3. loves ignorance

---

would be a problem here only if history books are viewed as archives of remembrance, as storage bins for information about the past. Obviously, an illiterate person is not going to look at a history book to help her remember something, and such a person would therefore be immune to the book's attempt to correct her thinking. Books can't jump off the shelf and make people read them, and people who can't read them wouldn't get much information out of them if they did. For this very reason, my own living memories of St. Patrick are blissfully immune to any facts about him contained in a seventh-century Gaelic tome—the book can't hurt me because I can't understand what it's saying. But even though I can't read that text, if some colleague from the history department were to tell me that it in fact proves definitively that Saint Patrick never drove any snakes out of Ireland, my cherished memories of that individual would be seriously threatened. This is the case because I live in a society where writing can perform a rhetorical function that transcends the value of its actual contents, and this function works just as well with illiterate people. Members of my society generally agree that debates about the past are settled when scholars state the facts on the basis of source documents, even source documents that we have never seen or heard of and could not read if we did.[22] So, while illiteracy does nullify the *archive* value of history books, it has no effect at all on the *symbolic* force of history books. In fact, *historical documents are often most effective at manipulating memory when people have no idea what they actually say.* Because this point is critical, I will elaborate on its implications a bit further.

As noted earlier, history books view the past as a neutral phenomenon from a degree-zero perspective. As such, they claim to transcend the values and ideals of specific memory groups. "History tells all who will listen what has happened and how things came to be as they are," and fearlessly invites every reader to review and challenge its claims.[23] This gives history books the appearance of objectivity, but it also makes it impossible for them to appeal to the clauses in the social contract of memory that call for the audience's sympathy. Instead, historians must anticipate an audience that is broad and possibly skeptical, and cannot assume the reader's foreknowledge of the events under consideration. Of course, in many cases the reader of a history narrative is aware of the ultimate outcome—the modern American who reads a biography of Abraham Lincoln at least knows that the subject is dead, and is probably also aware that Lincoln was president during the Civil War and was assassinated. The narrator of history, however, may not assume this knowledge, and certainly cannot assume that the reader could predict the logic of the book's plot as it ties the selected events of Lincoln's life together and explains why this life ended in violent tragedy. Because they are public rather than private, histories must appeal to the lowest common denominator of audience awareness.

Yet at the same time, because they do not rely on the reader's foreknowledge and sympathy, the rhetorical impact of written texts may be magnified by a phenomenon that David Lowenthal calls "the virtues of vagueness and ignorance." The past often provides a more effective foundation for group solidarity when less is known about it, and vague allusions to a general past that is accepted as true but rarely investigated carry no less weight on radio talk shows than quotations from academic experts. Through this strange loophole in the contract of memory, historical documents are sometimes more influential when people are less familiar with what they actually say. Lowenthal notes as an example that Americans regularly appeal to the U.S. Constitution when discussing their rights and national identity, even though many have never read it, or at least can't say when they did—probably sometime back in high school or college, two stages of life that many of us are trying to forget altogether.[24] This phenomenon is especially striking when popular memory misunderstands the actual contents of the text in question, for example, the belief held by most Americans that the U.S. Constitution calls for a strict "separation of church and state." In debates where the majority hold this view, the fact that such a phrase never actually appears in that document does not diminish the rhetorical force of arguments that appeal to this principle.

The Past in History Books: John's Solution

The Written Past . . .

1. Is universal and unitary
meaning that it transcends every individual representation of the past by swallowing all of them up into itself. In the process, the written text becomes a surrogate memory group for its reader, and replaces the reader's natural frameworks of memory with its own. History books thus become the ultimate authority and organizing principle in collective memory.

2. Is broken into permanent periods
meaning that its version of things can only be accepted or rejected, never negotiated or reconfigured. The division and arrangement of the past is frozen in history books, and they continue to express their original vision even after it is long obsolete from the perspective of contemporary problems and values. For this reason, history books sometimes challenge current notions and ideals simply by reminding people that they don't have to think the way that they do.

3. Loves ignorance
meaning that appeals to history books tend to be more powerful when people know less about their actual contents. This is especially true in societies that have low literacy rates but attribute a high level of symbolic value to documents. In such a culture, the persuasive power of appeals to "what the book says" is enhanced by the fact that most people can't check the book to challenge these claims.

   1.
+ 2.
+ 3.
+ John's illiterate culture
+ high symbolic value of documents in John's culture
= the answer to John's AntiChrist problem

As the survey above has suggested, memory and history books shape and present the past in distinct ways. Memories order the private past according to the social and ideological frameworks of the groups that preserve them; histories, by contrast, treat the past as public and organize the objectified past within the confines of narrative. For purposes of the present study, it is important to note that these natural differences would be magnified in the social setting in which the Fourth Gospel was produced. The Gospel of John was manufactured in an oral culture and represents a conscious shift from fluid memory to fixed written text. In John's context, the technology of writing would itself further distinguish memory from history by fixing the past in a medium that most people could not use and by presenting a vision that they could not negotiate. These aspects of writing would make a written Gospel especially appealing to John as a medium for his memory of Jesus.

Why John Wrote a Gospel

Why did John write a Gospel? Answers to this question will reflect one's view of the reasons why anyone would commit anything to writing. If writing is viewed primarily as an archive of speech, the Fourth Gospel was produced as an aid to memory, a storage bin for John's Jesus tradition. Under this model, John did not conceptualize an essential difference between his own preaching and public readings from his book. But while the Gospel of John has certainly functioned as an archive of Johannine tradition in the history of the church, the author's peculiar view of Christian memory makes it unlikely that this was his primary motive for writing a Gospel. Instead, it appears that John wished to capitalize on the rhetorical value of writing by converting the fluid memory of Jesus to a fixed history book, a move that would at once preserve his unique vision of Jesus, freeze that vision in a perpetually nonnegotiable medium, and assert the special authority of that vision against competing claims.

At least five related aspects of the shift from group memory to history book would have made the production of the Fourth Gospel especially suitable to John's purposes. By appeal to a written story about Jesus that most people could not read, John could effectively change the terms of his debate with the AntiChrists in a way that would acknowledge the Spirit's ongoing influence, while effectively denying their claims.

REASON #1: JESUS IN PUBLIC

I know that I was not present at Riverfront Stadium when Don Gullett hit a home run in the 1975 World Series, but I've always believed that I was. I know that I saw him hit a home run, and that this was very remarkable, because Don Gullett was the Cincinnati Reds' star pitcher. But I don't really know whether it was the World Series or just a regular-season baseball game, or whether it was 1975 or 1976 or 1977—I propose these dates because I think I was about ten years old at the time. None of those details really matters, however, so long as I choose to keep my memory private or share it only within a circle of close friends who might also cherish it but will not challenge it. Of course, this approach would be entirely inadequate if I wanted to write a biography of Don Gullett, because in that case my memory would have to stand the test of public scrutiny, of other people's memories and other records of the past. My recollection of Don Gullett's home run thus illustrates the key difference between memory and history: memory treats the past as personal experiences, while history books treat the past as public events.

The fact that memory tends to treat the past as personal experiences would be especially true in John's context, for his community viewed the memory of Jesus as a work of the Holy Spirit. As such, every person who possesses the Spirit can claim to be a remembrancer, able to recall Jesus and guided by the Paraclete in her interpretations of that memory. While the author of 1 John could appeal to this belief ad hominem to posture the Spirit/tradition as a special "anointing" that protects true Christians from the heretical teachings of the AntiChrists (1 John 2:20–27), John's charismatic approach to memory would also make it ultimately impossible for him to refute the AntiChrists' claims. As private spiritual experience, the AntiChrists' countermemory of Jesus would not be subject to historical inquiry and would not demand the objectivity that makes it possible for historians to proclaim their versions of the past "true." As inspired recollection, they could claim that their memories of Jesus were just as good as John's.

But John could counter the AntiChrists with a history book, one that would posture Jesus as a public figure and thus make all claims about his activity potentially subject to investigation. John points this out himself in texts such as John 19:35 and 21:24, which appeal to eyewitness testimony in the court of the reader's scrutiny. By moving Jesus into the public past, John creates an image that claims to transcend private faith experience in the same way that a biography of Don Gullett would transcend my private memory of his remarkable home run and treat that event as fact or fiction rather than nostalgia.

Of course, this does not mean that John sought to eradicate the influence of the Spirit. Were John thoroughly anticharismatic, passages such as John 14:26 and 16:13 would not have been included in his Gospel. It seems more likely that John wished to balance and supplement the Paraclete's "anointing" with a written text that could complement and define that ongoing spiritual experience. Believers could now refer to the text of the Fourth Gospel as a touchstone for pneumatic memory in the same way that they could "test the spirits" by appealing to the community's established christological creeds (see 1 John 4:1–6). Text and memory would henceforth work together to support John's witness to Jesus.

REASON #2: TRAPPED TIME

Meeting new people and sharing life stories with them is one of the major perks (and occupational hazards) of my job as a seminary professor. Many of my students are entering ministry as a second career, forcing them to significantly reconfigure the plot of their personal and professional autobiographies to explain how they came to this point in their lives. As they look for guideposts and precedents, they often interrogate me as to where my own path began. "When did you decide to become a professor?" they ask over a hamburger. "Did you always want to do this?" And the worst question, "So, do you think you're going to keep doing this, or will you end up doing something else?" Depending on the circumstances, people generally get one of two versions of my life history, the story of "Professor Tom" or the story of "Pastor Tom," both of which I have included on the next page in abbreviated form.

Obviously, a quick perusal of these two stories reveals a number of key differences, differences that might lead to charges of dishonesty. Yet each of these narratives is true in the sense that I could document all of the specific facts to which they refer. This being the case, I can, in good conscience, tell people whichever story supports the way I am feeling at any given moment about how my life will ultimately resolve itself. Because memory's image of the past is always shaped by the framework of our immediate values, memories change whenever these values change. In the process, new watersheds rise and are eventually replaced to continually break the flow of time into manageable periods, periods that in turn characterize the events and individuals who inhabit them. Experience demonstrates how quickly and how often we can reconfigure our memories to fit the rhetorical needs of the moment.

But such liberties, on which memory so often depends, do not extend to history books. If, for example, I were to write an autobiography, the written version of my life could not tolerate such contradictions, and would need to suppress, for sake of clarity and space limitations, those details that were not immediately relevant to, and supportive of, the story I chose to publish. In my written autobiography I would be Professor Tom *or* Pastor Tom—not one on one page and the other on the next—quite unlike the way that I can tell one story today and another tomorrow. Readers who happened to hear me telling someone the alternate version might even challenge the ethic of my presentation,

Life of Tom Version 1: "Professor Tom"

When I first became a Christian in high school, I didn't know anything about the Bible. I wasn't really raised in church, and only became interested in religion through my girlfriend's youth group. I was a very inquisitive person, always wanting to learn more about everything, so I tried to study the Bible and read theology books as much as I could. When I graduated from high school, I received a full-ride scholarship to the University of Cincinnati, and went there to study Classics. But after a year at U.C., I switched to a Bible college to major in biblical studies. By then I knew I wanted to teach at the college level, because the study of Scripture had always been so important to my own faith experience and I wanted to help other people develop their knowledge. When I finished my college degree I was married and my wife was still in school. We were dirt poor and used to living in the inner city by then, anyway, so I decided to just go ahead and get a seminary degree. During that time, people encouraged me to pursue a doctorate, so when I graduated I started a PhD and was able to teach some classes as an adjunct while my wife was working full time as a school teacher. About the time I finished that degree, my former seminary adviser went through a serious personal crisis and resigned suddenly two weeks before school started. I picked up some of his courses that year and then was hired to fill his slot the next. I like doing this for now, but don't know what I'll be doing in five years.

Life of Tom Version 2: "Pastor Tom"

When I finished high school, I felt called to some type of ministry, and wanted to attend a Bible college and start working in a church part time. But my parents objected because I had a full–ride scholarship to the University of Cincinnati. I went there for a year but really never felt comfortable, and transferred to finish a degree in ministry. I decided I wanted a Master of Divinity, so I went on to seminary while my wife finished her education degree. During that time we were heavily involved in church work. We served in every aspect of church life imaginable, often holding several positions at once, and I ended up being an elder and then a staff member. When I finished seminary, my wife was just starting her career, and we didn't want to have kids yet, so I decided to pursue a doctorate. I felt a PhD would better equip me for preaching and teaching, and I wanted to do a seminary doctorate so that I could keep my studies in dialogue with the church. But right before I finished that degree, an opening suddenly came up at my alma mater, and they needed someone to fill it fast. I taught there for a year and it went well, so I stayed on. But I've interviewed for, and turned down, several ministry positions, and am always open to offers. From time to time I wonder whether I really ought to be in pastoral work, especially urban ministry, but for now teaching gives me enough of a chance to "do ministry" with students. I don't know what I'll be doing in five years.

questioning why I had suppressed so much key information about my experiences and motives, and even the most lenient reviewers would have to recommend my inconsistent memoirs to obscurity.

Simply put, memories can change, books cannot. So long as the Johannine Jesus tradition was a tradition, it would maintain the fluid characteristics of a living memory. As such, the traditional story of Jesus and the image of his life and teaching could be revised and reworked indefinitely. But by producing a written Gospel, John could freeze one particular image of Jesus in the plot of a historical narrative on the physical surface of the inscribed page. This written text, and its organizational scheme, would endure over time, making it more difficult for opponents to reconfigure the elements of Jesus' memory, and also preventing the suppression and conflation of information stored within each category and period.

Regardless of the Paraclete's ongoing influence, within the text of the Fourth Gospel every moment of Jesus' life—every saying and sign—is forever distinct and discrete, shaped to fit the events that preceded it in the plot and those that will follow. These recorded events and sayings would remain valuable for teaching and meditative reflection, but would always derive their default meaning from the literary context rather than from private spiritual experience. As time has shown, a written version of John's memory of Jesus would preserve that portrait intact even when his image of Christ did not fit neatly into the church's evolving interests and social context.

REASON #3: A SHALLOW DATA POOL

When I was in sixth grade, my friend Steve Horsley and I wrote a number of songs in anticipation of a glamorous recording career. We performed these ditties frequently on the playground at Norwood View School, generally to rave reviews. Our trademark ballad, "Funky Honkey," was quite popular, along with the crowd favorites "You Is Ugly" and "Up Side the Head." We supplemented this musical repertoire with parodies of television commercials and brief comedy skits, most of which were reserved for underground venues (the alley behind Pepe's Pizza; the playground beside the reception hall of the Our Lady of the Holy Spirit Center) due to their extremely profane content. I preserved a number of these songs and skits on a Radio Shack cassette recorder with a built-in microphone, and now on those rare occasions when I am alone at the house I sometimes pull out these tapes and review the "Tom and Steve" corpus.

The Tom and Steve tapes, and the memories that they evoke, normally leave me in a state of bittersweet melancholy. As I listen, the sound of my own childish voice transports me back to days of school carnivals and playground baseball games and vinyl records and very primitive Atari video games. These clear images are pleasant to gaze upon but are always accompanied by a vast entourage of blurry ghosts that dance in and out of my peripheral vision. The constant presence of these shadowy figures confronts me with two disturbing realities. First, while these tapes are genuine artifacts of my childhood, they are not the whole puzzle, or even a small percentage of its pieces. Most of my childhood was unrecorded and therefore doomed to be forgotten. Second, and much more disconcerting, I realize that the few records on which my memory must rely actually work to obliterate everything that does not fall within their scope. I know, for example, that Steve and I wrote many more songs and jokes than what these tapes contain, but all the ones that were not recorded have disappeared behind these relics and been erased by them, following the principle that "when the perfect comes, the partial is displaced." Thus, the very database of memoirs that makes it possible for me to rebuild a vivid image of a small portion of my past also underscores the impossibility of recalling any significant percentage of my life, and in fact tends to take away my will to try. Over time, what was recorded is remembered, and what was not ceases to exist.

Following this principle, a written Gospel would preserve certain memories of Jesus in vivid color while at the same time erasing everything that lay outside its boundaries. The Jews, the AntiChrists, and other perceived opponents might challenge John's understanding of Jesus and might ban his Gospel from their synagogues and churches, but they could never expand or contract the database from which that image was built. All history books imply that what has been omitted from their database is irrelevant, and John in particular states this principle explicitly. Much to the dismay of modern scholars, John 20:30 and 21:25 both note, in a tone that is strikingly casual, that much more information could have been included in the story. John, however, has sorted through this bulk of data and has preserved everything necessary to produce and maintain genuine faith in Jesus, obviating the need for new revelations or further historical investigation. And if a quantitatively significant amount of Jesus tradition was thereby relegated to oblivion, John seems to feel no regret, but instead takes pride in knowing that such extraneous information will not confuse people in the future.[1] In this sense, the Gospel of John represents perhaps the earliest attempt to canonize a particular body of Christian teaching, to limit theological speculation to discussions of a written text.

REASON #4: THE LIVING WATERSHED

History books create the illusion of a fixed database and a fixed flow of time. Historians choose some events from the mass of the past and ignore others, shape those they have selected to fit tight narrative frameworks with delineated temporal periods, and remove this activity from the realm of negotiation by committing the results of their labors to writing. But as the past becomes more remote, later generations will have access to it only through these highly contrived texts, a fact that makes it possible to think of history books as themselves watershed moments in group development. This is especially the case for the first documents in any culture, whose appearance marks the dramatic transition from "the prehistoric period." John may have wished, then, not only to preserve one particular theory about how the past should be periodized, but also to create a document that would itself function as a watershed in his group's history.

Within John's oral context, the publication of a written memory of Jesus would draw a bold line between the former period of debate over what *Jesus said* and the new period of debate over what *the book says*. Whatever else might be said about the elusive Johannine community, its prehistoric period ended at the moment the Fourth Gospel was published. After this critical moment, John and his allies could point to the Fourth Gospel and say, "We are no longer talking about whether Jesus did X or Y; we are now talking about how to interpret what can be documented, what this book says he did." Whether or not John ever actually used this line of argument, Marcion almost certainly did use it some forty years later.

REASON #5: FAITH WITHOUT READING

As noted earlier, popular uses of memory frequently capitalize on the virtues of vagueness, the fact that beliefs about the past that are widely held but seldom investigated tend to be just as rhetorically effective as citations from well-documented historical treatises. In modern literate cultures, writing eliminates vagueness by presenting a public image of the past with claims that are subject to criticism and therefore must be verifiable. While the readers of history books seldom take time to check the footnotes or seriously investigate the presentation (or even to look up the meaning of words they don't know), they feel an inherent right to do so should they so choose. Memories, on the other hand, seek a sympathetic ear and hope that the audience will give the benefit of the doubt. In fact, from a functional/rhetorical point of view, memories rarely serve historical purposes, and as a result much less is invested in their truth claims.

For example, the library is closed right now, and I'm sitting in the Gallery, a study lounge at the College of Mt. St. Joseph, staring out the window while I work on this book. As I contemplate the snow-covered bushes, a young woman (apparently a student) and two older women (presumably faculty members) walk through during a break from class. One of the professors, making the small talk typical of such awkward occasions, says that she recently spoke to a 1963 graduate of the school, who "popped her head into my office" and said that, "Back in those days, if you wanted to date a boy from Xavier, you had to write a letter of request to the academic dean." Obviously, this recollection is intended to contrast the ancient world of 1963 with the world of today, a world where female college students typically and frequently explore a wide range of sexual experiences (not all of which involve boys). As such, it is clear that the teacher has invested less in the historical accuracy of this comment than in its rhetorical force. She was not, in other words, making a definitive statement about the history of Catholic colleges in Cincinnati, but was instead simply trying to amuse her student friend. It's a memory packaged as a joke; recognizing this, the student chuckles politely as the three move on down the hall and out of my range of hearing.

But after they leave, I find myself compelled to ponder the strange and exotic land of 1963 from which this memory emerged. Like the young coed, I have never lived in such a place, and therefore can neither confirm nor disprove this testimony. Could such a world have existed, and in the same physical location that I now inhabit? Despite my many doubts, in the end I decide to believe this claim and to concede that female Mount students in 1963 probably did need special permission to date boys from other colleges. Of course, I could presumably pursue the matter further by seeking out the source person for interview and/or by checking the Mount's student records, a relatively easy task because the memory reflects a time recently past, with many living witnesses and extant documents ready to hand. But I find no compulsion to do this, and I also find that the absence of hard evidence does not diminish my awe over the world of 1963. Whether the claim is true or not, I find it remarkable, and it feeds my imagination for several moments the same way that any passage from *Lord of the Rings* might. The memory challenges my thinking, but it is a negotiable challenge, negotiable because the reporter is not making an absolute historical claim but just trying to be funny and because I, her eavesdropping audience, am seeking an amusing diversion rather than hard facts. The memory works, in other words, simply because we leave it vague.

But of course, I would not be so gracious if I encountered this same piece of information in a history of the College of Mt. St. Joseph, which would repay my critical posture by clarifying all the details and leaving me no option to doubt whether the date were 1963 or whether we are talking about Xavier High School or Xavier University. The history book would, in other words, limit my interpretive options, even if I found the facts difficult to reconcile with the world in which I live. I could challenge its claims only by a more laborious reference to other history books and/or their sources, generally written texts as well. In this respect, the history book would, to paraphrase Foucault, close off "the space of freedom that I still enjoy"—freedom to negotiate the content and meaning of the past so long as the finished product satisfies the needs of the moment.[2]

Memories capitalize on vagueness and allude to the past for a variety of rhetorical purposes; history books, by contrast, ostensibly function to preserve the past and capitalize on specificity, hiding the historian's agenda behind a mask of objectivity. By producing a history book, John could eliminate and counter the vagueness of charismatic memory, challenging the AntiChrists' allusions to tradition and revelation by appeal to a written document. The claims of the history book would be less negotiable than those of memory, closing the range of interpretive options. Further, a written Gospel would be especially advantageous in John's context because it could exploit *at the same time* both the illusion of objectivity inherent in history books and the virtues of vagueness inherent in memory.

As public documents, history books make special claims that require special tools of objective analysis. Those who read history books enjoy the right to challenge these claims, but all challenges will, in turn, be subject to further scrutiny and review. The disgruntled historian may even retaliate with further documentation, new arguments, and a review of the review. This aspect of historiography ironically undermines history's attempt to create a public past, for most people are not qualified to conduct historiographic research, a fact that makes history texts immune to casual criticism. Obviously, even the most rudimentary inquiry into the veracity of a history book's claims would require a minimal familiarity with the specific contents of that document. In the case of the Fourth Gospel, this would mean that potential critics would need to study the text and raise counterarguments. *Yet most people in John's culture could not read*, a fact that would make it impossible for them even to discuss the actual contents of John's Gospel, much less to challenge its claims.

For this reason, John and his allies could exploit the virtues of vagueness inherent in memory even when using their written Gospel to counter opposing claims about Jesus. The rhetorical force of vagueness would be obvious to any ancient Jew due to the pervasive presence and influence of the Torah, a document that Jews viewed as essential to their identity and heritage, even though most of them could not read it. In a similar way, John must have been aware that most Christians and, indeed, the vast majority of the human race, were not sufficiently literate to read a document such as the Fourth Gospel—further evidence that he did not view his project as an archive of memory. The fact that most Christians could not read would, however, make the contents and interpretation of the text even less negotiable, as few would be in a position to challenge its vision. John's history book could thus capitalize on the mystique of a vague past without resolving that vagueness.

For all five of the reasons I have discussed here—and perhaps many more that would be obvious to a person immersed in an oral culture—a written Gospel would be the ideal weapon in John's conflict with the AntiChrists. Both John and the AntiChrists could appeal to the Spirit to validate their memories of Jesus, but John could now also appeal to the prestige of a book about Jesus, a book that further claimed to be based on eyewitness testimony. Such a book would become a touchstone for charismatic memory, limiting and controlling

Memory➜History		Tradition➜Gospel
Memory	**History Books**	**Why John Wrote a Gospel**
1. Treats the past as subjective, private experience.	**1.** Treat as the past as objective, public facts.	Claims about Jesus are subject to scrutiny, debate, and documentation.
2. Organizes the past around group values and shifts when those values shift.	**2.** Organize the past around a fixed historical narrative and cannot change, even when obsolete.	Portrait of Jesus cannot change or shift over time, making it immune to current values and experiences.
3. Uses a fluid database to construct a relevant image of the past.	**3.** Close the database of the past by erasing everything outside the scope of the story.	Pool of data about Jesus is limited to information contained in the text; new revelations from the Spirit can be ignored if irrelevant.
4. Allows debate both over "what happened" and how to interpret what happened.	**4.** End debate over "what happened" and limit discussion to the interpretation of what happened.	AntiChrists can no longer dispute whether or not Jesus did or said certain things; can only discuss the correct interpretation of the data in the text.
5. Assumes the audience's sympathy and foreknowledge.	**5.** Assume the audience's ignorance and skepticism.	Most people cannot challenge the claims of the Fourth Gospel, or John's claims based on appeals to that text, simply because they could not read it.

both the growth of the Johannine tradition and its interpretation. And since most people would be unable to read such a book, it would be impossible for most people to challenge its claims, or even to challenge arguments based on vague appeals to that text. If "general history starts only when tradition ends and the social memory is fading or breaking up," it may be said that John wrote a Gospel to erase his own memory.[3]

Postscript

The Original Quest
for a Historical Jesus

Returning to the guiding question of this book, I may now assert that John wrote a Gospel not to preserve a liquid memory of Jesus, but rather to replace that substance with something more solid. John did not, in other words, write a Gospel to help people remember information about Jesus, but rather to ensure that they remembered Jesus in a specific way, a way consistent with his own thinking about Christ. Very specifically, he sought to prevent the AntiChrists (or others like them) from expanding and reconfiguring the memory of Jesus, and he achieved this objective by encoding that memory in a written text, a text that would become a touchstone for genuine experience of the Spirit.

But in the course of this book, our discussion has raised many issues that go far beyond an answer to the question, Why did John write a Gospel? The implications of John's shift from living memory in the form of tradition to frozen memory in a written text are far-reaching, and while I don't have time to explore them in detail here, I want to outline at least three that seem fruitful for further discussion.

EVANGEL OR APOLOGY?

Even casual students of the Bible may be somewhat aware of the long-standing debate over the implications of the "purpose statement" of the Fourth Gospel, John 20:30–31. After the resurrected Jesus exposes his bloody wounds to Thomas, John breaks in to note that "Jesus did many other signs in the presence of his disciples that are not written in this book. But these things have been

157

written *so that you may believe* [either πιστεύσητε (past tense) or πιστεύητε (present tense), depending on which ancient manuscripts you prefer] that Jesus is the Christ the Son of God, and so that by believing you may have life in his name." Clearly, John wants his reader to come to a correct belief about Jesus. But what does he presuppose about this reader's current state of belief? Is John thinking of an unbelieving reader, a person of "the world" or a "Jew" who does not accept Jesus as the Christ and who therefore needs to repent so as to "have life"? Or does he presume that his readers are already Christians, yet Christians who need clarity about Christ's identity in view of the confusion caused by the Jews and the AntiChrists? The question is often stated in terms of the nature of the Gospel of John. Is this book an *evangelistic* document aimed at converting nonbelievers? Or is this book an *apologetic* document, one that seeks to justify and confirm the orthodox faith of people who are already members of John's churches? Or for those who do not wish to argue, is the Fourth Gospel *both* an evangelistic document and an apology, a cure-all for anyone who isn't entirely sure what to think about Jesus?[1]

My discussion here has not addressed this question directly, but it would certainly tip the scales in favor of the view that the Gospel of John is an apologetic text. The backdrop of the Fourth Gospel's production—a debate between two Christian groups over the correct memory of Jesus—strongly

---

John, Memory, and History: Implications

1. The Fourth Gospel is an apologetic treatise, not an evangelistic tract.

---

suggests that John wrote a Gospel primarily to combat the influence of the AntiChrists, who were leading believers away from the orthodox faith and thereby "destroying what we worked for" (2 John 8). In my view, the Fourth Gospel makes more sense when John 20:31 is interpreted alongside Luke 1:1–4, making the written text a reaffirmation of things that believers have been taught "from the beginning," at a point in time when their image of Christ was becoming blurred. As such, I would see the Gospel of John as a document aimed at Christian people with no specific evangelistic purpose, despite the ongoing usefulness of John 3:16 in bringing people to Christ.

But by saying this, I do not wish to suggest that John believed that most people in his churches would actually read his book. As I've said over and over, the evidence strongly suggests that only a small percentage of them would have been able to read anything at all. In fact, I do not know whether I could prove that John thought *anyone* in his churches would ever read his book about

Jesus. I suspect that he did not. But whether they ever read his book or not, and whether they could even read at all, John could expect most people in his churches to respect the authority of written texts, and could also expect them to see the obvious differences between the claims of the AntiChrists and the way that his own allies interpreted his written Gospel. The Fourth Gospel was a rhetorical fulcrum, a leveraging device for use by people like Demetrius (3 John 12), "the brothers" (3 John 5–8), and the "Elect Lady" (2 John 1), something they could point to in their debates with people like Diotrephes (3 John 9) as the final word on what Jesus did or did not do. As such, my argument here would support Robert Kysar's description of the Gospel of John as "an intra-church document . . . a Gospel intended for the family"—provided, of course, that we recognize that John's family was dysfunctional.[2]

THE SECOND, THIRD, FOURTH, OR FIFTH FOURTH GOSPEL?

A century from now, some doctoral student at Vanderbilt or Aberdeen will be writing a chapter in her dissertation that summarizes the major concerns of Johannine scholarship in the twentieth century (by the way, if you are that student and you are reading this book: Greetings to you from the past, and thanks for remembering me). Such a history of research, even if only a few pages long, will have to dedicate at least a paragraph or two to the "developmental approach" to the Fourth Gospel, because this issue has been one of the largest blips on the radar screen of Johannine studies—in fact, of biblical studies in general—in recent times.

For about forty years now, scholars have been debating whether the Gospel of John that we have in our Bibles is a "first edition" or the final volume in a series of revisions. According to the latter theory, some Johannine Christian wrote a book about Jesus in, say, 55 CE. That book was revised and expanded

---

John, Memory, and History: Implications

1. The Fourth Gospel is an apologetic treatise, not an evangelistic tract.

2. **The Fourth Gospel that we have today is most likely the first, or at most the second, edition of that book.**

---

in, say, 71 CE; the revised version was then revised again in 87 CE; a fourth edition was produced in 94 CE; this fourth edition was reworked one last time to produce the text of the Fourth Gospel as it exists today. Advocates of this theory explain these revisions in terms similar to our earlier discussion of living memory. Over time, the Johannine Christians faced new challenges or encountered new religious ideas in the world around them, making it necessary to reconsider and reconfigure traditional ways of thinking about Jesus and his teaching. Each time they encountered a major obstacle, they found it necessary to revise their book about Jesus in order to make it relevant to the new way of thinking. This theory is called "the developmental approach" because it argues that the Gospel of John as we have it today is the end product of this series of theological developments and revisions.

The more conservative versions of the developmental approach argue that our Gospel of John is a second edition, with chapter 21 added to the end of an earlier book that was already complete. Evidence for this conclusion may be drawn from the facts that (a) the Gospel of John comes to a logical end with the purpose statement at 20:30–31, (b) 21:25 seems to essentially repeat what 20:30 has already said, and (c) chapter 21 seems generally more interested in the fates of Peter and the Beloved Disciple than in Jesus (see 21:22–24). So it looks as if this chapter may have been added later, probably to explain why Jesus did not come back before the Beloved Disciple died. If this is the case, there must have been an earlier version of the Gospel of John that did not include chapter 21. But if chapter 21 represents a revised edition of the Gospel of John, could it be that there were other, earlier editions of the text that *predated* the edition to which chapter 21 was added? Many scholars think so, and argue that the Fourth Gospel may have gone through several revisions, some fairly thorough, before the final edition that we have today was released.[3]

While many things might be said about the relative merits and liabilities of the developmental approach, I will limit my remarks here to the observation that what I have said in this book probably works better if there were fewer editions of the Gospel of John, and works very well if there was only one. If John wrote a Gospel not to preserve the memory of Jesus but rather to replace it, and if his views of tradition and writing were fairly typical of the ways that other Johannine Christians thought about those same issues, it seems unlikely that the Johannine community would feel a need to produce a new version of the text every time they had some new insight or experience. This is not the place to discuss the issue in detail, but I will briefly note three arguments that point to this conclusion.

First, it seems odd to me that anyone would go to the trouble of revising a book that very few people could read, especially in view of the cost of producing a written document in John's time. When I reflect on the more complicated developmental theories—especially those that involve more than, say, three editions of the Fourth Gospel—I am led to wonder how many books in the history of the world have ever gone through more than two editions. And I would guess that a very high percentage of the books that have been revised more than twice are reference works. Of course, the Book of Mormon has gone through a great many editions, but this is a book that was written in modern times in a highly literate culture—it has been revised many times specifically because many people actually read it and pay close attention to what it says. Since it isn't clear that very many people could read the Gospel of John in the first place, one has to explain why Johannine Christians would find it logical and necessary to revise the text over and over rather than simply supplementing it with oral-traditional material and/or reinterpreting it to fit the new situation and understanding. In oral performances of all or some of the material in the book, it would be much easier just to add material ad hoc according to the immediate needs of the audience and the rhetorical situation than to write a new edition and quote it word for word.

This point has been, for me, the primary obstacle to embracing the developmental approach. John probably did not think that any great number of people were going to read his book, but was instead thinking that his allies could wave their hand toward it as needed to support their arguments against the AntiChrists. This being the case, it would be just as easy—*no, much easier*—to simply adjust the presentation or reinterpret the contents of the text than to produce a new edition of the document. Further, all the available evidence seems to suggest that people in oral cultures would be more likely just to supplement the extant text than to write a new one. The developmental approach needs, in other words, to explain why a person in a predominantly oral culture would behave in the way that this model suggests (i.e., why he/she would feel compelled to revise a Gospel), when the available anthropological and sociological data suggest, to me at least, that such a person would not have behaved in this fashion (i.e., she would not have felt compelled to do this).

Second, if there were indeed three or four editions of the Gospel of John, then we need to answer the guiding question of this book three or four times: Why did each of these four people write/revise a Gospel? In an oral culture, the transition from tradition to written text is a major social shift, and like all other major social shifts it requires a precipitating crisis. I have argued here that John wrote a Gospel under the precipitating crisis of the AntiChrists' claims, and that he responded to this crisis by writing a text because a written Gospel was uniquely suited to the specific challenges of fluid charismatic memory. But if John was only one of three, four, or five people who wrote or revised a Jesus book for the Johannine churches, it is necessary to explain the precipitating crisis that led each of them individually to feel that a new edition of a written text would be more effective than the sum of their charismatic memory of Jesus, plus their current version of the Gospel of John.

Of course, advocates of the developmental approach major in precipitating crises, discussing in great detail the various experiences of the Johannine community that led these Christians to change their theology again and again: John 1 and 3 reflect their struggle to convert disciples of John the Baptist; John 4 reveals that a number of Samaritans joined the church at some point; John 9 shows that some Johannine Christians were excommunicated from the synagogue; and so forth. As I noted way back in chapter 1, this approach builds on Culpepper's maxim that "theological developments are often precipitated by social crises."[4] But I also noted in chapter 1 that this maxim does not adequately explain the existence of any written document, such as the Gospel of John or a Signs Gospel. In terms of the present study, Culpepper's maxim, as applied by advocates of the developmental approach, accurately explains trends in the evolution of Johannine memory, because memory always attempts to shape its image of the past to meet the needs of the present. So if, for example, a bunch of Samaritans decided to join one of John's churches, we could call that event a precipitating crisis for a reconfiguration of the group's memory—they would now need to rethink Jesus' ministry and teaching in light of this new development. But this new development is *not* a precipitating crisis for *literacy*: there's no reason why you have to write, or rewrite, a Gospel because some Samaritans join your church. To claim that this event was a precipitating crisis for literacy, we would have to show that writing or revising a Gospel was somehow a logical response to that situation, and I am not aware that advocates of the developmental approach have done that.

Many Christians in John's time faced challenges that forced them seriously to rethink Jesus; Christians today face many of those same challenges. In the whole history of the first-century church, we know for certain that four people responded to these challenges by writing Gospels: Matthew, Mark, Luke, and John (assuming the Fourth Gospel was written before the year 100). The evidence suggests that there could have been six or seven more, depending on what you think about Q, L, M, the Signs Gospel, and possible early editions of the *Gospel of Thomas* and the *Gospel of Peter*. This takes us up to about ten early Gospels; for sake of discussion, let's quadruple that number and say that about forty Christians in John's day had written books about Jesus. If we accept Rodney Stark's claim that there were some 7,500 Christians in the Roman Empire at the end of the first century, these forty Gospel authors would represent 0.53 percent of the total Christian population.[5] So out of all the early Christians who faced serious personal and theological crises that challenged their thinking (which is to say, almost all of them), we must conclude that the number of them who responded to their situation by writing a Gospel was statistically insignificant.

Further, in the Johannine community specifically, the Elder who wrote the epistles dealt with his theological crisis, the AntiChrists, by writing letters that emphasized older community traditions and creeds; the Beloved Disciple (if not the same person as the Elder) apparently dealt with challenges by appealing to his own "witness," his claimed association with the historical Jesus. John is the only Johannine Christian who we know for certain wrote a book about Jesus. So even if the Johannine churches were a relatively small community of, say, 1,500 people (20 percent of Stark's estimated 7,500), John's decision to write a Gospel in response to his challenging situation would be statistically insignificant even within his own immediate group.

Because of this statistical insignificance, it is only with great difficulty that I have been able to explain, in the last eleven chapters, why John responded to his challenges by writing a Gospel. I have argued that the unique challenge of the AntiChrists' charismatic memory—or at least John's anticipation of the emergence of such a group—could be logically answered by a book about Jesus, and that John wrote his book because he was aware of the advantages of writing in such a dispute. Similarly, advocates of the developmental approach and proponents of the Signs Gospel need to explain why the hypothetical authors/editors who worked before John felt that a written Gospel was the logical way to respond to their situation, or why and how a new edition would be inherently better than the current one. They need, in other words, to answer the question, Why did all these people [re]write a Gospel? if they wish to get past the current impasse.

Third, I noted in an earlier chapter that history books continue to promote a rigid vision of the past, long after that vision has become obsolete and irrelevant. This attribute is perhaps the most significant difference between history books and living memories; living memory can change to meet the needs of new situations, but history books cannot. The history book will continue to proclaim its version of things forever, even when its contents challenge current perspectives. Societies acknowledge this fact tacitly or explicitly through "book burnings," violent attempts to erase certain memories and ideas by destroying the texts that preserve them. Any developmental theory must explain not only why and how multiple editions of the Gospel of John were produced, but also how each new editor (if there were more than one) *systematically destroyed every copy of previous editions so that these earlier editions could not challenge the new vision.*

In my view, the effort required to produce a revision of a written document in the first century would imply that the editor in question felt very, very strongly that the ideas promoted in the extant text were deficient. If the text was judged slightly deficient, it would be much easier to simply correct or paraphrase it in oral recitations—or, in extreme cases, to make written notes in the margin at key points—than to bother producing a new one. But if this new way of thinking was so different from earlier beliefs, and if the differences were so important as to justify a whole new edition of the sacred text, it is hard for me to imagine that an editor would be content to know that twenty copies of the old edition were sitting out in church libraries somewhere ready to challenge the new perspective. So long as these old copies existed, anyone with access to one of them could simply point out that "my Bible doesn't say that" or argue that the old way of thinking, still preserved with all its elements intact, was better. Memory can replace the old way of thinking simply by ignoring it and saying something else, under the principle that the values of today reshape the image of the past in a way that makes it hard to remember what the group wants to forget. But new versions of a history book can't do that—the old edition still proclaims its view of things loud and clear. Once writing enters the tradition equation, it becomes necessary to explain exactly how the old way of thinking could be eliminated, which means explaining how someone in the Johannine community could destroy every copy of the version of the text that he sought to replace.

This aspect of the problem relates to the interface between memory and community infrastructure, the question of who has the authority to change the way that a group thinks about the past. At the time that the Johannine Epistles were written, the infrastructure of the Johannine churches had broken down to a point where the Elder, mustering all his authority, could not get Diotrephes to give his representatives a glass of water. This being the case, I wonder how he could persuade Diotrephes to hand over his obsolete edition of the Gospel of John so that "the brothers" could burn it in his backyard? Of course, things may have been different at an earlier time, before the days of the AntiChrist crisis, when the Johannine network was tighter and worked more smoothly. I leave it to those who advocate developmental theories to show that this was the case, and to describe the Johannine infrastructure at the point in time when the revisions they propose were introduced and the old versions destroyed.

Again, I do not offer these points as a definitive refutation of the developmental approach, but only as observations about its limitations when viewed in the light of the interface between memory and writing in John's situation.

JOHN AND JESUS

Since the earliest days of the church, scholars have tended to view the Gospel of John as a christological treatise, admirable for its theological and literary depth but less concerned with the Jesus of history than Matthew, Mark, or Luke. Thus Clement of Alexandria (fl. 190s CE) argued that John, "knowing that the outward things had been set down in the [Synoptic] gospels . . . was moved by the Spirit to create a spiritual gospel" (*Eccl. Hist.* 6.14.7), and Bultmann asserted in 1958 that "the Gospel of John cannot be taken into account at all as a source for the teaching of Jesus."[6] Even John A. T. Robinson, who dedicated much of his career to the thesis that the Fourth Gospel "could take us as far back to source [= Jesus himself] as any other [Gospel]," admitted that John's presentation of his subject remains "the most [theologically] mature."[7]

But whether or not the Fourth Gospel portrays the Jesus of history accurately, John betrays a greater interest in a "historical Jesus" than any other primitive Christian author. The Gospel of John was born out of a desire to

---

John, Memory, and History: Implications

1. The Fourth Gospel is an apologetic treatise, not an evangelistic tract.

2. The Fourth Gospel that we have today is most likely the first, or at most the second, edition of that book.

3. **John shows more interest in a "historical Jesus" than Matthew, Mark, Luke, or anyone else in his time period.**

---

portray Jesus as a figure from the past and to keep him locked in that past, to draw a bold line between present Christian experience and the events of "the beginning," to suppress the living memory of Jesus and replace that memory with a fixed image of a person who lived and died decades earlier. The Jesus of the Fourth Gospel is an intentionally historical figure, one whose image is explicitly conflated with Christian faith and the Jewish Scriptures, but whose memory is no longer solely dependent on the work of the Spirit and no longer subject to the vicissitudes of tradition and the needs of the moment.

There is today, in Beaconsfield, England (some twenty-five miles northwest of London), a building made from wood supposedly taken from the *Mayflower*, the ship that carried the Pilgrims to the United States and that plays such a prominent role in American lore about the first Thanksgiving. Legend has it that the *Mayflower*, a mean cargo vessel before and after its famous voyage, returned to England and was offered at auction in 1624 after the death of its master and part owner, Christopher Jones. The ship, in a state of near ruin, sold for a fraction of its potential value, and was broken up, sawn apart, and incorporated into a barn. Considerable debate surrounds this story, but the skepticism of historians has not diminished the thriving tourist trade around the Mayflower Barn (now a reception hall) on the site of the historic Jordans Quaker community.

Assuming for a moment that the legends are true (or even if they are not), one may imagine that an enterprising American might purchase this barn, dismantle it, and bring the resultant pile of lumber back to Boston. He could then point to this pile with pride and say, "That used to be the *Mayflower*." But the Pilgrims didn't sail across the Atlantic Ocean on a pile of wood, and tourists wouldn't pay much to see one. This same entrepreneur might therefore hire historians to recreate the original plans of the *Mayflower* and then rebuild the ship from those materials, replacing the boards that couldn't be found or were too rotten to use and, of course, installing electric lighting and other conveniences essential to the tourist trade. And while such a careful restoration might be of considerable historical interest, and while it would no doubt capture the imagination of the many Americans who would visit with their children, the finished product would not be, and could not be, the original *Mayflower*.

The *Mayflower* was a product of its time, an inseparable combination of raw materials and the skill and toil of the early-seventeenth-century British shipbuilders. While the wood remains, the work and wisdom that gave that wood meaningful form was lost four centuries ago; it would, indeed, be impossible even to list the names of the original craftsmen. New minds could guess at the original plan by comparison with other known vessels from that time period, and new hands could build a replica with the old pieces, making the barn into a boat once more. But these exertions would represent not a move backward in time, but rather a move forward—not to an old boat, but rather to a new boat that had never existed before. The "restoration" would thus represent a move forward to a third phase in the life of the *Mayflower*, not a move back to the first phase. And while such a move might draw many tourists, it would take us no closer to the past than if we were to enter that barn at Jordans and lay our hand on the wall and say, "Someone who sailed on the *Mayflower* once touched this very same piece of wood that I'm touching now." For many people, in fact, this experience might offer a much more significant link to the Pilgrims than any restored tourist attraction complete with flush toilets. I would include myself among that number.

In a similar way, John's candid comments underscore the impossibility of "going back behind" the Gospels—at least, behind his Gospel—to what historians today would call an "original memory of Jesus," to a simple recall of his deeds and words that could somehow provide a virtual experience of his "real" person. If such a thing ever existed, it is now gone forever, and comes to us embedded in a combination of recollections, Scriptures, and theological conclusions. It would never be possible, in other words, to go backward to a point when the raw materials for the Jesus quest were truly "raw." John would doubtless ask why anyone would want to. And while modern attempts to subtract early Christian interpretation and faith from the extant sources might produce a small pile of factoids, it must be understood that any image of Jesus built from those pieces would not be a "re-creation" but rather an entirely new Jesus—a third phase, Frankenstein Jesus, a Jesus who might speak meaningfully to modern spiritual tourists but who should not be confused with the person who lived in Galilee in the early first century.

The Gospels, especially John's Gospel, will be most helpful in this restoration project when they are viewed as artifacts and relics rather than databases for a forensic memory of Jesus that never actually existed. John's Gospel invites us to lay our hand on the wall and meditate on the fact that some other person, twenty centuries ago, touched that same page; some person who lived not very long after Jesus died and knew people who claimed to have known him; some person whose memory of Jesus was, like ours, shaped to meet the needs of a personal crisis. And this person invites us now to remember Jesus just the way he did, to see the object of our common interest through his own eyes. Thus, every time we read, John welcomes us back to our old table at that small café in Ephesus, and in that moment and in that way the Gospel of John becomes both memory and history.

"... this building has become
the subject and the scene
of many wild and extraordinary
traditions.

"One of them I have been enabled,
by a personal acquaintance with an eye–witness of the events,
to trace to its origin;

"and yet

"it is hard to say
whether the events which I am about to record
appear more strange or improbable
as seen through the distorting medium of tradition,
or in the appalling dimness of uncertainty
which surrounds
the reality."

—J. Sheridan LeFanu, *The Purcell Papers*, 15

Abbreviations

AB	Anchor Bible
IEJ	*Israel Exploration Journal*
JAAR	*Journal of the American Academy of Religion*
JSJ	*Journal for the Study of Judaism in the Persian, Hellenistic, and Roman Periods*
LCL	Loeb Classical Library
NICNT	New International Commentary on the New Testament
NIGTC	New International Greek Testament Commentary
NTS	*New Testament Studies*
SBLDS	Society of Biblical Literature Dissertation Series
SBLMS	Society of Biblical Literature Monograph Series
TSAJ	Texte und Studien zum Antiken Judentum
WBC	Word Biblical Commentary

Notes

Prescript

1. Graham Stanton, "Form Criticism Revisited," in *What About the New Testament? Essays in Honour of Christopher Evans* (London: SCM Press, 1975), 16.
2. Ernst Käsemann, *The Testament of Jesus: A Study of the Gospel of John in the Light of Chapter 17*, trans. Gerhard Krodel (Philadelphia: Fortress, 1968), 13.
3. See, for example, Leon Morris, *The Gospel according to John: The English Text with Introduction, Exposition and Notes*, NICNT (Grand Rapids: Eerdmans, 1971), 8–30, 35–40; D. A. Carson, *The Gospel according to John* (Grand Rapids: Eerdmans, 1991), 68–81, 87–95.
4. For example, Robert Fortna, the most significant proponent of this position today, argues that much of the Fourth Gospel was drawn from a more primitive Signs Gospel, yet still attributes much of the current text to John's editorial expansions and other community traditions (see his *The Fourth Gospel and Its Predecessor: From Narrative Source to Present Gospel* [Philadelphia: Fortress, 1988], 1–9).

Chapter 1: Why Did John Write a Gospel?

1. The name "John" will be used throughout this study to refer to that individual who was primarily responsible for the publication of the Fourth Gospel as it exists today. The term is synonymous here with the designation "the Fourth Evangelist." The masculine pronoun "he" will be used to refer to this author in agreement with the gender of the English name John.
2. R. Alan Culpepper, *The Gospel and Letters of John*, Interpreting Biblical Texts (Nashville: Abingdon, 1998), 14.
3. Culpepper, 43–44.
4. Culpepper, 54.
5. Culpepper, 88–89.
6. Culpepper, 58.
7. Culpepper, 58.

Chapter 2: Writing as Archive

1. David Lowenthal, *The Past Is a Foreign Country* (Cambridge: Cambridge University Press, 1985), 252.
2. Augustine, *The Confessions* 10.8.12, 10.9.16, in *The Works of St. Augustine: A Translation for the 21st Century*, trans. Maria Boulding (New York: New City Press, 1997), 245, 247. Augustine's complete discussion of memory covers *Confessions* 10.8.12–10.19.28.
3. Augustine, 10.14.22, in *Works of St. Augustine*, 251.
4. Quote from Barbie Zelizer, "Reading the Past against the Grain: The Shape of Memory Studies," *Critical Studies in Mass Communication* 12 (1995): 218.
5. Paul Connerton, *How Societies Remember*, Themes in the Social Sciences (Cambridge: Cambridge University Press, 1989), 22.
6. Quote from James Fentress and Chris Wickham, *Social Memory*, New Perspectives on the Past (Cambridge, MA: Blackwell, 1992), 8–9.
7. Zelizer, 218.
8. Quote from David Lowenthal, *Possessed by the Past: The Heritage Crusade and the Spoils of History* (New York: Free Press, 1996), 107.
9. Plato, *Phaedrus* 274–75. All citations of *Phaedrus* are from *Plato in Twelve Volumes*, trans. Harold North Fowler, LCL (Cambridge, MA: Harvard University Press, 1982). Note that Fowler translates the phrase μνήμης φάρμακον as "elixir of memory."
10. Schnackenburg asserts that "no other can be intended" than the Beloved Disciple, based on both the immediate context and the similar reference at John 21:20–24 (*The Gospel according to St. John*, trans. Kevin Smyth [New York: Crossroad, 1987], 3.290). See also Rudolf Bultmann, *The Gospel of John: A Commentary*, trans. G. R. Beasley-Murray, R. W. N. Hoare, and J. K. Riches (Philadelphia: Westminster, 1971), 677–79; C. K. Barrett, *The Gospel according to St. John: An Introduction with Commentary and Notes on the Greek Text*, 2nd ed. (Philadelphia: Westminster, 1978), 557–58; F. F. Bruce, *The Gospel of John: Introduction, Exposition, and Notes* (Grand Rapids: Eerdmans, 1983), 376–77; D. A. Carson, *The Gospel according to John* (Grand Rapids: Eerdmans, 1991), 625.
11. C. H. Dodd, *Historical Tradition in the Fourth Gospel* (Cambridge: Cambridge University Press, 1963), 14. See also Barrett, 557–58; Schnackenburg, 3.290–91; Raymond E. Brown, *The Gospel according to John: A New Translation with Introduction and Commentary*, AB (Garden City, NY: Doubleday, 1966, 1970), 2.936–37.
12. Carson, 626; see also Leon Morris, who is more cautious in his evaluation, *The Gospel according to John: The English Text with Introduction, Exposition and Notes*, NICNT (Grand Rapids: Eerdmans, 1971), 820–22.
13. Or, in terms of Carson's reading: "*I* saw this happen, and now *I* am pulling the images of what *I* saw out of *my* brain and showing them to you." Still here, "memory" is understood as recall, and the text of the Fourth Gospel is treated as a surrogate memory of empirical experience.
14. Brown, 2.1123.
15. See discussion of the causal view in Brown, 2.1123, and Schnackenburg, 3.372–74.
16. Bruce, 376; Carson, 681–82; Morris, 880–81. Carson explains v. 23 by suggesting that "the circulating rumor is making the rounds while the beloved disciple is still alive, but advancing in years, and he is determined to stifle it as well as he can for fear of the damage that would be done if he died before the Lord's

return" (682). If this is the case, the written text would have functioned as a parallel memory alongside the living memory of the Beloved Disciple, the two forms of witness mutually supporting one another.

17. Brown, 2.1119.
18. Schnackenburg, 3.371.
19. Bultmann, 717.
20. Barrett, 583–84. "It is to be understood," Schnackenburg argues, "that the editors [who added the comment at 24b] want to draw upon his [the Beloved Disciple's] authority for the written work as well, into which his oral tradition and testimonies have been put" (3.373). Bultmann also argues that the editor who added 21:24b sought "to set the present [written] Gospel under the authority of the oldest witness" to Jesus (716).

Chapter 3: The Persistence of John's Memory

1. See D. A. Carson, *The Gospel according to John* (Grand Rapids: Eerdmans, 1991), 182–83; Leon Morris, *The Gospel according to John: The English Text with Introduction, Exposition and Notes*, NICNT (Grand Rapids: Eerdmans, 1971), 201–5.
2. In Barrett's words, "During the ministry [of Jesus] the disciples, in spite of their call and their belief in Jesus . . . understood his words little more than his adversaries" (*The Gospel according to St. John: An Introduction with Commentary and Notes on the Greek Text*, 2nd ed. [Philadelphia: Westminster, 1978], 201). While John partially alleviates this confusion at 16:29–30, Barrett's comment certainly applies to the flow of the narrative at John 2.
3. Morris explains that "they [the crowd] thought of Him as King in a wrong sense [at the time of the event]. After the glorification the disciples thought of Him as King in a right sense" under the guiding insight of the Paraclete (587–88).
4. John may be referring to "the Scripture" (τῇ γραφῇ; singular) quoted at v. 17, Psalm 69:9, which in its original context describes the psalmist's persecution because of his concern for God's house. Brown and Schnackenburg both raise this possibility briefly but do not give it serious consideration, and Barrett calls it as "a very strained interpretation" because the citation in v. 17 seems intended to explain Jesus' "zealous" actions in the temple rather than his death (201; see Raymond E. Brown, *The Gospel according to John: A New Translation with Introduction and Commentary*, AB [Garden City, NY: Doubleday, 1966, 1970], 1.116; Rudolf Schnackenburg, *The Gospel according to St. John*, trans. Kevin Smyth [New York: Crossroad, 1987], 1.353).
5. "Misunderstanding" and irony are now widely recognized as dominant themes in the Fourth Gospel's Christology. For extended discussions of these motifs from varying methodological perspectives, see Herbert LeRoy, *Rätsel und Missverständnis: Ein Beitrag zur Formgeschichte des Johannesevangeliums* (Bonn: Peter Hanstein, 1968); R. Alan Culpepper, *Anatomy of the Fourth Gospel: A Study in Literary Design* (Philadelphia: Fortress, 1983); Gail R. O'Day, *Revelation in the Fourth Gospel: Narrative Mode and Theological Claim* (Philadelphia: Fortress, 1986); Tom Thatcher, *The Riddles of Jesus in John: A Study in Tradition and Folklore*, SBLMS (Atlanta: Society of Biblical Literature, 2000).
6. Arthur J. Dewey, "The Eyewitness of History: Visionary Consciousness in the Fourth Gospel," in *Jesus in Johannine Tradition*, ed. Robert T. Fortna and Tom Thatcher (Louisville, KY: Westminster John Knox, 2001), 68.
7. See the survey and discussion in Brown, 2.1135–43, and Max Turner, "Holy

Spirit," in *The Dictionary of Jesus and the Gospels*, ed. Joel B. Green, Scot McKnight, and I. Howard Marshall (Downers Grove, IL: InterVarsity Press, 1992), 341–51.

8. Is John referring to Jesus' return from the dead, or to Jesus' second coming, or does he mean that Jesus will come to his disciples in the form of the Spirit? Brown equates the indwelling Paraclete with Jesus himself and translates John 14:18 as "I shall not leave you as orphans: I [as the Paraclete] am coming back to you," insisting that "not two presences but the same presence is involved" (2.637, 640, 644–46; see also Rudolf Bultmann, *The Gospel of John: A Commentary*, trans. G. R. Beasley-Murray, R. W. N. Hoare, and J. K. Riches [Philadelphia: Westminster, 1971], 617–18). Carson, however, argues that "it is not at all clear that John ever speaks of the coming of Jesus in the Spirit," and concludes that Jesus "is referring to his departure in death and his [personal] return after the resurrection," making John 20:19 the fulfillment of 14:18 (501; see also Barrett, 463–64; Morris, 651).

9. F. F. Bruce, *The Gospel of John: Introduction, Exposition, and Notes* (Grand Rapids: Eerdmans, 1983), 305.

10. All quotes Schnackenburg, 3.144, 3.83, 3.142, see also 3.138–54; Barrett, 467–68; Brown, 2.715–16; Bultmann, 575.

11. See the neutral discussion in Raymond E. Brown, *The Epistles of John: A New Translation with Introduction and Commentary*, AB (Garden City, NY: Doubleday, 1982), 345–47. For the view that the anointing is the indwelling Holy Spirit, see Rudolf Schnackenburg, *The Johannine Epistles: Introduction and Commentary*, trans. Reginald Fuller and Ilse Fuller (New York: Crossroad, 1992), 141–43; David Rensberger, *1 John, 2 John, 3 John*, Abingdon New Testament Commentaries (Nashville: Abingdon, 1997), 79–80.

12. Maurice Halbwachs, *On Collective Memory*, ed. and trans. Lewis Coser (Chicago: University of Chicago Press, 1992), 39. Pages 41–189 of this volume are selected translations from *The Social Frameworks of Memory* [Les cadres sociaux de la mémoire, 1952 edition]; pages 193–235 are a translation of the final chapter of *The Legendary Topography of the Holy Land: A Study in Collective Memory* (La topographie légendaire des évangiles en terre sainte: Étude de mémoire collective, 1941 edition].

Chapter 4: Writing as Rhetoric

1. Rosalind Thomas, *Literacy and Orality in Ancient Greece* (Cambridge: Cambridge University Press, 1992), 74.

2. All citations of Herodotus are from the Loeb edition, trans. A. D. Godley (Cambridge, MA: Harvard University Press, 1960).

3. The emergence of this trend was highlighted in John A. T. Robinson's landmark 1957 paper, "The New Look on John" (now pages 94–106 in Robinson's *Twelve New Testament Studies* [London: SCM Press, 1962]), and it has remained the majority view ever since.

4. William V. Harris, *Ancient Literacy* (Cambridge, MA: Harvard University Press, 1989), 24; on urbanization and literacy, 17; on availability of written materials, 14; on writing and economic systems, 18–19.

5. Harris, 11, 15–17, quote 15.

6. Harris, 13, 22. Harris notes that "nowhere, under the Roman Empire, was there any elaborate network of schools" (17). See also Ann Ellis Hanson, "Ancient Illiteracy," in *Literacy in the Roman World*, ed. J. H. Humphrey, Journal of Roman Archaeology Supplementary Series (Ann Arbor: University of Michigan, 1991), 159–98.

7. Meir Bar-Ilan, "Illiteracy in the Land of Israel in the First Centuries C.E.," in *Essays in the Social Scientific Study of Judaism and Jewish Society*, ed. Simcha Fishbane, Stuart Schoenfeld, and Alain Goldschläger (Hoboken, NJ: KTAV Publishing, 1992), 2.55. Bar-Ilan's estimate of 3 percent literacy encompasses the total Jewish population in first–century Palestine. In some rural areas, however, literacy rates would be below 1 percent, and it is possible that in some towns not one person could read (54–55). Catherine Hezser's extensive study of Jewish literacy in Roman Palestine concludes that, regardless of the specific percentages and differing definitions of "literacy," "the average Jewish literacy rate (of whatever degree) [in Roman Palestine] must be considered to have been lower than the average Roman [literacy] rate" estimated by William Harris (10–15 percent) (*Jewish Literacy in Roman Palestine*, TSAJ [Tübingen: Mohr-Siebeck, 2001], 496).

8. Martin Goodman, "Texts, Scribes and Power in Roman Judaea," in *Literacy and Power in the Ancient World*, ed. Alan K. Bowman and Greg Woolf (New York: Cambridge University Press, 1994), 99. While Goodman's comment focuses on Roman Palestine, Avigdor Shinan asserts that "the public reading and study of Scripture was a feature of all brands of Second Temple period Judaism" ("Synagogues in the Land of Israel: The Literature of the Ancient Synagogue and Synagogue Archaeology," in *Sacred Realm: The Emergence of the Synagogue in the Ancient World*, ed. Steven Fine [New York: Oxford University Press, 1996], 132).

9. All citations of Josephus's *Against Apion* are from the Loeb edition, trans. H. St. J. Thackeray (Cambridge, MA: Harvard University Press, 1966).

10. See complete text with translation and notes in Eric M. Meyers, "Ancient Synagogues: An Archaeological Introduction," in *Sacred Realm: The Emergence of the Synagogue in the Ancient World*, 9.

11. All citations of Philo's *Embassy to Gaius* are from the Loeb edition, trans. F. H. Colson (Cambridge, MA: Harvard University Press, 1971). All citations of Philo's *Life of Moses* are from the Loeb edition, trans. F. H. Colson (Cambridge, MA: Harvard University Press, 1950).

12. Josephus also portrays the public reading of Scripture as a dominant feature of ancient Jewish community life. For example, when the Ionian Jews appealed to Marcus Agrippa (63–12 BCE) for protection of their ancestral customs, they insisted that Sabbath observance is not a sign of laziness, for "we give every seventh day over to the study of our customs and law" (*Antiquities* 16.43; trans. Ralph Marcus and Allen Wickgren, LCL [Cambridge, MA: Harvard University Press, 1963]). This same practice continued in Josephus's own day, on the basis of Moses' decree "that every week men should desert their other occupations and assemble to listen to the Law and obtain a thorough and accurate knowledge of it" (*Against Apion* 2.175).

13. All citations of Josephus's *Jewish War* are from the Loeb edition, trans. H. St. J. Thackeray (Cambridge, MA: Harvard University Press, 1961).

14. See the texts of the letters and critical notes in "Jews of Palestine in the Zenon Papyri," in *Corpus Papyrorum Judaicarum*, ed. Victor Tcherikover and Alexander Fuks (Cambridge, MA: Harvard University Press, 1957).

15. Yigael Yadin, "The Expedition to the Judean Desert, 1960: Expedition D," *IEJ* 11 (1961): 40–50.

16. Yigael Yadin, "The Expedition to the Judean Desert, 1961: Expedition D," *IEJ* 12 (1962): 231–35. The critical edition of the Babatha Archive appears in *The Documents from the Bar Kokhba Period in the Cave of Letters: Greek Papyri, Aramaic and Nabatean Signatures and Subscriptions*, ed. Naphtali Lewis (Jerusalem: Hebrew University, 1989).

17. See Yadin 1961, 248–57.
18. The ancient Jews' awareness of the social power of written texts is also evident in their attitudes toward public archives, official repositories of significant documents. It seems that late Second Temple Jews, literate and illiterate, realized that written texts filed in public archives were critical for legal protection and even, in some cases, for establishing personal identity and status. For discussion and documentation, see Tom Thatcher, "Literacy, Textual Communities, and Josephus' *Jewish War*," *JSJ* 29 (1998): 123–42.
19. Mary Beard, "Writing and Religion: Ancient Literacy and the Function of the Written Word in Roman Religion," in *Literacy in the Roman World*, 39.
20. See the balanced discussion in Joseph Fitzmeyer, *The Gospel according to Luke*, 2nd ed., AB (Garden City, NY: Doubleday, 1981), 1.292. Luke apparently means to give this impression even if he does not thereby intend to disparage his predecessors. If, as Marshall and others have suggested, Luke actually seeks to affirm the validity of these other authors, his comments would still function to give his own account a higher status: "theirs was good, mine is better" (see I. Howard Marshall, *The Gospel of Luke: A Commentary on the Greek Text*, NIGTC [Grand Rapids: Eerdmans, 1978], 40–43).

Chapter 5: John's Memory Framework

1. Maurice Halbwachs, *The Collective Memory*, trans. Francis J. Ditter Jr. and Vida Yazdi Ditter (New York: Harper & Row, 1980), 52. This translation is based on the 1950 French edition of *La mémoire collective* (Paris: Presses Universitaires de France).
2. Maurice Halbwachs, *On Collective Memory*, ed. and trans. Lewis Coser (Chicago: University of Chicago Press, 1992), 45. Pages 41–189 of this volume are selected translations from *The Social Frameworks of Memory* [Les cadres sociaux de la mémoire, 1952 edition]; pages 193–235 are a translation of the final chapter of *The Legendary Topography of the Holy Land: A Study in Collective Memory* [La topographie légendaire des évangiles en terre sainte: Étude de mémoire collective, 1941 edition].
3. Halbwachs 1980, 56.
4. Halbwachs 1992, 60.
5. Halbwachs 1992, 38.
6. Halbwachs 1992, 45.
7. Eviatar Zerubavel, *Time Maps: Collective Memory and the Social Shape of the Past* (Chicago: University of Chicago Press, 2003), 15–25.
8. Irenaeus, *Against Heresies* 3.3.4; Eusebius, *Eccl. Hist.* 3.1.1, 3.23.3–4, 3.39.6. See discussion in Martin Hengel, *The Johannine Question*, trans. John Bowden (Philadelphia: Trinity Press, 1989), 30–31.
9. David Rensberger, *1 John, 2 John, 3 John*, Abingdon New Testament Commentaries (Nashville: Abingdon, 1997), 78.
10. See Raymond Brown's exhaustive survey of possible backgrounds for the concept in *The Epistles of John*, AB (Garden City, NY: Doubleday, 1982), 332–36.
11. John Painter, "The Farewell Discourses and the History of Johannine Christianity," *NTS* 27 (1981): 531, 540–41.

Chapter 6: One Way Back to Two Places

1. David Rensberger, *1 John, 2 John, 3 John*, Abingdon New Testament Commentaries (Nashville: Abingdon, 1997), 24. See also Raymond Brown, *The Community of the Beloved Disciple: The Life, Loves, and Hates of an Individual*

Church in New Testament Times (New York: Paulist Press, 1979), 138–42; Gary Burge, *The Anointed Community: The Holy Spirit in the Johannine Tradition* (Grand Rapids: Eerdmans, 1987), 218–19.

2. Eric Hobsbawm, "Introduction: Inventing Traditions," in *The Invention of Tradition*, ed. Eric Hobsbawm and Terence Ranger, Canto Edition (Cambridge: Cambridge University Press, 1992), 1–2.

3. Note Marianne Meye Thompson's cautious appraisal, which reflects the current trend away from the Gnostics as an easy answer to the AntiChrist question: "[W]hile striking parallels can be adduced between early known heresies and the epistles of John, none of these heresies perfectly mirrors the false teachings of 1 and 2 John" (*1–3 John*, IVP New Testament Commentary [Downers Grove, IL: InterVarsity, 1992], 18; see also Rensberger, 22–24).

4. The term "countermemory" is derived from Michel Foucault, "Nietzsche, Genealogy, and History," in *Language, CounterMemory, Practice*, ed. Donald F. Bouchard, trans. Donald F. Bouchard and Sherry Simon (Ithaca, NY: Cornell University Press, 1977), 160.

5. Rudolf Schnackenburg, *The Johannine Epistles: Introduction and Commentary*, trans. Reginald Fuller and Ilse Fuller (New York: Crossroad, 1992), 286. See also Rudolf Bultmann, *The Johannine Epistles*, trans. R. Philip O'Hara, with Lane C. McGaughy and Robert W. Funk, Hermeneia (Philadelphia: Fortress, 1973), 113.

6. See Rensberger, 24–25; John Painter, *The Quest for the Messiah: The History, Literature, and Theology of the Johannine Community*, 2nd ed. (Nashville: Abingdon, 1993), 438–39; Stephen Smalley, *1, 2, 3 John*, WBC (Waco, TX: Word Books, 1984), xxiii–xxv.

7. In my view, 1 John 4:5 does not contradict this conclusion. Specifically, I take the statement, "They [the AntiChrists] are from the world; for this reason they speak from the world and the world hears them" to be a qualitative evaluation of the current status of the AntiChrists and their followers, not a statement about the origin of their views. Because the AntiChrists disagree with John, they fall into the same category as other nonbelievers, members of "the world." First John 4:5 thus reflects the Elder's estimate of the AntiChrists' ontological status as enemies of God, and therefore does not conflict with the more explicit remarks about their origins at 2:19.

8. Foucault, first quote 144–45, second quote 146.

9. Foucault, 160.

10. Ann Burlein, *Lift High the Cross: Where White Supremacy and the Christian Right Converge* (Durham, NC: Duke University Press, 2002), 4.

11. Burlein, 217; see also 7.

12. Maurice Halbwachs, *On Collective Memory*, ed. and trans. Lewis Coser (Chicago: University of Chicago Press, 1992), 160; see also 120–22. Pages 41–189 of this volume are selected translations from *The Social Frameworks of Memory* [Les cadres sociaux de la mémoire, 1952 edition]; pages 193–235 are a translation of the final chapter of *The Legendary Topography of the Holy Land: A Study in Collective Memory* [La topographie légendaire des évangiles en terre sainte: Étude de mémoire collective, 1941 edition].

13. Halbwachs 1992, 85–86.

Chapter 7: Jesus Now and Then

1. Maurice Halbwachs, *On Collective Memory*, ed. and trans. Lewis Coser (Chicago: University of Chicago Press, 1992), 90–92, quote 92. Pages 41–189 of this volume are selected translations from *The Social Frameworks of Memory*

(Les cadres sociaux de la mémoire, 1952 edition); pages 193–235 are a translation of the final chapter of *The Legendary Topography of the Holy Land: A Study
in Collective Memory* (La topographie légendaire des évangiles en terre sainte:
Étude de mémoire collective, 1941 edition).

2. Halbwachs's discussion of religious memory focuses almost exclusively on
   European church history and alludes to other faith systems only to contrast or
   highlight aspects of Christian thought. As such, while his remarks are appropriate to the discussion here, they may not entirely characterize the memory
   frameworks of other religions.
3. Halbwachs 1992, 93–100.
4. Halbwachs 1992, 112–13.
5. Halbwachs 1992, 100.
6. All quotes Halbwachs 1992, 88.
7. Halbwachs 1992, 88.
8. Halbwachs 1992, 103.
9. Halbwachs 1992, 115.

Chapter 8: AntiChristian Mystical Memory

1. See the Our Lady of the Holy Spirit Center's Web site, www.olhsc.org.
2. Monte Leach, "Miracle at Cold Spring" (*Share International* [1992]); cited here
   from the Our Lady of the Holy Spirit Center Web site, www.olhsc.org.
3. All quotes Maurice Halbwachs, *On Collective Memory*, ed. and trans. Lewis
   Coser (Chicago: University of Chicago Press, 1992), 104, 106, 107. Pages
   41–189 of this volume are selected translations from *The Social Frameworks of
   Memory* [Les cadres sociaux de la mémoire, 1952 edition]; pages 193–235 are a
   translation of the final chapter of *The Legendary Topography of the Holy Land: A
   Study in Collective Memory* [La topographie légendaire des évangiles en terre
   sainte: Étude de mémoire collective, 1941 edition].
4. Halbwachs 1992, 106–7.
5. Halbwachs 1992, 105, 110–11.
6. Halbwachs 1992, 105.
7. Halbwachs 1992, 111–12.
8. R. Alan Culpepper, *1 John, 2 John, 3 John*, Knox Preaching Guides (Atlanta:
   John Knox, 1985), 52.
9. Barry Schwartz, "Social Change and Collective Memory: The Democratization of George Washington," *American Sociological Review* 56 (1991): 232. This
   theme permeates much of Schwartz's work. See also Michael Schudson, "The
   Present in the Past Versus the Past in the Present," *Communication* 11 (1989):
   107, 112.

Chapter 9: "Everything That Rises Must Converge"

1. A. J. Hill, *Under Pressure: The Final Voyage of the Submarine S-5* (New York: Free
   Press, 2002). Hill's very interesting book is not a study in social memory, and
   my review here is not intended as a negative critique of his presentation.
2. Maurice Halbwachs, *The Collective Memory*, trans. Francis J. Ditter Jr. and Vida
   Yazdi Ditter (New York: Harper & Row, 1980), 51.
3. David Lowenthal, *Possessed by the Past: The Heritage Crusade and the Spoils of History* (New York: Free Press, 1996), 120.
4. Lowenthal 1996, 120.
5. David Rensberger, *1 John, 2 John, 3 John*, Abingdon New Testament Commentaries (Nashville: Abingdon, 1997), 24.

6. Paul Connerton, *How Societies Remember*, Themes in the Social Sciences (Cambridge: Cambridge University Press, 1989), 19–20.

7. Roy Rosenzweig and David Thelen, *The Presence of the Past: Popular Uses of History in American Life* (New York: Columbia University Press, 1998), 8–22, 68.

8. Barbie Zelizer, "Reading the Past against the Grain: The Shape of Memory Studies," *Critical Studies in Mass Communication* 12 (1995): 221.

9. David Lowenthal, *The Past Is a Foreign Country* (Cambridge: Cambridge University Press, 1985), 208.

10. Halbwachs 1980, 86–87.

11. Eviatar Zerubavel, *Time Maps: Collective Memory and the Social Shape of the Past* (Chicago: University of Chicago Press, 2003), 14–15.

12. Lowenthal 1985, 128–29.

13. See discussion in Eviatar Zerubavel, *The Fine Line: Making Distinctions in Everyday Life* (Chicago: University of Chicago Press, 1993), 27–31.

14. Maurice Halbwachs, *On Collective Memory*, ed. and trans. Lewis Coser (Chicago: University of Chicago Press, 1992), 222–23. Pages 41–189 of this volume are selected translations from *The Social Frameworks of Memory* [Les cadres sociaux de la mémoire, 1952 edition]; pages 193–235 are a translation of the final chapter of *The Legendary Topography of the Holy Land: A Study in Collective Memory* [La topographie légendaire des évangiles en terre sainte: Étude de mémoire collective, 1941 edition].

15. James Fentress and Chris Wickham, *Social Memory*, New Perspectives on the Past (Cambridge, MA: Blackwell, 1992), 32.

16. Zelizer, 231.

17. Fentress and Wickham, 55–57.

Chapter 10: Beyond the Scope of the Present Study

1. Roy Rosenzweig and David Thelen, *The Presence of the Past: Popular Uses of History in American Life* (New York: Columbia University Press, 1998), 37–38.

2. Yosef Hayim Yerushalmi, *Zakhor: Jewish History and Jewish Memory* (New York: Schocken Books, 1989), 95.

3. First quote Maurice Halbwachs, *The Collective Memory*, trans. Francis J. Ditter Jr. and Vida Yazdi Ditter (New York: Harper & Row, 1980), 84; second quote David Lowenthal, *Possessed by the Past: The Heritage Crusade and the Spoils of History* (New York: Free Press, 1996), 11.

4. Halbwachs 1980, 83; Yerushalmi 94–95, 114.

5. Roland Barthes, *Writing Degree Zero*, trans. Annette Lavers and Colin Smith (London: Jonathan Cape, 1967), 54.

6. Eviatar Zerubavel, *The Fine Line: Making Distinctions in Everyday Life* (Chicago: University of Chicago Press, 1993), 1.

7. E. Zerubavel 1993, 3.

8. Eviatar Zerubavel, *Time Maps: Collective Memory and the Social Shape of the Past* (Chicago: University of Chicago Press, 2003), 84–85; see also Yael Zerubavel, *Recovered Roots: Collective Memory and the Making of Israeli National Tradition* (Chicago: University of Chicago Press, 1995), 8.

9. Yerushalmi, 11.

10. See discussion in David Lowenthal, *The Past Is a Foreign Country* (Cambridge: Cambridge University Press, 1985), 218; Stephen Owen, *Remembrances: The Experience of the Past in Classical Chinese Literature* (Cambridge, MA: Harvard University Press, 1986), 53–54, 103–4.

11. Lowenthal 1985, 217–18.

12. Lowenthal 1985, 234.
13. Y. Zerubavel, 221.
14. E. Zerubavel 2003, 93–97.
15. See E. Zerubavel 1993, 12–13; Y. Zerubavel, 221.
16. Plato, *Phaedrus* 275. All citations of *Phaedrus* are from *Plato in Twelve Volumes*, trans. Harold North Fowler, LCL (Cambridge, MA: Harvard University Press, 1982).
17. Y. Zerubavel, 84–95, 147–77.
18. E. Zerubavel 2003, 34. Zerubavel uses this analogy to describe a "rigid" mode of thinking but does not apply it specifically to historical memory. Using his terms, I am proposing that all history books have a "rigid mind."
19. First quote Paul Connerton, *How Societies Remember*, Themes in the Social Sciences (Cambridge: Cambridge University Press, 1989), 75; second quote Lowenthal 1996, 146.
20. Peter Burke, "History as Social Memory," in *Memory: History, Culture, and the Mind*, ed. Thomas Butler (New York: Basil Blackwell, 1989), 110.
21. E. Zerubavel 2003, 87–88.
22. See Rosenzweig and Thelen, 102–4.
23. Lowenthal 1996, 128–29.
24. Lowenthal 1996, 134–36.

Chapter 11: Why John Wrote a Gospel

1. If the comment at John 21:25 was added by a later editor (i.e., a person other than John), this would simply illustrate the extent to which John's disciples continued to depend on the notion of a limited data pool in their ongoing debates over Jesus' identity.
2. Rux Martin, "Truth, Power, Self: An Interview with Michel Foucault (October 25, 1982)," in *Technologies of the Self*, ed. Luther H. Martin, Huck Gutman, and Patrick H. Hutton (Amherst, MA: University of Massachusetts Press, 1988), 11.
3. Maurice Halbwachs, *The Collective Memory*, trans. Francis J. Ditter Jr. and Vida Yazdi Ditter (New York: Harper & Row, 1980), 78.

Postscript

1. For the view that the Fourth Gospel is primarily an evangelistic document, see C. H. Dodd, *The Interpretation of the Fourth Gospel* (Cambridge: Cambridge University Press, 1953), 9; Leon Morris, *The Gospel according to John: The English Text with Introduction, Exposition and Notes* (Grand Rapids: Eerdmans, 1971), 39–40. For the view that the Fourth Gospel is primarily an apologetic document, see Robert Kysar, *John: The Maverick Gospel* (Atlanta: John Knox, 1976), 17; Rudolf Schnackenburg, *The Gospel according to St. John*, trans. Kevin Smyth (New York: Crossroad, 1987), 3.338–39. For the view that the Fourth Gospel was intended to serve both evangelistic and apologetic purposes, see C. K. Barrett, T*he Gospel according to St. John: An Introduction with Commentary and Notes on the Greek Text*, 2nd ed. (Philadelphia: Westminster, 1978), 26, 575; Rudolf Bultmann, *The Gospel of John: A Commentary*, trans. G. R. Beasley-Murray, R. W. N. Hoare, and J. K. Riches (Philadelphia: Westminster, 1971), 698–99.
2. Kysar, 17.
3. Milestone studies in the evolution of the developmental approach include J. Louis Martyn's *History and Theology in the Fourth Gospel* (1968; 2nd ed.,

Nashville: Abingdon, 1979); R. Alan Culpepper's *The Johannine School: An Evaluation of the Johannine-School Hypothesis Based on an Investigation of the Nature of Ancient Schools*, SBLDS (Missoula, MT: Scholars Press, 1975); Raymond Brown's *The Community of the Beloved Disciple: The Life, Loves, and Hates of an Individual Church in New Testament Times* (New York: Paulist, 1979); and John Painter's *The Quest for the Messiah: The History, Literature, and Theology of the Johannine Community*, 2nd ed. (Nashville: Abingdon, 1993).

4. R. Alan Culpepper, *The Gospel and Letters of John*, Interpreting Biblical Texts (Nashville: Abingdon, 1998), 58.

5. Rodney Stark, *The Rise of Christianity: How the Obscure, Marginal Jesus Movement Became the Dominant Religious Force in the Western World in a Few Centuries* (San Francisco: HarperSanFrancisco, 1997), 4–13.

6. Rudolf Bultmann, *Jesus and the Word*, trans. Louise Pettibone Smith and Erminie Huntress Lantero (New York: Scribners, 1958), 12.

7. John A. T. Robinson, *The Priority of John*, ed. J. F. Coakley (London: SCM, 1985), 21–22, 298, 342.

Works Cited

Augustine. *The Confessions*. Trans. Maria Boulding. *The Works of St. Augustine: A Translation for the 21st Century*. New York: New City Press, 1997.

Bar-Ilan, Meir. "Illiteracy in the Land of Israel in the First Centuries C.E." In *Essays in the Social Scientific Study of Judaism and Jewish Society*, ed. Simcha Fishbane, Stuart Schoenfeld, and Alain Goldschläger, 2.46–61. Hoboken, NJ: KTAV Publishing, 1992.

Barrett, C. K. *The Gospel according to St. John: An Introduction with Commentary and Notes on the Greek Text*. 2nd ed. Philadelphia: Westminster, 1978.

Barthes, Roland. *Writing Degree Zero*. Trans. Annette Lavers and Colin Smith. London: Jonathan Cape, 1967.

Beard, Mary. "Writing and Religion: Ancient Literacy and the Function of the Written Word in Roman Religion." In *Literacy in the Roman World*, ed. J. H. Humphrey, 35–58. Journal of Roman Archaeology Supplementary Series. Ann Arbor: University of Michigan, 1991.

Brown, Raymond E. *The Community of the Beloved Disciple: The Life, Loves, and Hates of an Individual Church in New Testament Times*. New York: Paulist Press, 1979.

———. *The Epistles of John: A New Translation with Introduction and Commentary*. AB. Garden City, NY: Doubleday, 1982.

———. *The Gospel according to John: A New Translation with Introduction and Commentary*. AB. Garden City, NY: Doubleday, 1966, 1970.

Bruce, F. F. *The Gospel of John: Introduction, Exposition, and Notes*. Grand Rapids: Eerdmans, 1983.

Bultmann, Rudolf. *The Gospel of John: A Commentary*. Trans. G. R. Beasley-Murray, R. W. N. Hoare, and J. K. Riches. Philadelphia: Westminster, 1971.

———. *Jesus and the Word*. Trans. Louise Pettibone Smith and Erminie Huntress Lantero. New York: Scribners, 1958.

———. *The Johannine Epistles*. Trans. R. Philip O'Hara, with Lane C. McGaughy and Robert W. Funk. Hermeneia. Philadelphia: Fortress, 1973.

Burge, Gary. *The Anointed Community: The Holy Spirit in the Johannine Tradition*. Grand Rapids: Eerdmans, 1987.

183

Burke, Peter. "History as Social Memory." In *Memory: History, Culture, and the Mind*, ed. Thomas Butler, 97–113. New York: Basil Blackwell, 1989.

Burlein, Ann. *Lift High the Cross: Where White Supremacy and the Christian Right Converge*. Durham, NC: Duke University Press, 2002.

Carson, D. A. *The Gospel according to John*. Grand Rapids: Eerdmans, 1991.

Connerton, Paul. *How Societies Remember*. Themes in the Social Sciences. Cambridge: Cambridge University Press, 1989.

Crossan, John Dominic. *Who Killed Jesus?: Exposing the Roots of AntiSemitism in the Gospel Story of the Death of Jesus*. San Francisco: HarperSanFrancisco, 1995.

Culpepper, R. Alan. *Anatomy of the Fourth Gospel: A Study in Literary Design*. Philadelphia: Fortress, 1983.

———. *1 John, 2 John, 3 John*. Knox Preaching Guides. Atlanta: John Knox, 1985.

———. *The Gospel and Letters of John*. Interpreting Biblical Texts. Nashville: Abingdon, 1998.

———. *The Johannine School: An Evaluation of the Johannine–School Hypothesis Based on an Investigation of the Nature of Ancient Schools*. SBLDS. Missoula, MT: Scholars Press, 1975.

Dewey, Arthur J. "The Eyewitness of History: Visionary Consciousness in the Fourth Gospel." In *Jesus in Johannine Tradition*, ed. Robert T. Fortna and Tom Thatcher, 59–70. Louisville, KY: Westminster John Knox, 2001.

Dodd, C. H. *Historical Tradition in the Fourth Gospel*. Cambridge: Cambridge University Press, 1963.

———. *The Interpretation of the Fourth Gospel*. Cambridge: Cambridge University Press, 1953.

Eusebius. *The Ecclesiastical History*. Trans. Kirsopp Lake. LCL. Cambridge, MA: Harvard University Press, 1964–65.

Fentress, James, and Chris Wickham. *Social Memory*. New Perspectives on the Past. Cambridge, MA: Blackwell, 1992.

Fitzmeyer, Joseph. *The Gospel according to Luke*. 2nd ed. AB. Garden City, NY: Doubleday, 1981.

Fortna, Robert T. *The Fourth Gospel and Its Predecessor: From Narrative Source to Present Gospel*. Philadelphia: Fortress, 1988.

Foucault, Michel. "Nietzsche, Genealogy, and History." In *Language, CounterMemory, Practice*, ed. Donald F. Bouchard, trans. Donald F. Bouchard and Sherry Simon, 139–64. Ithaca, NY: Cornell University Press, 1977.

Goodman, Martin. "Texts, Scribes and Power in Roman Judaea." In *Literacy and Power in the Ancient World*, ed. Alan K. Bowman and Greg Woolf, 99–108. New York: Cambridge University Press, 1994.

Halbwachs, Maurice. *The Collective Memory*. Trans. Francis J. Ditter Jr. and Vida Yazdi Ditter. New York: Harper & Row, 1980.

———. *On Collective Memory*. Ed. and trans. Lewis Coser. Chicago: University of Chicago Press, 1992. Pages 41–189 of this volume are selected translations from *The Social Frameworks of Memory* [Les cadres sociaux de la mémoire, 1952 edition]; pages 193–235 are a translation of the final chapter of *The Legendary Topography of the Holy Land: A Study in Collective Memory* [La topographie légendaire des évangiles en terre sainte: Étude de mémoire collective, 1941 edition].

Hanson, Ann Ellis. "Ancient Illiteracy." In *Literacy in the Roman World*, ed. J. H. Humphrey, 159–98. Journal of Roman Archaeology Supplementary Series. Ann Arbor: University of Michigan, 1991.

Harris, William V. *Ancient Literacy*. Cambridge, MA: Harvard University Press, 1989.

Hengel, Martin. *The Johannine Question*. Trans. John Bowden. Philadelphia: Trinity Press, 1989.

Herodotus. *Histories*. Trans. A. D. Godley. LCL. Cambridge, MA: Harvard University Press, 1966.

Hezser, Catherine. *Jewish Literacy in Roman Palestine*. TSAJ. Tübingen: Mohr–Siebeck, 2001.

Hill, A. J. *Under Pressure: The Final Voyage of the Submarine* S-Five. New York: Free Press, 2002.

Hobsbawm, Eric. "Introduction: Inventing Traditions." In *The Invention of Tradition*, ed. Eric Hobsbawm and Terence Ranger, 1–14. Canto Edition. Cambridge: Cambridge University Press, 1992.

Ignatius. *Letters*. In *The Apostolic Fathers*, trans. Kirsopp Lake. LCL. New York: Macmillan, 1912–13.

Irenaeus. *Against Heresies*. In *The Apostolic Fathers*, trans. J. B. Lightfoot. London: Macmillan, 1893.

Josephus. *Against Apion*. Trans. H. St. J. Thackeray. LCL. Cambridge, MA: Harvard University Press, 1966.

———. *Jewish Antiquities*. Trans. Ralph Marcus and Allen Wickgren. LCL. Cambridge, MA: Harvard University Press, 1963.

———. *The Jewish War*. Trans. H. St. J. Thackeray. LCL. Cambridge, MA: Harvard University Press, 1961.

Käsemann, Ernst. *The Testament of Jesus: A Study of the Gospel of John in the Light of Chapter 17*. Trans. Gerhard Krodel. Philadelphia: Fortress, 1968.

Kysar, Robert. *John: The Maverick Gospel*. Atlanta: John Knox, 1976.

LeFanu, Joseph Sheridan. *The Purcell Papers*. Ed. August Derleth. Sauk City, WI: Arkham House, 1975.

LeRoy, Herbert. *Rätsel und Missverständnis: Ein Beitrag zur Formgeschichte des Johannesevangeliums*. Bonn: Peter Hanstein, 1968.

Lewis, Naphtali, ed. *The Documents from the Bar Kokhba Period in the Cave of Letters: Greek Papyri, Aramaic and Nabatean Signatures and Subscriptions*. Jerusalem: Hebrew University, 1989.

Lowenthal, David. *The Past Is a Foreign Country*. Cambridge: Cambridge University Press, 1985.

———. *Possessed by the Past: The Heritage Crusade and the Spoils of History*. New York: Free Press, 1996.

Marshall, I. Howard. *The Gospel of Luke: A Commentary on the Greek Text*. NIGTC. Grand Rapids: Eerdmans, 1978.

Martin, Rux. "Truth, Power, Self: An Interview with Michel Foucault (October 25, 1982)." In *Technologies of the Self*, ed. Luther H. Martin, Huck Gutman, and Patrick H. Hutton, 9–15. Amherst: University of Massachusetts Press, 1988.

Martyn, J. Louis. *History and Theology in the Fourth Gospel*. 2nd ed. Nashville: Abingdon, 1979.

Meyers, Eric M. "Ancient Synagogues: An Archaeological Introduction." In *Sacred Realm: The Emergence of the Synagogue in the Ancient World*, ed. Steven Fine, 3–20. New York: Oxford University Press, 1996.

Morris, Leon. *The Gospel according to John: The English Text with Introduction, Exposition and Notes*. NICNT. Grand Rapids: Eerdmans, 1971.

O'Day, Gail R. *Revelation in the Fourth Gospel: Narrative Mode and Theological Claim*. Philadelphia: Fortress, 1986.

Owen, Stephen. *Remembrances: The Experience of the Past in Classical Chinese Literature*. Cambridge, MA: Harvard University Press, 1986.

Painter, John. "The Farewell Discourses and the History of Johannine Christianity." *NTS* 27 (1981): 525–43.

———. *The Quest for the Messiah: The History, Literature, and Theology of the Johannine Community*. 2nd ed. Nashville: Abingdon, 1993.

Philo. *Embassy to Gaius*. Trans. F. H. Colson. LCL. Cambridge, MA: Harvard University Press, 1971.

———. *Life of Moses*. Trans. F. H. Colson. LCL. Cambridge, MA: Harvard University Press, 1950.

Plato. *Phaedrus*. Trans. Harold North Fowler. LCL. Cambridge, MA: Harvard University Press, 1982.

Rensberger, David. *1 John, 2 John, 3 John*. Abingdon New Testament Commentaries. Nashville: Abingdon, 1997.

Robinson, John A. T. "The New Look on John." In *Twelve New Testament Studies*, 94–106. London: SCM Press, 1962.

———. *The Priority of John*. Ed. J. F. Coakley. London: SCM, 1985.

Rosenzweig, Roy, and David Thelen. *The Presence of the Past: Popular Uses of History in American Life*. New York: Columbia University Press, 1998.

Schnackenburg, Rudolf. *The Gospel according to St. John*. Trans. Kevin Smyth. New York: Crossroad, 1987.

———. *The Johannine Epistles: Introduction and Commentary*. Trans. Reginald Fuller and Ilse Fuller. New York: Crossroad, 1992.

Schudson, Michael. "The Present in the Past Versus the Past in the Present." *Communication* 11 (1989): 105–13.

Schwartz, Barry. "Social Change and Collective Memory: The Democratization of George Washington." *American Sociological Review* 56 (1991): 221–36.

Shinan, Avigdor. "Synagogues in the Land of Israel: The Literature of the Ancient Synagogue and Synagogue Archaeology." In *Sacred Realm: The Emergence of the Synagogue in the Ancient World*, ed. Steven Fine, 130–52. New York: Oxford University Press, 1996.

Smalley, Stephen. *1, 2, 3 John*. WBC. Waco, TX: Word Books, 1984.

Stanton, Graham. "Form Criticism Revisited." In *What About the New Testament? Essays in Honour of Christopher Evans*, 13–27. London: SCM Press, 1975.

Stark, Rodney. *The Rise of Christianity: How the Obscure, Marginal Jesus Movement Became the Dominant Religious Force in the Western World in a Few Centuries*. San Francisco: HarperSanFrancisco, 1997.

Tcherikover, Victor, and Alexander Fuks, eds. *Corpus Papyrorum Judaicarum*. Cambridge, MA: Harvard University Press, 1957.

Thatcher, Tom. "Literacy, Textual Communities, and Josephus' Jewish War." *JSJ* 29 (1998): 123–42.

———. *The Riddles of Jesus in John: A Study in Tradition and Folklore*. SBLMS. Atlanta: Society of Biblical Literature, 2000.

Thomas, Rosalind. *Literacy and Orality in Ancient Greece*. Cambridge: Cambridge University Press, 1992.

Thompson, Marianne Meye. *1–3 John*. IVP New Testament Commentary. Downers Grove, IL: InterVarsity, 1992.

Turner, Max. "Holy Spirit." In *The Dictionary of Jesus and the Gospels*, ed. Joel B. Green, Scot McKnight, and I. Howard Marshall, 341–51. Downers Grove, IL: InterVarsity Press, 1992.

Yadin, Yigael. "The Expedition to the Judean Desert, 1960: Expedition D." *IEJ* 11 (1961): 40–50.

———. "The Expedition to the Judean Desert, 1961: Expedition D." *IEJ* 12 (1962): 231–35.

Yerushalmi, Yosef Hayim. *Zakhor: Jewish History and Jewish Memory*. New York: Schocken Books, 1989.

Zelizer, Barbie. "Reading the Past against the Grain: The Shape of Memory Studies." *Critical Studies in Mass Communication* 12 (1995): 214–39.

Zerubavel, Eviatar. *The Fine Line: Making Distinctions in Everyday Life*. Chicago: University of Chicago Press, 1993.

———. *Time Maps: Collective Memory and the Social Shape of the Past*. Chicago: University of Chicago Press, 2003.

Zerubavel, Yael. *Recovered Roots: Collective Memory and the Making of Israeli National Tradition*. Chicago: University of Chicago Press, 1995.

Index